SCIENCE&
RELIGION

OPPOSING VIEWPOINTS®

Other Books of Related Interest in the Opposing Viewpoints Series:

Biomedical Ethics
Civil Liberties
Constructing a Life Philosophy
Death and Dying
The Environmental Crisis

Additional Books in the Opposing Viewpoints Series:

Abortion
AIDS
American Foreign Policy
American Government
The American Military
American Values
America's Elections
America's Prisons
The Arms Race
Censorship
Central America
Chemical Dependency
Crime & Criminals
Criminal Justice
The Death Penalty
Drug Abuse
Economics in America
Latin America and U.S. Foreign Policy
Male/Female Roles
The Mass Media
The Middle East
Nuclear War
The Political Spectrum
Poverty
Problems of Africa
Sexual Values
Social Justice
The Soviet Union
Teenage Sexuality
Terrorism
The Vietnam War
War and Human Nature

SCIENCE & RELIGION

OPPOSING VIEWPOINTS®

David L. Bender & Bruno Leone, *Series Editors*

Janelle Rohr, *Book Editor*

Bonnie Szumski, *Assistant Editor*

OPPOSING VIEWPOINTS SERIES ®

Greenhaven Press, Inc.   P.O. Box 289009   San Diego, CA 92128-9009

215
S416
1988

Library of Congress Cataloging-in-Publication Data

Science & religion : opposing viewpoints / Janelle Rohr, book editor;
  Bonnie Szumski, assistant editor.
     P.   cm. — (Opposing viewpoints series)
  Bibliography: p.
  Includes index.
  Summary: Presents opposing viewpoints about the relationship between religion and science, both historically and in the present.
  ISBN 0-89908-431-1. ISBN 0-89908-406-0 (pbk.)
    1. Religion and science—1946-   [1. Religion and science.]
I. Rohr, Janelle, 1963-   . II. Szumski, Bonnie, 1958-
III. Title: Science and religion. IV. Series.
BL240.2.S323 1988
215—dc19
                                   87-38066
                                        CIP
                                        AC

"Congress shall make no law... abridging the freedom of speech, or of the press."

First Amendment to the US Constitution

The basic foundation of our democracy is the first amendment guarantee of freedom of expression. The *Opposing Viewpoints Series* is dedicated to the concept of this basic freedom and the idea that it is more important to practice it than to enshrine it.

Contents

Why Consider Opposing Viewpoints?

"It is better to debate a question without settling it than to settle a question without debating it."

Joseph Joubert (1754-1824)

The Importance of Examining Opposing Viewpoints

The purpose of the Opposing Viewpoints books, and this book in particular, is to present balanced, and often difficult to find, opposing points of view on complex and sensitive issues.

Probably the best way to become informed is to analyze the positions of those who are regarded as experts and well studied on issues. It is important to consider every variety of opinion in an attempt to determine the truth. Opinions from the mainstream of society should be examined. But also important are opinions that are considered radical, reactionary, or minority as well as those stigmatized by some other uncomplimentary label. An important lesson of history is the eventual acceptance of many unpopular and even despised opinions. The ideas of Socrates, Jesus, and Galileo are good examples of this.

Readers will approach this book with their own opinions on the issues debated within it. However, to have a good grasp of one's own viewpoint, it is necessary to understand the arguments of those with whom one disagrees. It can be said that those who do not completely understand their adversary's point of view do not fully understand their own.

9

A persuasive case for considering opposing viewpoints has been presented by John Stuart Mill in his work *On Liberty*. When examining controversial issues it may be helpful to reflect on this suggestion:

> The only way in which a human being can make some approach to knowing the whole of a subject, is by hearing what can be said about it by persons of every variety of opinion, and studying all modes in which it can be looked at by every character of mind. No wise man ever acquired his wisdom in any mode but this.

Analyzing Sources of Information

The Opposing Viewpoints books include diverse materials taken from magazines, journals, books, and newspapers, as well as statements and position papers from a wide range of individuals, organizations and governments. This broad spectrum of sources helps to develop patterns of thinking which are open to the consideration of a variety of opinions.

Pitfalls To Avoid

A pitfall to avoid in considering opposing points of view is that of regarding one's own opinion as being common sense and the most rational stance and the point of view of others as being only opinion and naturally wrong. It may be that another's opinion is correct and one's own is in error.

Another pitfall to avoid is that of closing one's mind to the opinions of those with whom one disagrees. The best way to approach a dialogue is to make one's primary purpose that of understanding the mind and arguments of the other person and not that of enlightening him or her with one's own solutions. More can be learned by listening than speaking.

It is my hope that after reading this book the reader will have a deeper understanding of the issues debated and will appreciate the complexity of even seemingly simple issues on which good and honest people disagree. This awareness is particularly important in a democratic society such as ours where people enter into public debate to determine the common good. Those with whom one disagrees should not necessarily be regarded as enemies, but perhaps simply as people who suggest different paths to a common goal.

Developing Basic Reading and Thinking Skills

In this book carefully edited opposing viewpoints are purposely placed back to back to create a running debate; each viewpoint is preceded by a short quotation that best expresses the author's main argument. This format instantly plunges the reader into the midst of a controversial issue and greatly aids that reader in mastering the basic skill of recognizing an author's point of view.

A number of basic skills for critical thinking are practiced in the activities that appear throughout the books in the series. Some of the skills are:

Evaluating Sources of Information   The ability to choose from among alternative sources the most reliable and accurate source in relation to a given subject.

Separating Fact from Opinion   The ability to make the basic distinction between factual statements (those that can be demonstrated or verified empirically) and statements of opinion (those that are beliefs or attitudes that cannot be proved).

Identifying Stereotypes   The ability to identify oversimplified, exaggerated descriptions (favorable or unfavorable) about people and insulting statements about racial, religious or national groups, based upon misinformation or lack of information.

Recognizing Ethnocentrism   The ability to recognize attitudes or opinions that express the view that one's own race, culture, or group is inherently superior, or those attitudes that judge another culture or group in terms of one's own.

It is important to consider opposing viewpoints and equally important to be able to critically analyze those viewpoints. The activities in this book are designed to help the reader master these thinking skills. Statements are taken from the book's viewpoints and the reader is asked to analyze them. This technique aids the reader in developing skills that not only can be applied to the viewpoints in this book, but also to situations where opinionated spokespersons comment on controversial issues. Although the activities are helpful to the solitary reader, they are most useful when the reader can benefit from the interaction of group discussion.

Using this book and others in the series should help readers develop basic reading and thinking skills. These skills should improve the readers' ability to understand what they read. Readers should be better able to separate fact from opinion, substance from rhetoric and become better consumers of information in our media-centered culture.

This volume of the Opposing Viewpoints books does not advocate a particular point of view. Quite the contrary! The very nature of the book leaves it to the reader to formulate the opinions he or she finds most suitable. My purpose as publisher is to see that this is made possible by offering a wide range of viewpoints which are fairly presented.

David L. Bender
Publisher

Introduction

> *"The Bible was written to show us how to go to heaven, not how the heavens go."*
>
> Galileo Galilei (1564-1642)

In the spring of 1633, Galileo Galilei, an Italian scientist, was delivered before the dreaded Roman Inquisition to be tried on charges of heresy. He was denounced, according to a formal statement, "for holding as true the false doctrine . . . that the sun is the center of the world and immovable, and that the earth moves." The statement went on to read that "the proposition that the sun is the center of the world and does not move from its place is absurd and . . . heretical, because it is expressly contrary to the Holy Scripture." Galileo was found guilty and forced to renounce his views. Ill and broken in spirit, he was sentenced to a life of perpetual imprisonment and penance.

Throughout history, Galileo has been joined by others in what is viewed by many as an ongoing conflict between science and religion. Roger Bacon, a thirteenth-century English priest, spent the final fourteen years of his life in a dungeon for writing that in the quest for truth, experimentation and observation are valid challenges to the uncritical acceptance of spiritual and secular authorities. In the nineteenth century, Charles Darwin was mocked and maligned for claiming that all living things evolved from lower life forms. And in 1925, John Scopes, a high school biology teacher from Dayton, Tennessee, was accused and convicted of violating a state law which specified that only divine creation as an explanation for the origin of life could be taught in Tennessee public schools. Chapter 1 of this anthology presents documents from three of these important historical incidents: Galileo versus the Inquisition; Darwin versus Hugh Miller, a fellow nineteenth-century scientists; and the two opposing attorneys in the Scopes trial, Clarence Darrow and William Jennings Bryan.

Today, in an age in which science and technology have become such dominant forces in human progress, these examples may seem like barbaric remnants of an unenlightened past. The truth, however, is that the conflict between science and religion is still being waged. The "battlefield" has changed, the "weapons" have been updated and the "wounds" inflicted are generally less gaping. But the battle goes on.

All of this would seem to raise two very relevant questions. First, why are science and religion at odds? And second, have they always been and will they continue to be antagonists?

The answer to the first question is apparent. Both science and religion seek to provide answers to some very fundamental questions related to the physical world. How did life originate? In what direction is life heading? Can we define human nature and satisfactorily explain human behavior? The fact that scientists and theologians frequently arrive at different answers to these and similar questions is not the problem. Scientists often heatedly disagree even among themselves over basic questions of cause and effect. The same is true of theologians. Rather, the difficulty lies in the vastly different approaches employed by each in finding answers to these seminal questions. Science climbs the ladder of reason in its search for truth while religion kneels before the altar of faith. The methodology of science includes observation and experimentation while religion embraces divine revelation. Thus as the physical anthropologist attempts to explain human origins in terms of progressive evolution, the religious scholar may look to the creative act described in Genesis I. Similarly, as the psychologist explains warfare as a species "death wish," the theologian explains it as the price paid for "original sin."

The reader should not conclude from the above that science and religion cannot be reconciled. For centuries religion has had many staunch defenders in the scientific community and vice versa. As a brief survey of the readings in this book makes clear, some scientists find that their research increases their religious faith and some theologians incorporate science into their belief systems.

Science and Religion: Opposing Viewpoints is a new edition of a 1981 title of the same name. The five topics examined in this anthology are Great Historical Debates on Science and Religion, Are Science and Religion Compatible? How Did the Universe Originate? How Did Life Originate? and Should Ethical Values Limit Scientific Research? The editors have compiled readings from a broad range of contributors including scientists, clergy, philosophers, teachers, and journalists. Both past and current debates on science and religion suggest that the issues in conflict are too heated to be easily or quickly resolved.

Great Historical Debates on Science and Religion

Chapter Preface

When viewing the past, it is easy to find beliefs, ideas, and attitudes that seem absurd to a modern observer. An obvious example is the fear medieval sailors had of falling off the edge of the earth if they sailed too far away from land. In the face of these seemingly absurd beliefs, readers benefit from trying to understand the context in which they arise, particularly while reading the following chapter, which includes six historical essays.

British author James Burke tells an interesting anecdote that explains why understanding the context of another culture's belief is important. "Someone once observed to the eminent philosopher Wittgenstein how stupid medieval Europeans . . . must have been that they could have looked at the sky and thought that the sun was circling the earth." According to Burke, Wittgenstein is said to have replied, "I agree. But I wonder what it would have looked like if the sun *had* been circling the earth." Burke argues it would have looked the same. In the context of a culture guided by and based on Christianity, it made sense for medieval Europeans to look at the sky and see proof that they were the center of a God-directed universe.

The medieval world is by no means unique in having firmly-held beliefs that are abandoned only with reluctance. Examples of this can be found in every century, including our own. When the Wright brothers first invented an airplane, they had to overcome the conviction that it was absurd to think that humans could fly. The twentieth century, with its rockets and space stations, has clearly made a great leap from even the Wright brothers' experiments. A hundred years from now, what will people think of our first probes into space?

The following viewpoints are important historical sources in the debate between science and religion. The authors write from their own individual perspectives and cultures, an important factor to consider while reading their viewpoints.

"In discussions of physical problems we ought to begin not from the authority of scriptural passages, but from sense-experiences and necessary demonstrations."

The Church Should Not Have Final Authority in Science

Galileo Galilei

For centuries, Europeans believed that the earth was the center of the universe and that the sun revolved around it. Nicolaus Copernicus was the first European astronomer to challenge this view. Copernicus avoided controversy during his lifetime by delaying publication of his findings until he was on his deathbed. In contrast, Italian astronomer Galileo Galilei incurred the wrath of the Roman Catholic Church by supporting the Copernican theory as factual. The following viewpoint is an excerpt from a letter Galileo wrote to the Grand Duchess Christina in 1614. When Galileo learned that he was under investigation by the Inquisition, he forwarded this letter to the Vatican to defend himself.

As you read, consider the following questions:

1. What reasons does Galileo give for relying upon observation instead of Scripture when describing the physical universe?
2. Why would it be wrong to ban Copernicus's teachings, according to the author?

Galileo Galilei, "Letter to the Grand Duchess Christina," 1614.

The reason produced for condemning the opinion that the earth moves and the sun stands still is that in many places in the Bible one may read that the sun moves and the earth stands still. Since the Bible cannot err, it follows as a necessary consequence that anyone takes an erroneous and heretical position who maintains that the sun in inherently motionless and the earth movable.

With regard to this argument, I think in the first place that it is very pious to say and prudent to affirm that the Holy Bible can never speak untruth—whenever its true meaning is understood. But I believe that nobody will deny that it is often very abstruse, and may say things which are quite different from what its bare words signify. Hence in expounding the Bible if one were always to confine oneself to the unadorned grammatical meaning, one might fall into error. Not only contradictions and propositions far from true might thus be made to appear in the Bible, but even grave heresies and follies. Thus it would be necessary to assign to God feet, hands and eyes, as well as corporeal and human affections, such as anger, repentance, hatred and sometimes even the forgetting of things past and ignorance of those to come. These propositions uttered by the Holy Ghost were set down in that manner by the sacred scribes in order to accommodate them to the capacities of the common people, who are rude and unlearned. For the sake of those who deserve to be separated from the herd, it is necessary that wise expositors should produce the true senses of such passages, together with the special reasons for which they were set down in these words. This doctrine is so widespread and so definite with all theologians that it would be superfluous to adduce evidence for it.

The Bible's Audience

Hence I think that I may reasonably conclude that whenever the Bible has occasion to speak of any physical conclusion (especially those which are very abstruse and hard to understand), the rule has been observed of avoiding confusion in the minds of the common people which would render them contumacious toward the higher mysteries. Now the Bible, merely to condescend to popular capacity, has not hesitated to obscure some very important pronouncements, attributing to God himself some qualities extremely remote from (and even contrary to) His essence. Who, then, would positively declare that this principle has been set aside, and the Bible has confined itself rigorously to the bare and restricted sense of its words, when speaking but casually of the earth, of water, of the sun, or of any other created thing? Especially in view of the fact that these things in no way concern the primary purpose of the sacred writings, which is the service of God and the salvation of souls—matters infinitely beyond the comprehension of the common people.

This being granted, I think that in discussions of physical problems we ought to begin not from the authority of scriptural passages, but from sense-experiences and necessary demonstrations; for the Holy Bible and the phenomena of nature proceed alike from the divine Word, the former as the dictate of the Holy Ghost and the latter as the observant executrix of God's commands. It is necessary for the Bible, in order to be accommodated to the understanding of every man, to speak many things which appear to differ from the absolute truth so far as the bare meaning of the words is concerned. But Nature, on the other hand, is inexorable and immutable; she never transgresses the laws imposed upon her, or cares a whit whether her abstruse reasons and methods of operation are understandable to men. For that reason it appears that nothing physical which sense-experience sets before our eyes, or which necessary demonstrations prove to us, ought to be called in question (much less condemned) upon the testimony of biblical passages which may have some different meaning beneath their words. For the Bible is not chained in every expression to conditions as strict as those which govern all physical effects; nor is God any less excellently revealed in Nature's actions than in sacred statements of the Bible. Perhaps this is what Tertullian meant by these words. 'We conclude that God is known first through Nature, and then again, more particularly, by doc-

Galileo before the Inquisition

trine; by Nature in His words, and by doctrine in His revealed word.'

From this I do not mean to infer that we need not have an extraordinary esteem for the passages of holy Scripture. On the contrary, having arrived at any certainties in physics, we ought to utilize these as the most appropriate aids in the true exposition of the Bible and in the investigation of those meanings which are necessarily contained therein, for these must be concordant with demonstrated truths. I should judge that the authority of the Bible was designed to persuade men of those articles and propositions which, surpassing all human reasoning, could not be made credible by science, or by any other means than through the very mouth of the Holy Spirit.

The Authority of the Bible

Yet even in those propositions which are not matters of faith, this authority ought to be preferred over that of all human writings which are supported only by bare assertions or probable arguments, and not set forth in a demonstrative way. This I hold to be necessary and proper to the same extent that divine wisdom surpasses all human judgement and conjecture.

But I do not feel obliged to believe that that same God who has endowed us with senses, reason, and intellect has intended to forgo their use and by some other means to give us a knowledge which we can attain by them. He would not require us to deny sense and reason in physical matters which are set before our eyes and minds by direct experience or necessary demonstrations. This must be especially true in those sciences of which but the faintest trace (and that consisting of conclusions) is to be found in the Bible. Of astronomy, for instance, so little is found that none of the planets except Venus are so much as mentioned, and this only once or twice under the name of 'Lucifer.' If the sacred scribes had any intention of teaching people certain arrangements and motions of the heavenly bodies, or had they wished us to derive such knowledge from the Bible, then in my opinion they would not have spoken of these matters so sparingly in comparison with the infinite number of admirable conclusions which are demonstrated in that science. Far from pretending to teach us the constitution and motions of the heavens and the stars, with their shapes, magnitudes, and distances, the authors of the Bible intentionally forebore to speak of these things, though all were quite well known to them. . . .

How One Goes to Heaven

From these things it follows as a necessary consequence that, since the Holy Ghost did not intend to teach us whether heaven moves or stands still, whether its shape is spherical or like a discus or extended in a plane, nor whether the earth is located at its center or off to one side, then so much the less was it intended to settle for us any other conclusion of the same kind. And the motion or rest of the earth and the sun is so closely linked with the things just named, that without a determination of the one, neither side can be taken in the other matters. Now if the Holy Spirit has purposely neglected to teach us propositions of this sort as irrelevant to the highest goal (that is, to our salvation), how can anyone affirm that it is obligatory to take sides on them, and that one belief is required by faith, while the other side is erroneous? Can an opinion be heretical and yet have no concern with the salvation of souls? Can the Holy Ghost be asserted not to have intended teaching us something that does concern our salvation? I would say here something that was heard from an ecclesiastic of the most eminent degree: 'That the intention of the Holy Ghost is to teach us how one goes to heaven, not how heaven goes.' . . .

Matters of Faith

Take note, theologians, that in your desire to make matters of faith out of propositions relating to the fixity of sun and earth you run the risk of eventually having to condemn as heretics those who would declare the earth to stand still and the sun to change position—eventually, I say, at such a time as it might be physically or logically proved that the earth moves and the sun stands still.

Galileo Galilei, note in his copy of *Dialogue Concerning the Two Chief World Systems—Ptolemaic & Copernican*, 1632.

To command that the very professors of astronomy themselves see to the refutation of their own observations and proofs as mere fallacies and sophisms is to enjoin something that lies beyond any possibility of accomplishment. For this would amount to commanding that they must not see what they see and must not understand what they know, and that in searching they must find the opposite of what they actually encounter. Before this could be done they would have to be taught how to make one mental faculty command another, and the inferior powers the superior, so that the imagination and the will might be forced to believe the opposite of what the intellect understands. I am referring at all times to merely physical propositions, and not to supernatural things which are matters of faith. . . .

Suppressing the Truth

If in order to banish the opinion [of Copernicus] in question from the world it were sufficient to stop the mouth of a single man—as perhaps those men persuade themselves who, measuring the minds of others by their own, think it impossible that this doctrine should be able to continue to find adherents—then that would be very easily done. But things stand otherwise. To carry out such a decision it would be necessary not only to prohibit the book of Copernicus and the writings of other authors who follow the same opinion, but to ban the whole science of astronomy. Furthermore, it would be necessary to forbid men to look at the heavens, in order that they might not see Mars and Venus sometimes quite near the earth and sometimes very distant, the variation being so great that Venus is forty times and Mars sixty times as large at one time as another. And it would be necessary to prevent Venus being seen round at one time and forked at another, with very thin horns; as well as many other sensory observations which can never be reconciled with the Ptolemaic system in any way, but are very strong arguments for the Copernican. And to ban Copernicus now that his doctrine is daily reinforced by many new observations and by the learned applying themselves to the reading of his book, after this opinion has been allowed and tolerated for those many years during which it was less followed and less confirmed, would seem in my judgement to be a contravention of truth, and an attempt to hide and suppress her the more as she revealed herself the more clearly and plainly. Not to abolish and censure his whole book, but only to condemn as erroneous this particular proposition, would (if I am not mistaken) be a still greater detriment to the minds of men, since it would afford them occasion to see a proposition proved that it was heresy to believe. And to prohibit the whole science would be but to censure a hundred passages of holy Scripture which teach us that the glory and greatness of Almighty God are marvelously discerned in all his works and divinely read in the open book of heaven. For let no one believe that reading the lofty concepts written in that book leads to nothing further than the mere seeing of the splendor of the sun and the stars and their rising and setting, which is as far as the eyes of brutes and the vulgar can penetrate. Within its pages are couched mysteries so profound and concepts so sublime that the vigils, labors, and studies of hundreds upon hundreds of the most acute minds have still not pierced them, even after continual investigations for thousands of years.

"The proposition that the sun is the centre of the world and does not move from its place is absurd and false philosophically and formally heretical."

The Church Should Have Final Authority in Science

The Roman Curia

The medieval Inquisition was an office in the Vatican charged with defending and advancing the Roman Catholic faith. When Galileo Galilei was suspected of teaching heretical doctrines, the Inquisition investigated him. Its first investigation, held in 1615, was dropped without charges. Galileo was prohibited, however, from teaching as a fact that the sun was the center of the universe. Yet in 1632, Galileo published *Dialogue Concerning the Two Chief World Systems: Ptolemaic and Copernican.* As a result of the book, he was investigated again by the Inquisition and found guilty by the Roman Curia, the ruling body of the Church. The following viewpoint is the Roman Curia's sentence that was read to Galileo.

As you read, consider the following questions:

1. Name three things Galileo did that the Roman Curia criticizes.
2. Why do the authors object to Galileo's publishing *Dialogue Concerning the Two Chief World Systems*?
3. What is the Curia's response to Galileo's claim that he meant to present both sides and not draw a conclusion in his *Dialogue Concerning the Two Chief World Systems*?

Document in Karl Von Gebler, *Galileo Galilei and the Roman Curia.* Merrick, NY: Richwood Publishing Company, 1879.

[We] by the grace of God, cardinals of the Holy Roman Church, Inquisitors General, by the Holy Apostolic see specially deputed, against heretical depravity throughout the whole Christian Republic.

Wheras you, Galileo, son of the late Vincenzo Galilei, Florentine, aged seventy years, were in the year 1615 denounced to this Holy Office for holding as true the false doctrine taught by many, that the sun is the centre of the world and immovable, and that the earth moves, and also with a diurnal motion; for having disciples to whom you taught the same doctrine; for holding correspondence with certain mathematicians of Germany concerning the same; for having printed certain letters, entitled "On the Solar Spots," wherein you developed the same doctrine as true; and for replying to the objections from the Holy Scriptures, which from time to time were urged against it, by glossing the said Scriptures according to your own meaning: and whereas there was thereupon produced the copy of a document in the form of a letter, purporting to be written by you to one formerly your disciple, and in this diverse propositions are set forth, following the hypothesis of Copernicus, which are contrary to the true sense and authority of Holy Scripture:

This Holy Tribunal being therefore desirous of proceeding against the disorder and mischief thence resulting, which went on increasing to the prejudice of the Holy Faith, by command of his Holiness and of the most eminent Lords Cardinals of this supreme and universal Inquisition, the two propositions of the stability of the sun and the motion of the earth were by the theological "Qualifiers" qualified as follows:

The proposition that the sun is the centre of the world and does not move from its place is absurd and false philosophically and formally heretical, because it is expressly contrary to the Holy Scripture.

The proposition that the earth is not the centre of the world and immovable, but that it moves, and also with a diurnal motion, is equally absurd and false philosophically, and theologically considered, at least erroneous in faith.

The Vatican's Previous Order

But whereas it was desired at that time to deal leniently with you, it was decreed at the Holy Congregation held before his Holiness on the 25th February, 1616, that his Eminence the Lord Cardinal Bellarmine should order you to abandon altogether the said false doctrine, and, in the event of your refusal, that an injunction should be imposed upon you by the Commissary of the Holy Office, to give up the said doctrine, and not to teach it to others, nor to defend it, nor even discuss it; and failing your acquiescence in this injunction, that you should be imprisoned. And

24

This chart from 1660 shows a cross section of the spherical universe in which Aristotle and most other ancients believed. The earth is in the center, surrounded by concentric, glasslike spheres on which the sun, the moon, and the other planets revolve. There is a fine, distant sphere for the stars.

in execution of this decree, on the following day, at the Palace, and in the presence of his Eminence, the said Lord Cardinal Bellarmine, after being gently admonished by the said Lord Cardinal, the command was intimated to you by the Father Commissary of the Holy Office for the time before a notary and witnesses, that you were altogether to abandon the said false opinion, and not in future to defend or teach it in any way whatsoever, neither verbally nor in writing; and upon your promising to obey you were dismissed.

And in order that a doctrine so pernicious might be wholly

rooted out and not insinuate itself further to the grave prejudice of Catholic truth, a decree was issued by the Holy Congregation of the Index, prohibiting the books which treat of this doctrine, and declaring the doctrine itself to be false and wholly contrary to sacred and divine Scripture.

A Most Grievous Error

And whereas a book appeared here recently, printed last year at Florence, the title of which shows that you were the author, this title being: "Dialogue of Galileo Galilei on the Two Principal Systems of the World, the Ptolemaic and the Copernican"; and whereas the Holy Congregation was afterwards informed that through the publication of the said book, the false opinion of the motion of the earth and the stability of the sun was daily gaining ground; the said book was taken into careful consideration, and in it there was discovered a patent violation of the aforesaid injunction that had been imposed upon you, for in this book you have defended the said opinion previously condemned and to your face declared to be so, although in the said book you strive by various devices to produce the impression that you leave it undecided, and in express terms as probable: which however is a most grievous error, as an opinion can in no wise be probable which has been declared and defined to be contrary to Divine Scripture:

Therefore by our order you were cited before this Holy Office, where, being examined upon your oath, you acknowledged the book to be written and published by you. You confessed that you began to write the said book about ten or twelve years ago, after the command had been imposed upon you as above; that you requested licence to print it, without however intimating to those who granted you this licence that you had been commanded not to hold, defend, or teach in any way whatever the doctrine in question.

The False Side

You likewise confessed that the writing of the said book is in various places drawn up in such a form that the reader might fancy that the arguments brought forward on the false side are rather calculated by their cogency to compel conviction than to be easy of refutation; excusing yourself for having fallen into an error, as you alleged, so foreign to your intention, by the fact that you had written in dialogue, and by the natural complacency that every man feels in regard to his own subtleties, and in showing himself more clever than the generality of men, in devising, even on behalf of false propositions, ingenious and plausible arguments.

And a suitable term having been assigned to you to prepare your defence, you produced a certificate in the handwriting of his Eminence the Lord Cardinal Bellarmine, procured by you, as you asserted, in order to defend yourself against the calumnies of your enemies, who gave out that you had abjured and had been punished by the Holy Office; in which certificate it is declared that you had not abjured and had not been punished, but merely that the declaration made by his Holiness and published by the Holy Congregation of the Index, had been announced to you, wherein it is declared that the doctrine of the motion of the earth and the stability of the sun is contrary to the Holy Scriptures, and therefore cannot be defended or held. And as in this certificate there is no mention of the two articles of the injunction, namely, the order not "to teach" and "in any way," you represented that we ought to believe that in the course of fourteen or sixteen years you had lost all memory of them; and that this was why you said nothing of the injunction when you requested permission to print your book. And all this you urged not by way of excuse for your error, but that it might be set down to a vainglorious ambition rather than to malice. But this certificate produced by you in your defence has only aggravated your delinquency, since although it is there stated that the said opinion is contrary to Holy Scripture, you have nevertheless dared to discuss and defend it and to argue its probability; nor does the licence artfully and cunningly extorted by you avail you anything, since you did not notify the command imposed upon you.

Aristotle's Authority

The reasons Aristotle gives . . . to affirm the truth, it is not my intention to relate here; because it is quite enough . . . to know on his great authority that this earth is immovable, and does not revolve, and that, with the sea, it is the centre of the heavens.

Dante Alighieri, *The Banquet.*

And whereas it appeared to us that you had not stated the full truth with regard to your intention, we thought it necessary to subject you to a rigorous examination, at which (without prejudice, however, to the matters confessed by you, and set forth as above, with regard to your said intention) you answered like a good Catholic. Therefore, having seen and maturely considered the merits of this your cause, together with your confessions and excuses above mentioned, and all that ought justly to be seen and considered, we have arrived at the underwritten final sentence against you:

Invoking, therefore, the most holy name of our Lord Jesus Christ and of His most glorious Mother, and ever Virgin Mary, by this our final sentence, which sitting in judgment, with the counsel

27

and advice of the Reverend Masters of sacred theology and Doctors of both Laws, our assessors, we deliver in these writings, in the cause and causes presently before us between the magnificent Carlo Sinceri, Doctor of both Laws, Proctor Fiscal of this Holy Office, of the one part, and you Galileo Galilei, the defendant, here present, tried and confessed as above, of the other part,—we say, pronounce, sentence, declare, that you, the said Galileo, by reason of the matters adduced in process, and by you confessed as above, have rendered yourself in the judgment of this Holy Office vehemently suspected of heresy, namely, of having believed and held the doctrine—which is false and contrary to the sacred and divine Scriptures—that the sun is the centre of the world and does not move from east to west, and that the earth moves and is not the centre of the world; and that an opinion may be held and defended as probable after it has been declared and defined to be contrary to Holy Scripture; and that consequently you have incurred all the censures and penalties imposed and promulgated in the sacred canons and other constitutions, general and particular, against such delinquents. From which we are content that you be absolved, provided that first, with a sincere heart, and unfeigned faith, you abjure, curse, and detest the aforesaid errors and heresies, and every other error and heresy contrary to the Catholic and Apostolic Roman Church in the form to be prescribed by us.

"Dialogues" Prohibited

And in order that this your grave and pernicious error and transgression may not remain altogether unpunished, and that you may be more cautious for the future, and an example to others, that they may abstain from similar delinquencies—we ordain that the book of the *"Dialogues of Galileo Galilei"* be prohibited by public edict.

We condemn you to the formal prison of this Holy Office during our pleasure, and by way of salutary penance, we enjoin that for three years to come, you repeat once a week the seven penitential Psalms.

Reserving to ourselves full liberty to moderate, commute, or take off, in whole or in part, the aforesaid penalties and penance.

And so we say, pronounce, sentence, declare, ordain, condemn and reserve, in this and any other better way and form which we can and may lawfully employ.

"The facts and considerations have thoroughly convinced me that species have been modified, during a long course of descent."

Species Evolved by Natural Selection

Charles Darwin

Charles Darwin first published *On the Origin of Species* in 1859. Although other nineteenth-century scientists had speculated that living creatures had evolved from extinct species, Darwin was the first to suggest a plausible way in which this had happened. In the following viewpoint, Darwin argues that natural selection explains how species have evolved and cites evidence for his theory. He concludes that evolution gives humans a secure and positive future. Since natural selection works for the good of each creature, Darwin contends, all beings are progressing toward perfection.

As you read, consider the following questions:

1. Why does Darwin believe that his theory should not challenge anyone's religious feelings?
2. What conclusions does the author draw from his study of embryos and organs?
3. According to Darwin, in what ways is evolution beneficial?

Charles Darwin, *On the Origin of Species*, 1859.

The facts and considerations have thoroughly convinced me that species have been modified, during a long course of descent. This has been effected chiefly through the natural selection of numerous successive, slight, favourable variations; aided in an important manner by the inherited effects of the use and disuse of parts; and in an unimportant manner, that is in relation to adaptive structures, whether past or present, by the direct action of external conditions, and by variations which seem to us in our ignorance to arise spontaneously. It appears that I formerly underrated the frequency and value of these latter forms of variation, as leading to permanent modifications of structure independently of natural selection. But as my conclusions have lately been much misrepresented, and it has been stated that I attribute the modification of species exclusively to natural selection, I may be permitted to remark that in the first edition of this work, and subsequently, I placed in a most conspicuous position—namely, at the close of the Introduction—the following words: "I am convinced that natural selection has been the main but not the exclusive means of modification." This had been of no avail. Great is the power of steady misrepresentation; but the history of science shows that fortunately this power does not long endure.

A Satisfactory Explanation

It can hardly be supposed that a false theory would explain, in so satisfactory a manner as does the theory of natural selection, the several large classes of facts above specified. It has recently been objected that this is an unsafe method of arguing; but it is a method used in judging the common events of life, and has often been used by the greatest natural philosophers. The undulatory theory of light has thus been arrived at; and the belief in the revolution of the earth on its own axis was until lately supported by hardly any direct evidence. It is no valid objection that science as yet throws no light on the far higher problem of the essence or origin of life. Who can explain what is the essence of the attraction of gravity? No one now objects to following out the results consequent on this unknown element of attraction; notwithstanding that Leibnitz formerly accused Newton of introducing "occult qualities and miracles into philosophy."

I see no good reason why the views given in this volume should shock the religious feelings of any one. It is satisfactory, as showing how transient such impressions are, to remember that the greatest discovery ever made by man, namely, the law of the attraction of gravity, was also attacked by Leibnitz, "as subversive of natural, and inferentially of revealed, religion." A celebrated author and divine has written to me that "he has gradually learnt to see that it is just as noble a conception of the Deity to believe that He created a few original forms capable of self-development into other needful forms, as to believe that He required a fresh act of creation to supply the voids caused by the action of His laws.". . .

Resistance to the Theory

The chief cause of our natural unwillingness to admit that one species has given birth to clear and distinct species, is that we are always slow in admitting great changes of which we do not see the steps. The difficulty is the same as that felt by so many geologists, when Lyell first insisted that long lines of inland cliffs had been formed, and great valleys excavated, by the agencies which we see still at work. The mind cannot possibly grasp the full meaning of the term of even a million years; it cannot add up and perceive the full effects of many slight variations, accumulated during an almost infinite number of generations. . . .

Undeniable Facts

Astronomers and geologists have made it exceedingly probable that this earth on which we live has been brought to its present condition by passing through a succession of changes from an original state of great heat and fluidity, perhaps even from a mixture mainly consisting of gases. . . .

If we begin, as it were, at the other end, and trace things backwards from the present, instead of forwards from the remote past, it cannot be denied that Darwin's investigations have made it exceedingly probable that the vast variety of plants and animals have sprung from a much smaller number of original forms.

Frederick Temple, *The Relations Between Religion and Science,* 1884.

It may be asked how far I extend the doctrine of the modification of species. The question is difficult to answer, because the more distinct the forms are which we consider, by so much the arguments in favour of community of descent become fewer in number and less in force. But some arguments of the greatest weight extend very far. All the members of whole classes are connected together by a chain of affinities, and all can be classed on the same principle, in groups subordinate to groups. Fossil remains sometimes tend to fill up very wide intervals between existing order.

Evidence for Evolution

Organs in a rudimentary condition plainly show that an early progenitor had the organ in a fully developed condition; and this in some cases implies an enormous amount of modification in the descendants. Throughout whole classes various structures are formed on the same pattern, and at a very early age the embryos closely resemble each other. Therefore I cannot doubt that the theory of descent with modification embraces all the members of the same great class or kingdom. I believe that animals are descended from at most only four or five progenitors, and plants from an equal or lesser number.

Analogy would lead me one step farther, namely, to the belief that all animals and plants are descended from some one prototype. But analogy may be a deceitful guide. Nevertheless all living things have much in common, in their chemical composition, their cellular structure, their laws of growth, and their liability to injurious influences. We see this even in so trifling a fact as that the same poison often similarly affects plants and animals; or that the poison secreted by the gall fly produces monstrous growths on the wild rose or oak-tree. With all organic beings excepting perhaps some of the very lowest, sexual production seems to be essentially similar. With all, as far as is at present known the germinal vesicle is the same; so that all organisms start from a common origin. If we look even to the two main divisions—namely, to the animal and vegetable kingdoms—certain low forms are so far intermediate in character that naturalists have disputed to which kingdom they should be referred. As Professor Asa Gray has remarked, "the spores and other repoductive bodies of many of the lower algae may claim to have first a characteristically animal, and then an unequivocally vegetable existence." Therefore, on the principle of natural selection with divergence of character, it does not seem incredible that, from such low and intermediate forms, both animals and plants may have been developed; and, if we admit this, we must likewise admit that all the organic beings which have ever lived on this earth may be descended from some one primordial form. But this inference is chiefly grounded on analogy and it is immaterial whether or not it be accepted. . . .

A Boon to Natural History

When the views advanced by me in this volume . . . or when analogous views on the origin of species are generally admitted, we can dimly foresee that there will be a considerable revolution in natural history. Systematists will be able to pursue their labours as at present; but they will not be incessantly haunted by the shadowy doubt whether this or that form be a true species. This, I feel sure and I speak after experience, will be not slight relief. The endless disputes whether or not some fifty species of British brambles are good species will cease. Systematists will have only to decide (not that this will be easy) whether any form be sufficiently constant and distinct from other forms, to be capable of definition; and if definable, whether the differences be sufficiently important to deserve a specific name. This latter point will become a far more essential consideration than it is at present; for differences, however slight, between any two forms if not blended by intermediate gradations, are looked at by most naturalists as sufficient to raise both forms to the rank of species. . . .

A Clear and Firm Principle

The main conclusion here arrived at, and now held by many naturalists who are well competent to form a sound judgment, is that man is descended from some less highly organised form. The grounds upon which this conclusion rests will never be shaken, for the close similarity between man and the lower animals in embryonic development, as well as in innumerable points of structure and constitution, both of high and of the most trifling importance,—the rudiments which he retains, and the abnormal reversions to which he is occasionally liable,—are facts which cannot be disputed. They have long been known, but until recently they told us nothing with respect to the origin of man. Now when viewed by the light of our knowledge of the whole organic world, their meaning is unmistakable. The great principle of evolution stands up clear and firm, when these groups or facts are considered in connection with others, such as the mutual affinities of the members of the same group, their geographical distribution in past and present times, and their geological succession. It is incredible that all these facts should speak falsely. He who is not content to look, like a savage, at the phenomena of nature as disconnected, cannot any longer believe that man is the work of a separate act of creation.

Charles Darwin, *The Descent of Man*, 1871.

When we feel assured that all the individuals of the same species, and all the closely allied species of most genera, have within a not very remote period descended from one parent, and have migrated from some one birth-place; and when we better know the many means of migration, then, by the light which geology now throws, and will continue to throw, on former changes of climate and of the level of the land, we shall surely be enabled to trace in an admirable manner the former migrations of the inhabitants of the whole world. Even at present, by comparing the differences between the inhabitants of the sea on the opposite sides of a continent, and the nature of the various inhabitants on that continent, in relation to their apparent means of immigration, some light can be thrown on ancient geography.

The noble science of Geology loses glory from the extreme imperfection of the record. The crust of the earth with its imbedded remains must not be looked at as a well-filled museum, but as a poor collection made at hazard and at rare intervals. The ac-

33

cumulation of each great fossiliferous formation will be recognised as having depended on an unusual concurrence of favourable circumstances, and the blank intervals between the successive stages as having been of vast duration. But we shall be able to gauge with some security the duration of these intervals by a comparison of the preceding and succeeding organic forms. . . .

Progress Towards Perfection

Authors of the highest eminence seem to be fully satisfied with the view that each species has been independently created. To my mind it accords better with what we know of the laws impressed on matter by the Creator, that the production and extinction of the past and present inhabitants of the world should have been due to secondary causes, like those determining the birth and death of the individual. When I view all beings not as special creations, but as the lineal descendants of some few beings which lived long before the first bed of the Cambrian system was deposited, they seem to me to become ennobled. Judging from the past, we may safely infer that not one living species will transmit its unaltered likeness to a distant futurity. And of the species now living very few will transmit progeny of any kind to a far distant futurity; for the manner in which all organic beings are grouped, shows that the greater number of species in each genus, and all the species in many genera, have left no descendants, but have become utterly extinct. We can so far take a prophetic glance into futurity as to foretell that it will be the common and widely-spread species, belonging to the larger and dominant groups within each class, which will ultimately prevail and procreate new and dominant species. As all the living forms of life are the lineal descendants of those which lived long before the Cambrian epoch, we may feel certain that the ordinary succession by generation has never once been broken, and that no cataclysm has desolated the whole world. Hence we may look with some confidence to a secure future of great length. And as natural selection works solely by and for the good of each being, all corporeal and mental endowments will tend to progress towards perfection.

"It [is] . . . palpably absurd to ask us to believe in a succession *of beings that was thus infinitely earlier than any of the beings themselves which composed the succession."*

Species Did Not Evolve

Hugh Miller

Hugh Miller was a popular geological writer in nineteenth-century England. The following viewpoint is an excerpt from Miller's 1857 book, *The Testimony of the Rocks,* which had sold over forty thousand copies by the turn of the century. Miller believes that geology proved the existence of God. By looking at fossils in rock strata, he argues, geologists can see that each being was created and then became extinct. Miller writes that this evidence challenges scientists who believe that creatures are part of a series that evolved over time.

As you read, consider the following questions:

1. How does the author believe geology adds to the study of natural theology?
2. What conclusion does Miller draw after he describes mollusk fossils found in rock strata?
3. Why are humans uniquely special as creations of God, according to Miller?

Hugh Miller, "The Testimony of the Rocks, or Geology in Its Bearing on the Two Theologies, Natural & Revealed," Lecture Fifth, 1857.

The science of the geologist seems destined to exert a marked influence on that of the natural theologian. For not only does it greatly add to the materials on which the natural theologian founds his deductions, by adding to the organisms, plant and animal, of the present creation the extinct organisms of the creations of the past, with all their extraordinary display of adaptation and design; but it affords him, besides, materials peculiar to itself, in the history which it furnishes both of the appearance of these organisms in time, and of the wonderful order in which they were chronologically arranged. Not only—to borrow from [William] Paley's illustration—does it enable him to argue on the old grounds, from the contrivance exhibited in the *watch* found on the moor, that the watch could not have lain upon the moor for ever; but it establishes further, on different and more direct evidence, that there was a time when absolutely the watch was not there; nay, further, so to speak, that there was a previous time in which no watches existed at all, but only water-clocks; yet further, that there was a time in which there were not even water-clocks, but only sun-dials; and further, an earlier time still in which sun-dials were not, nor any measurers of time of any kind. And this is distinct ground from that urged by Paley. For, besides holding that each of these contrivances must have had in turn an originator or contriver, it adds historic fact to philosophic inference. Geology takes up the master volume of the greatest of the natural theologians, and, after scanning its many apt instances of palpable design, drawn from the mechanism of existing plants and animals, authoritatively decides that not one of these plants or animals had begun to be in the times of the Chalk; nay, that they all date their origin from a period posterior to that of the Eocene. And the fact is, of course, corroborative of the inference. 'That well constructed edifice,' says the natural theologian, 'cannot be a mere *lusus naturae* [sport of nature], or chance combination of stones and wood; it must have been erected by a builder.' 'Yes,' remarks the geologist, 'it was erected some time during the last nine years. I passed the way ten years ago, and saw only a blank space where it now stands.' Nor does the established fact of an absolute beginning of organic being seem more pregnant with important consequences to the science of the natural theologian than the fact of the peculiar order in which they begin to be.

Absurd Atheistic Assertions

The importance of the now demonstrated fact, that all the living organisms which exist on earth had a beginning, and that a time was when they were not, will be best appreciated by those who know how much, and, it must be added, how unsuccessfully, writers on the evidences have laboured to convict of an absurdity, on this special head, the atheistic asserters of an infinite series of beings. Even Robert Hall (in his famous Sermon on Modern Infidelity) could but play, when he attempted grappling with the subject, upon the words *time* and *eternity*, and strangely argue, that as each member of an infinite series must have begun in *time*, while the succession itself was *eternal*, it was palpably absurd to ask us to believe in a *succession* of beings that was thus infinitely earlier than any of the beings themselves which composed the succession. And [Richard] Bentley, more perversely ingenious still, could assert, that as each of the individuals in an infinite series must have consisted of many parts,—that as each man in such a series, for instance, must have had ten fingers and ten toes,—it was palpably absurd to ask us to believe in an infinity which thus comprised many infinities,—ten infinities of fingers, for example, and ten infinities of toes. The infidels had the better in this part of the argument. It was surely easy enough to show against the great preacher on the one hand, that *time* in such a question is but a mere word that means simply a certain limited or definite period which had a beginning, whereas eternity means an unlimited and undefinable period which had no beginning;—that his seeming argument was no argument, but merely a sort of verbal play on this difference of signification in the words. . . .

A Fundamentally Different Creature

The lesson then concerning man, which we seem to gather from nature as revealed to us in our own consciousness and as externally observed, is that man differs fundamentally from every other creature which presents itself to our senses. That he differs absolutely, and therefore differs in origin also. . . .

He is manifestly "animal," with the reflex functions, feelings, desires, and emotions of an animal. Yet equally manifest is it that he has a special nature "looking before and after" which constitutes him "rational." Ruling, comprehending, interpreting, and completing much in nature, we also see in him that which manifestly points above nature.

St. George Mivart, *Lessons from Nature, as Manifested in Mind and Matter*, 1876.

A line infinitely produced is capable of being divided into—i.e., consists of—an infinity of given parts; a plane infinitely extended is capable of being divided into an infinity of infinitely divisible lines; and a cube—i.e., a solid infinitely expanded—is capable of being divided into an infinity of infinitely divisible planes. In fine, metaphysic theology furnishes no argument against the infinite series of the atheist. But geology does. Every plant and animal that now lives upon earth began to be during the great Tertiary period, and had no place among the plants and animals of the great

Secondary division. We can trace several of our existing quadrupeds, such as the badger, the hare, the fox, the red deer, and the wild cat, up till the earlier times of the Pleistocene; and not a few of our existing shells, such as the great pecten, the edible oyster, the whelk, and the Pelican's-foot shell, up till the greatly earlier times of the Coraline Crag. But at certain definite lines in the deposits of the past, representative of certain points in the course of time, the existing mammals and molluscs cease to appear, and we find their places occupied by other mammals and molluscs. Even such of our British shells as seem to have enjoyed as species the longest term of life cannot be traced beyond the times of the Pliocene deposits. We detect their remains in a perfect state of keeping in almost every shell-bearing bed, till we reach the Red and Coraline Crags, where we find them for the last time; and, on passing into older and deeper lying beds, we see their places taken by other shells, of species altogether distinct. . . .

A Beginning and an End

We thus know, that in certain periods, nearer or more remote, all our existing molluscs *began* to exist, and that they had no existence during the previous periods; which were, however, richer in animals of the same great molluscan group than the present time. Our British group of recent marine shells falls somewhat short of *four* hundred species; whereas the group characteristic of the older Miocene deposits, largely developed in those districts of France which border on the Bay of Biscay, and more sparingly in the south of England, near Yarmouth, comprises more than *six* hundred species. Nearly an equal number of still older shells have been detected in a single deposit of the Paris basin,—the *Calcaire grossier*; and a good many more in a more ancient formation still, the London Clay. On entering the Chalk, we find a yet older group of shells, wholly unlike any of the preceding ones; and in the Oolite and Lias yet other and different groups. And thus group proceeded group throughout all the Tertiary, Secondary, and Palaeozoic periods; some of them remarkable for the number of species which they contained, others for the profuse abundance of their individual specimens, until, deep in the rocks at the base of the Silurian system, we detect what seems to be the primordial group, beneath which only a single animal organism is known to occur,— the *Oldhamia antiqua*,—a plant-like zoophyte, akin apparently to some of our recent sertulariae. Each of the extinct groups had, we find, a beginning and an end;—there is not in the wide domain of physical science a more certain fact; and every species of the group which now exists had, like all their predecessors on the scene, their beginning also. The 'infinite series' of the atheists of former times can have no place in modern science: all organic existences, recent or extinct, vegetable or animal, have had their beginning;—there was a time when they were not. . . .

In order to prove the absurdity of 'man's conceiting himself the final cause of creation', proof of an ulterior cause,—of a higher end and aim,—must be adduced; and of aught higher than man, the geologist, as such, knows nothing. The long vista opened up by his science closes with the deputed lord of creation,—with man as he at present exists; and when, casting himself full upon revelation, the veil is drawn aside, and an infinitely grander vista stretches out before him into the future, he sees man—no longer, however, the natural, but the Divine man—occupying what is at once its terminal point and its highest apex. Such are some of the bearings of geologic science on the science of natural theology. Geology had disposed effectually and for ever of the oft-urged assumption of an infinite series; it deals as no other science could have dealt with the assertion of the sceptic, that creation is a 'singular effect.' . . . Yet further, it exhibits in a new aspect the argument founded on design, and invests the place and standing of man in *creation* with a peculiar significancy and importance, from its relation to the future. . . . The character of man as a fellow-worker with his Creator in the material province has still to be considered in the light of geology. Man was the first, and is still the only creature of whom we know anything, who has set himself to carry on and improve the work of the world's original framer,—who is a planter of woods, a tiller of fields, and a keeper of gardens,—and who carries on his work of mechanical contrivance on obviously the same principles as those on which the Divine designer wrought of old, and on which He works still. It may not be wholly unprofitable to acquaint ourselves, through evidence furnished by the rocks, with the remarkable fact, that the Creator imparted to man the Divine image before He united to man's the Divine nature.

"*[The Bible] is a book primarily of religion and morals. It is not a book of science.*"

Evolution Should Be Taught in Public Schools

Clarence Darrow

In 1925 the Tennessee legislature passed a law that outlawed teaching evolution in public schools. When biology teacher John T. Scopes challenged the law and taught evolution, the resulting trial became a national media event. Scopes was defended by a trio of lawyers: Clarence Darrow, the nation's foremost criminal lawyer at the time; Arthur Garfield Hays, counsel to the American Civil Liberties Union; and Dudley Field Malone, a liberal Catholic lawyer. In the following viewpoint, an excerpt from a speech at the trial, Darrow argues that the principles of intellectual and religious freedom are at stake. The trial concluded with Scopes being found guilty and fined $100.

As you read, consider the following questions:

1. For what reasons does Darrow object to using the Bible to guide science?
2. What caused the conflict in Tennessee over evolution, according to the author?
3. In Darrow's opinion, what dangerous precedent is set by making it a crime to teach evolution in schools?

Clarence Darrow, "You Can't Teach That!" speech given in Dayton, Tennessee on July 13, 1925 at the Scopes trial.

This case we have to argue is a case at law, and hard as it is for me to bring my mind to conceive it, almost impossible as it is to put my mind back into the sixteenth century, I am going to argue it as if it was serious, and as if it was a death struggle between two civilizations.

What Liberty Means

We have been informed that the legislature has the right to prescribe the course of study in the public schools. Within reason, they no doubt have. They could not prescribe a course of study, I am inclined to think, under your constitution, which omitted arithmetic and geography and writing. Neither, under the rest of the constitution, if it shall remain in force in the state, could they prescribe it if the course of study was only to teach religion; because several hundred years ago, when our people believed in freedom, and when no men felt so sure of their own sophistry that they were willing to send a man to jail who did not believe them, the people of Tennessee adopted a constitution, and they made it broad and plain, and said that the people of Tennessee should always enjoy religious freedom in its broadest terms. So I assume that no legislature could fix a course of study which violated that. For instance, suppose the legislature should say, "We think the religious privileges and duties of the citizens of Tennessee are much more important than education; we agree with the distinguished governor of the state, if religion must go, or learning must go, why, let learning go." I do not know how much it would have to go, but let it go. "And therefore, we will establish a course in the public schools of teaching that the Christian religion, as unfolded in the Bible, is true, and that every other religion, or mode or system of ethics, is false; and to carry that out, no person in the public schools shall be permitted to read or hear anything except Genesis, *Pilgrim's Progress*, Baxter's *Saint Rest*, and *In His Image*." Would that be constitutional? If it is, the Constitution is a lie and a snare and the people have forgotten what liberty means. . . .

What is the Bible? Your Honor, I have read it myself. I might read it more or more wisely. Others may understand it better. Others may think they understand it better when they do not. But in a general way I know what it is. I know there are millions of people in the world who look on it as being a divine book, and I have not the slightest objection to it. I know there are millions of people in the world who derive consolation in their times of trouble and solace in times of distress from the Bible. I would be pretty near the last one in the world to do anything or take any action to take it away. I feel just exactly the same toward the religious creed of every human being who lives. If anybody finds anything in this life that brings them consolation and health and

Mike Peters. Reprinted by permission of United Feature Syndicate, Inc.

happiness I think they ought to have it, whatever they get. I haven't any fault to find with them at all. But what is it?

The Bible is not one book. The Bible is made up of 66 books written over a period of about 1,000 years, some of them very early and some of them comparatively late. It is a book primarily of religion and morals. It is not a book of science. Never was and was never meant to be. Under it there is nothing prescribed that would tell you how to build a railroad or a steamboat or to make anything that would advance civilization. It is not a textbook or a text on chemistry. It is not big enough to be. It is not a book on geology; they knew nothing about geology. It is not a book on biology; they knew nothing about it. It is not a work on evolution; that is a mystery. It is not a work on astronomy. The man who looked out at the universe and studied the heavens had no thought but that the earth was the center of the universe. But we know better than that. We know that the sun is the center of the solar system. And that there are an infinity of other systems around about us. They thought the sun went around the earth and gave us light and gave us night. We know better. We know the earth turns on its axis to produce days and nights. They thought the earth was created 4,004 years before the Christian Era. We know better. I doubt if there is a person in Tennessee who does not know better. They told it the best they knew. And while suns may change all you may learn of chemistry, geometry and mathematics, there are no doubt certain primitive, elemental instincts in the organs of man that remain the same. He finds out what he can and yearns to know more and supplements his knowledge with hope and faith.

That is the province of religion and I haven't the slightest fault to find with it. Not the slightest in the world. One has one thought and one another, and instead of fighting each other as in the past, they should support and help each other. . . .

Let us see. Here is the state of Tennessee, living peacefully, surrounded by its beautiful mountains, each one of which contains evidence that the earth is millions of years old, people quiet, not all agreeing upon any one subject, and not necessary. If I could not live in peace with people I did not agree with, why, what? I could not live. Here is the state of Tennessee going along in its own business, teaching evolution for years, state boards handing out books on evolution, professors in colleges, teachers in schools, lawyers at the bar, physicians, ministers, a great percentage of the intelligent citizens of the state of Tennessee evolutionists, have not even thought it was necessary to leave their church. They believed that they could appreciate and understand and make their own simple and human doctrine of the Nazarene, to love their neighbor, be kindly with them, not to place a fine on and not try to send to jail some man who did not believe as they believed, and got along all right with it, too, until something happened. They have not thought it necessary to give up their church, because they believed that all that was here was not made on the first six days of creation, but that it had come by a slow process of developments extending over the ages, that one thing grew out of another. There are people who believed that organic life and the plants and the animals and man and the mind of man, and the religion of man are the subjects of evolution, and they have not got through, and that the God in which they believed did not finish creation on the first day, but that He is still working to make something better and higher still out of human beings, who are next to God, and that evolution has been working forever and will work forever—they believe it.

The Fundamentalists' Challenge

And along comes somebody who says "we have got to believe it as I believe it. It is a crime to know more than I know." And they publish a law to inhibit learning. Now, what is in the way of it? First, what does the law say? This law says that it shall be a criminal offense to teach in the public schools any account of the origin of man that is in conflict with the divine account in the Bible. It makes the Bible the yardstick to measure every man's intellect, to measure every man's intelligence and to measure every man's learning. Are your mathematics good? Turn to Elijah 1:2 [sic]. Is your philosophy good? See II Samuel 3. Is your astronomy good? See Genesis 2:7. Is your chemistry good? See—well, chemistry, see Deuteronomy 3:6, or anything that tells about

43

brimstone. Every bit of knowledge that the mind has must be submitted to a religious test. Now, let us see, it is a travesty upon language, it is a travesty upon justice, it is a travesty upon the constitution to say that any citizen of Tennessee can be deprived of his rights by a legislative body in the face of the constitution. . . .

All Sides of Every Question

Truth cannot be established by vote of the courts any more than by vote of the legislature. In the end, a sustained public opinion will have its way. We can hardly question the right of any people to decide how and what the youth in its schools shall be taught. We ought to contest not the right but the wisdom of any limitation which prevents the teacher from presenting all sides of every question, of opening up for the young mind every possible avenue to truth. In this day it ought not to be necessary—but it is—to argue for the scientific method, for the right to research and experiment, with the fearless publication of the findings to all, in school or out. Any other course will take us straight back to the Middle Ages, when scientific truth was determined by vote of ecclesiastical councils and the wisdom of Greece and Rome was lost amid casuistry, obscurantism, and the Inquisition.

The Nation, July 8, 1925.

If today you can take a thing like evolution and make it a crime to teach it in the public school, tomorrow you can make it a crime to teach it in the private school, and the next year you can make it a crime to teach it from the hustings or in the church. At the next session you may ban books and the newspapers. Soon you may set Catholic against Protestant and Protestant against Protestant, and try to foist your own religion upon the minds of men. If you can do one you can do the other. Ignorance and fanaticism is ever busy and needs feeding. Always it is feeding and gloating for more. Today it is the public-school teachers, tomorrow the private. The next day the preachers and the lecturers, the magazines, the books, the newspapers. After a while, Your Honor, it is the setting of man against man and creed against creed until, with flying banners and beating drums, we are marching backward to the glorious ages of the sixteenth century when bigots lighted fagots to burn the men who dared to bring any intelligence and enlightenment and culture to the human mind.

"Evolution . . . disputes the truth of the Bible account of man's creation and shakes faith in the Bible as the Word of God."

Evolution Should Not Be Taught in Public Schools

William Jennings Bryan

William Jennings Bryan was a candidate for the US presidency twice and was the secretary of state under Woodrow Wilson. Bryan, an evangelical Christian, was also a fervent opponent of evolution. When Tennessee teacher John T. Scopes was brought to trial for teaching evolution, Bryan offered his assistance to the prosecution. The following viewpoint is an excerpt from a concluding statement he planned to make to the jury. Both the defense and the prosecution agreed to forgo concluding statements, however. Byran's address was never delivered but was published after his death.

As you read, consider the following questions:

1. In what circumstances do states have the right to control what is taught in public schools, according to the author?
2. What are Bryan's objections to evolution?
3. How does the author believe teaching evolution affects children's minds?

William Jennings Bryan, proposed address in Scopes case, 1925.

Demosthenes, the greatest of ancient orators, in his "Oration on the Crown," the most famous of his speeches, began by supplicating the favor of all the gods and goddesses of Greece. If, in a case which involved only his own fame and fate, he felt justified in petitioning the heathen gods of his country, surely we, who deal with the momentous issues involved in this case, may well pray to the Ruler of the universe for wisdom to guide us in the performance of our several parts in this historic trial. . . .

Let us now separate the issues from the misrepresentations, intentional or unintentional, that have obscured both the letter and the purpose of the law. This is not an interference with freedom of conscience. A teacher can think as he pleases and worship God as he likes, or refuse to worship God at all. He can believe in the Bible or discard it; he can accept Christ or reject Him. This law places no obligations or restraints upon him. And so with freedom of speech; he can, so long as he acts as an individual, say anything he likes on any subject. This law does not violate any right guaranteed by any constitution to any individual. It deals with the defendant, not as an individual, but as an employee, an official or public servant, paid by the state, and therefore under instructions from the state.

State Control of Public Schools

The right of the state to control the public schools is affirmed in the recent decision in the Oregon case, which declares that the state can direct what shall be taught and also forbid the teaching of anything "manifestly inimical to the public welfare." The above decision goes even farther and declares that the parent not only has the right to guard the religious welfare of the child, but is in duty bound to guard it. That decision fits this case exactly. The state had a right to pass this law, and the law represents the determination of the parents to guard the religious welfare of their children.

It need hardly be added that this law did not have its origin in bigotry. It is not trying to force any form of religion on anybody. The majority is not trying to establish a religion or to teach it—it is trying to protect itself from the effort of an insolent minority to force irreligion upon the children under the guise of teaching science. What right has a little irresponsible oligarchy of self-styled "intellectuals" to demand control of the schools of the United States, in which, 25,000,000 children are being educated at an annual expense of nearly $2,000,000,000? . . .

Religion and Learning

Religion is not hostile to learning; Christianity has been the greatest patron learning has ever had. But Christians know that "the fear of the Lord is the beginning of wisdom" now just as it has been in the past, and they therefore oppose the teaching of guesses that encourage godlessness among the students.

Neither does Tennessee undervalue the service rendered by science. The Christian men and women of Tennessee know how deeply mankind is indebted to science for benefits conferred by the discovery of the laws of nature and by the designing of machinery for the utilization of these laws. Give science a fact and it is not only invincible, but it is of incalculable service to man. If one is entitled to draw from society in proportion to the service that he renders to society, who is able to estimate the reward earned by those who have given to us the use of steam, the use of electricity, and enabled us to utilize the weight of water that flows down the mountainside? Who will estimate the value of the service rendered by those who invented the phonograph, the telephone and the radio? Or, to come more closely to our home life, how shall we recompense those who gave us the sewing machine, the harvester, the threshing machine, the tractor, the automobile and the method now employed in making artificial ice? The department of medicine also opens an unlimited field for invaluable service. Typhoid and yellow fever are not feared as they once were. Diphtheria and pneumonia have been robbed of some of their terrors, and a high place on the scroll of fame still awaits the discoverer of remedies for arthritis, cancer, tuberculosis and other dread diseases to which mankind is heir.

On the Side of Religion

Why, if the court please, have we not the right to interpret our Bible as we see fit? Why, have we not the right to bar the door to science when it comes within the four walls of God's church upon this earth? Have we not the right? Who says that we have not? Show me the man who will challenge it. We have the right to pursue knowledge—we have the right to participate in scientific investigation, but, if the court please, when science strikes at that upon which man's eternal hope is founded, then I say the foundation of man's civilization is about to crumble. They say this is a battle between religion and science. If it is, I want to serve notice now, in the name of the great God, that I am on the side of religion.

A.T. Stewart, speech at *Scopes* trial, July 16, 1925.

Christianity welcomes truth from whatever source it comes, and is not afraid that any real truth from any source can interfere with the divine truth that comes by inspiration from God Himself. It is not scientific truth to which Christians object, for true science is classified knowledge, and nothing therefore can be scientific unless it is true.

Evolution is not truth; it is merely an hypothesis—it is millions of guesses strung together. It had not been proven in the days of Darwin; he expressed astonishment that with two or three million species it had been impossible to trace any species to any other species. It had not been proven in the days of Huxley, and it has not been proven up to today. It is less than four years ago that Prof. Bateson came all the way from London to Canada to tell the American scientists that every effort to trace one species to another had failed—every one. He said he still had faith in evolution, but had doubts about the origin of species. But of what value is evolution if it cannot explain the origin of species? While many scientists accept evolution as if it were a fact, they all admit, when questioned, that no explanation has been found as to how one species developed into another.

Darwin suggested two laws, sexual selection and natural selection. Sexual selection has been laughed out of the class room, and natural selection is being abandoned, and no new explanation is satisfactory even to scientists. Some of the more rash advocates of evolution are wont to say that evolution is as firmly established as the law of gravitation or the Copernican theory. The absurdity of such a claim is apparent when we remember that anyone can prove the law of gravitation by throwing a weight into the air, and that anyone can prove the roundness of the earth by going around it, while no one can prove evolution to be true in any way whatever. . . .

The Power of Christ

But while the wisest scientists cannot prove a pushing power, such as evolution is supposed to be, there is a lifting power that any child can understand. The plant lifts the mineral up into a higher world, and the animal lifts the plants up into a world still higher. So, it has been reasoned by analogy, man rises, not by a power within him, but only when drawn upward by a higher power. There is a spiritual gravitation that draws all souls toward heaven, just as surely as there is a physical force that draws all matter on the surface of the earth towards the earth's center. Christ is our drawing power; He said, "I, if I be lifted up from the earth, will draw all men unto Me," and His promise is being fulfilled daily all over the world. . . .

It is not a laughing matter when one considers that evolution not only offers no suggestions as to a Creator but tends to put the creative act so far away as to cast doubt upon creation itself. And while it is shaking faith in God as a beginning, it is also creating doubt as to a heaven at the end of life. Evolutionists do not feel that it is incumbent upon them to show how life began or at what point in their long-drawn-out scheme of changing species man became endowed with hope and promise of immortal life. God may be a matter of indifference to the evolutionists and a life beyond may have no charm for them, but the mass of mankind will continue to worship their Creator and continue to find comfort in the promise of their Savior that He has gone to prepare a place for them. Christ has made of death a narrow, star-lit strip between the companionship of yesterday and the reunion of tomorrow; evolution strikes out the stars and deepens the gloom that enshrouds the tomb. . . .

A Threat to the Bible's Truth

Our first indictment against evolution is that it disputes the truth of the Bible account of man's creation and shakes faith in the Bible as the Word of God. This indictment we prove by comparing the processes described as evolutionary with the text of Genesis. It not only contradicts the Mosaic record as to the beginning of human life, but it disputes the Bible doctrine of reproduction according to kind—the greatest scientific principle known.

Our second indictment is that the evolutionary hypothesis, carried to its logical conclusion, disputes every vital truth of the Bible. Its tendency, natural, if not inevitable, is to lead those who really accept it, first to agnosticism and then to atheism. Evolutionists attack the truth of the Bible, not openly at first, but by using weasel-words like "poetical," "symbolical" and "allegorical" to suck the meaning out of the inspired record of man's creation. . . .

Who Is the Ignoramus?

Evolution is not a theory, but a hypothesis. . . . Today there is not a scientist in all the world who can trace one single species to any other, and yet they call us ignoramuses and bigots because we do not throw away our Bible and accept it as proved that out of two or three million species not a one is traceable to another. And they say that evolution is a fact when they cannot prove that one species came from another, and if there is such a thing, all species must have come, commencing as they say, commencing in that one lonely cell down there in the bottom of the ocean that just evolved and evolved until it got to be a man. And they cannot find a single species that came from another, and yet they demand that we allow them to teach this stuff to our children, that they may come home with their imaginary family tree and scoff at their mother's and father's Bible.

William Jennings Bryan, speech at *Scopes* trial, July 16, 1925.

How can any teacher tell his students that evolution does not tend to destroy his religious faith? How can an honest teacher conceal from his students the effect of evolution upon Darwin himself? And is it not stranger still that preachers who advocate evolution never speak of Darwin's loss of faith, due to his belief in evolution? The parents of Tennessee have reason enough to fear the effect of evolution on the minds of their children. Belief in evolution cannot bring to those who hold such a belief any compensation for the loss of faith in God, trust in the Bible, and belief in the supernatural character of Christ. It is belief in evolution that has caused so many scientists and so many Christians to reject the miracles of the Bible, and then give up, one after another, every vital truth of Christianity. They finally cease to pray and sunder the tie that binds them to their Heavenly Father.

The miracle should not be a stumbling block to any one. It raises but three questions: First, could God perform a miracle? Yes, the God who created the universe can do anything He wants to with it. He can temporarily suspend any law that He has made or He may employ higher laws that we do not understand.

Second—Would God perform a miracle? To answer that question in the negative one would have to know more about God's plans and purposes than a finite mind can know, and yet some are so wedded to evolution that they deny that God would perform a miracle merely because a miracle is inconsistent with evolution.

If we believe that God can perform a miracle and might desire to do so, we are prepared to consider with open mind the third question, namely, Did God perform the miracles recorded in the Bible? The same evidence that establishes the authority of the Bible establishes the truth of the record of miracles performed. . . .

Let us, then, hear the conclusion of the whole matter. Science is a magnificent material force, but it is not a teacher of morals. It can perfect machinery, but it adds no moral restraints to protect society from the misuse of the machine. It can also build gigantic intellectual ships, but it constructs no moral rudders for the control of storm-tossed human vessels. It not only fails to supply the spiritual element needed but some of its unproven hypotheses rob the ship of its compass and thus endangers its cargo. . . .

Christianity Must Be Defended

It is for the jury to determine whether this attack upon the Christian religion shall be permitted in the public schools of Tennessee by teachers employed by the state and paid out of the public treasury. This case is no longer local, the defendant ceases to play an important part. The case has assumed the proportions of a battle-royal between unbelief that attempts to speak through so-called science and the defenders of the Christian faith, speaking through the legislators of Tennessee.

a critical thinking activity

Evaluating Primary Sources

Historians typically distinguish between primary and secondary sources. Primary sources are documents or artifacts produced by the people witnessing or participating in an event. The account written by a person who saw people rioting for bread during the French Revolution would be a primary source. Secondary sources are based on primary sources—they explain or interpret these events. History textbooks are secondary sources.

Primary sources are essential to the study of history. They are our basis for what we know about the past. A primary source may tell what happened, how people felt about it, and what the consequences were. But just as one must be careful when reading accounts about today's events, careful historians and critical readers must be discriminating when they use primary sources.

It is helpful to consider the following concepts when evaluating historical documents:

a. author's position to observe—two factors should be considered: was the author an eyewitness to what is being described? Eyewitness accounts can be the most objective and valuable or they can be tainted with bias. Second, how is the author an authority on the subject? Are the author's conclusions based on careful study or are they general statements?

b. hidden agenda—the author may purposely or unwittingly tell only part of the story. The excerpt may seem to be a straightforward description of a situation, yet the author has selected which facts, details, and language to record. These may have been chosen to advance professional or political goals or to defend a firmly-held belief.

c. bias—the author's statements may be based on personal bias, rather than a reasoned conclusion based on facts. One clue that this is happening is noticing when the author uses exaggerated language or quickly dismisses opponents' arguments.

These concepts are not meant to suggest that primary sources are invalid. Even if the author tries to advance a hidden agenda, the source can give essential information about the author's time and culture.

Below are excerpts paraphrased from the viewpoints in this chapter. The author's name and the viewpoint number follow each excerpt. Evaluate the following sources using the three concepts listed above. Base your answers on what you know from reading the viewpoints themselves and from the biographical information about the author on the first page of the viewpoint. *Mark the letter(s) of one or more of the above concepts that should be evaluated to determine the validity of the excerpt.* It is important to remember that a historian would not determine a source's reliability based on so short an excerpt. This is done here only to offer practice in using this skill. Two examples are done for you, with explanations for the answers.

Examples:

All living things have much in common, in their chemical composition, their laws of growth, and their liability to injurious influences. Therefore I cannot doubt the theory of descent with modification [evolution].—*Charles Darwin*, viewpoint 3

Answer: a, c. Darwin is in a good position to make this observation: as a biologist, he spent years researching and studying his theory before publishing it. This extract is reasoned, not biased—he cites evidence to support his conclusion.

Evolutionists attack the truth of the Bible, not honestly or openly, but by using weazel-words like "poetical," "symbolical," and "allegorical" to suck the meaning out of the inspired record of man's creation.—*William Jennings Bryan*, viewpoint 6

Answer: c, maybe b. Bryan's statement seems to be based on bias. He uses inflammatory expressions—"weazel-words" and 'suck the meaning out of the inspired record" in addition to dismissing evolutionists as sneaky and dishonest. It could be argued that since he is a lawyer defending banning the teaching of evolution, he has a hidden agenda in this excerpt.

1. To ban the teaching that the sun is the center of the universe, it would be necessary to ban astronomy. It would be necessary to forbid men to look at the heavens, in order that they might not see Mars and Venus sometimes quite near the earth and sometimes distant.—*Galileo Galilei*, viewpoint 1

2. The proposition that the sun is the centre of the world and does not move from its place is absurd and false philosophically. The proposition that the earth is not the centre of the world and that it moves is equally absurd.—*The Roman Curia*, viewpoint 2

3. At certain definite lines in the deposits of the past, the existing mammals and mollusks cease to appear. Our British shells cannot be traced beyond the Pliocene deposits. In certain time periods, all our existing mollusks began to exist, and they had no existence in the previous period.—*Hugh Miller*, viewpoint 4

4. If evolution is banned, preachers, lecturers, books, will be censored. After a while, creed against creed will be set against each other until, with flying banners and beating drums, we are marching backward to the sixteenth century when bigots lighted faggots to burn the men who dared to bring intelligence and culture to the human mind.—*Clarence Darrow*, viewpoint 5

Are Science and Religion Compatible?

Chapter Preface

In Lewis Carroll's book *Through the Looking Glass,* the Queen of Hearts admonishes Alice for not believing in impossible things: "I dare say you haven't had much practice. When I was your age I always did it for half an hour a day. Why, sometimes I've believed as many as six impossible things before breakfast." Alice and the Queen were not talking about science and religion, but their contrasting philosophies—Alice's skepticism and the Queen's belief in the impossible—echo the debate over the compatibility of science and religion.

One view is that science and religion are not compatible; they are based on two very different perceptions of reality. Religion is a field based on belief in impossible things; it is founded on faith in improbable events, such as the birth of a savior who died and returned to life. Science is based on extensive experiments leading to proven conclusions; scientific facts are accepted as such only after data has been collected and repeated experiments have proven their validity. Therefore, the conclusion drawn by those who hold this separatist view is that science and religion inevitably clash.

The opposing view is that science and religion are compatible and share many characteristics. Religious believers contend that religion, like science, has objective proof for its conclusions. Religious faith tends to be based on real-life experiences and can be deepened by reading venerated sacred writings, such as the Old and New Testaments, the Koran, or the Vedas. And just as skeptics may criticize religion for its subjectivity, many scholars argue that science, too, can be subjective. In 1912, a skull, jawbone, and tooth were found in a quarry near Sussex, England. The three items had features that convinced scientists they had proven the theory of evolution—they believed the finding (named Piltdown Man) was the missing link between primates and humans. More than thirty years later, newly developed tests on the remains indicated that the bones were from the Middle Ages. They had been stained with iron to look old and the tooth had been filed and painted brown. Why did the scientists in 1912 fail to notice the iron stain and the paint when they had tests to identify them? Many have concluded that the scientists' subjective desire to prove evolution superseded their commitment to objectivity. These examples show that both science and religion depend to some extent on belief in impossible things, hence they may be compatible when both sides acknowledge that fact.

The following chapter contains seven viewpoints that discuss the relationship between science and religion, an issue that has long divided philosophers.

"The world of belief and the world of science are complementary, interdependent worlds."

Science and Religion Are Complementary

Harald Fritzsch

Harald Fritzsch is a West German physicist who teaches at the University of Munich and at the Max Planck Institute. In the following viewpoint, Fritzsch defines science's role as that of exploring and explaining natural phenomena. But describing phenomena does not give a complete picture of the world, he contends. Fritzsch concludes that religion provides an intuitive sense of the unity and purpose of the cosmos.

As you read, consider the following questions:

1. What does Fritzsch define as "religiosity"?
2. What function does the author believe religiosity performs?
3. How do Eastern religions express an understanding of the universe that complements science, according to Fritzsch?

What about the existence of God in our world of science? Is there room for God in a world that seemingly can dispense with His intervention in the processes of the universe? And what about God if the universe of the mind ultimately also disappears and nothing is left but an increasingly hot or cold gas of photons, neutrinos, and other particles? Are religion and science an irreconcilable contradiction?

Two Approaches to Reality

I do not believe that such a contradiction exists nor ever existed. The scientific method of exploration concerns the creation of appropriate concepts to describe natural phenomena and the establishment of connections between these phenomena. We feel our way along this "road of ideas," along chains of causality. We open up reality by attempting to construct a logical "road network" free of contradictions, one which we then clap on to reality. I . . . [caution] the reader against confusing the network of scientific concepts—our picture of reality—with the real world. Many of the mistakes and much of the tragically flawed reasoning of our time are based on just this fallacy. The world is more than merely such a network of roads. It is a continuum that cannot be completely encompassed by even the most finely spun net of one-dimensional "roads of causality." Only through the intuitive feeling of the unity of the cosmos will we be able to glimpse the continuum outside the "roads." This intuitive sense for the unity of the universe in my opinion warrants the designation *religiosity*. . . .

I do not think of science and religion as adversaries. Quite the contrary. They are two complementary sides of our view of the cosmos. They are interdependent. In Einstein's words: "Science without religion is lame, religion without science, blind."

When I speak of the complementarity of science and religion I do not mean to imply that science has made religion obsolete. Naive reliance on progress is a thing of the past. Gone are the days when we thought that accumulating knowledge and harnessing nature would bring us more profound insight into the meaning of life and lead automatically to a better world. Nothing is worse than the sort of vulgar belief that sees the meaning of human existence *only* in the acquisition of material values, the permanent expansion of technical possibilities and an ever deeper involvement of science in all aspects of life.

Death of the Universe

We have seen that the universe forms a unity, that it has a history, and that it will die. I must confess that to a large extent the appeal the cosmos holds for me lies in these aspects. Since Einstein and Hubble and the discoveries of particle physicists, the universe has become less alien to us.

56

We know that the evolution of the cosmos during the past 20 billion years has been a continuous process marked by the creation of new structures as well as the death of old ones. Nothing lasts forever. Death, including our own death, is an intrinsic part of the processes taking place in the eighth epoch.

Finding Meaning in Life

Religiosity is well able to lend meaning to life and provide a structure for ethical values and norms. What [French philosophers Albert] Camus and [Jacques] Monod failed to find in the cold, rational world of quarks and galaxies can be found in the necessity for human beings to see themselves as part of the cosmos. We are neither rulers nor slaves of the world surrounding us, but are embedded in the inexhaustible continuum of possibilities and relations the eighth epoch holds out to us. We are the product of that epoch and carry within us the traces of its varied history since the Big Bang. At the same time our actions allow us to shape the course of history. All our actions are unique in the cosmos, just as every second is unique. Therein lies the meaning: in living; in the experience of the cosmic unity that transcends the individual; in the self-consciousness of the acting individual aware of his or her limits and from this awareness deriving the confidence essential to the acceptance of life.

Incomplete Enterprises

Science and religion are complementary and dialectical. Whatever their histories, neither is logically dependent on the other; and yet neither, despite the integrity of each, is complete without the other. Science discovers intelligible causes, but limps at discovering meanings; religion discovers intelligible meanings, but defers to science about causes. Both are theory-laden enterprises that need ever and critically to review their driving assumptions.

Holmes Rolston III, *Commonweal*, May 22, 1987.

God is therefore also the unity of the universe in its eighth epoch, which reveals itself to us in diversity. He, like ourselves, is a part of the eighth epoch. Thus if we understand *eternal* in its temporal-physical sense, there is no eternal God, just as there is no eternal life.

Eastern Religions

Starting from this vantage point, when I look at the religions of the world I am struck by the similarity between this conception and the ideas of the major Eastern religions, of Hinduism, Buddhism, and Taoism. Hinduism has thousands of gods, all of them ultimately different embodiments of one and the same divine reality expressed in the unity of the cosmos. The most famous of these gods, Shiva, is the god of creation and annihilation—the symbol of the dynamics of life processes.

Buddhism's road to self-realization, the way to the achievement of a divine state of consciousness, of Nirvana, is, like the evolution of the universe, eightfold. Detachment from the individual, the experience of wholeness, are essential features of Buddhism.

It is illuminating to find that the Taoism of ancient China preempted significant insights of modern science. Thus Taoism teaches that reality is constant change marked by the emergence of stable structures. Taoism sees the dynamics of the world as a constant interchange between conflicting positions, between yin and yang, as expressed by this aphorism in Lao Tzu's *Way*:

> To remain whole, be twisted!
> To become straight, let yourself be bent.
> To become full, be hollow.
> Be tattered, that you may be renewed.

All Eastern religions have in common an awareness of the unity of the cosmos and its significance. They recognize that the division, or "dissection," of the cosmos is a human construct, not an inherent property of the universe. Hinduism even goes so far as to see the human trait of differentiating, of categorizing, as a sickness to be cured through meditation.

Christianity

A comparison between Eastern religions and Christianity points up an interesting difference. The suffering individual seeking forgiveness, one of the leitmotifs of Christianity, plays only a minor role in Eastern religions. The God of Christianity has human features; He concerns Himself with the suffering and sorrows of the individual. Therein lie both the power and success as well as the weakness of Christianity. I believe the Eastern religions can be brought into harmony with the insights of modern science; I see problems with Christianity. The God of Spinoza and Einstein, the God of unity in diversity, is quite compatible with the Eastern religious concept of God, but not so readily with the God of Christianity.

For almost four hundred years, since the Vatican's trial of Galileo, science and the Church have been at odds. . . . Today's world is also the world of science and technology. It is only a question of time before everyone, not only those involved in research, will become concerned about the relationship of science and religion. The time of reciprocal exclusion, or division into discrete competencies, is past.

The world of belief and the world of science are complementary, interdependent worlds. To draw a sharp dividing line between them, as many theologians have done in the past and still do today, is absurd.

"Science and religion are diametrically opposed at their deepest philosophical levels."

Science and Religion Are Opponents

Norman F. Hall and Lucia K.B. Hall

In the following viewpoint, Norman F. Hall and Lucia K.B. Hall contrast science's view of the universe with religion's view. They assert that religion cannot be reconciled with science because it assumes the existence of a supernatural Being who guides the planet. This assumption is a direct contradiction of science's assumption that research can decipher the workings of the universe, they argue. Norman F. Hall is a scientist at the Scripps Institute of Oceanography in San Diego, California. Writer Lucia K.B. Hall has done professional research in biochemistry.

As you read, consider the following questions:

1. According to the authors, what assumption do religious persons make about the universe?
2. What do the Halls mean when they write that the scientist must be able to "trust the universe"?
3. What values and ethics does science contain, according to the authors?

Norman F. Hall and Lucia K.B. Hall, "Is the War Between Science and Religion Over?" This article first appeared in THE HUMANIST issue of May/June 1986 and is reprinted by permission.

The CBS television news report, "For Our Times," which covered a two-week conference on "Faith, Science, and the Future" held at the Massachusetts Institute of Technology, left the viewer with the feeling that the long conflict between science and religion is at an end. Hundreds of scientists and theologians gathered to discuss issues of science and ethics and proceeded from the assumption that science and religion were two non-conflicting bodies of knowledge, equally valuable complementary paths leading toward an ultimate understanding of the world and our place in it. The conflicts of the past were said to be due to excessive zeal and misunderstanding on both sides. Peaceful coexistence and even a measure of syncretism are now assumed to be possible as long as each concedes to the other's authority in their separate worlds of knowledge: that of matter and facts for science, and that of the spirit and values for religion.

Nonsense

Let us be blunt. While it may appear open-minded, modest, and comforting to many, this conciliatory view is nonsense. Science and religion are diametrically opposed at their deepest philosophical levels. And, because the two worldviews make claims to the same intellectual territory—that of the origin of the universe and humankind's relationship to it—conflict is inevitable.

Transcending the Material World

It is possible, of course, to define a nonsupernatural "religious" worldview that is not in conflict with science. But in all of its traditional Western forms, the *supernatural* religious worldview makes the assumption that the universe and its inhabitants have been designed and created—and, in many cases, are guided—by "forces" or beings which transcend the material world. The material world is postulated to reflect a mysterious plan originating in these forces or beings, a plan which is knowable by humans only to the extent that it has been revealed to an exclusive few. Criticizing or questioning any part of this plan is strongly discouraged, especially where it touches on questions of morals or ethics.

Science, on the other hand, assumes that there are no transcendent, immaterial forces and that all forces which do exist within the universe behave in an ultimately objective or random fashion. The nature of these forces, and all other scientific knowledge, is revealed only through human effort in a dynamic process of inquiry. The universe as a whole is assumed to be neutral to human concerns and to be open to any and all questions, even those concerning human ethical relationships. Such a universe does not come to us with easy answers; we must come to it and be prepared to work hard.

In order to understand how scientific observations are made, let's follow a hypothetical scientist into his or her laboratory. Suppose this scientist's task is to measure the amount of protein in a biological fluid—a common procedure in research laboratories, hospitals, and school science classes. The scientist will proceed by carefully measuring out into test tubes both several known volumes of the fluid and also several different volumes of a "standard" solution he or she has prepared by dissolving a weighed quantity of pure protein. The scientist will add water to bring all the tubes to the same volume and then add a reagent which reacts with protein to produce a blue color. After the solutions in all the test tubes have reacted for a specified period of time, the scientist will measure the intensity of the blue color with a spectrophotometer. By comparing the color intensity of the unknown solutions with that of the known standard protein solutions, he or she will be able to calculate how much standard protein is needed to produce the same color reaction as the unknown, and this, the scientist will conclude, is the amount of protein in the unknown sample.

Natural Adversaries

Now that science has won immense prestige and has become a major factor of social progress, the experts of religion are inclined to forget the forms of damning it that were used in the past and agree to all kinds of compromises. But no matter what forms the relations between science and religion take, it is clear to any sober-minded person that religion has always struggled and continues to struggle against science as its natural adversary.

Yuri Pishchik, *American Atheist*, March 1987.

What our hypothetical scientist has done is to perform a controlled experiment. He or she must report it honestly and completely, including a description or a reference to the method. He or she must also be prepared to say that all variables which could have affected the reported result, to the best of his or her knowledge and belief, have been kept constant (for example, by using a water bath to maintain a constant temperature) or have been measured (as were the different volumes of the unknown solution and standard solution) or are random (measurement errors or perhaps proteinaceous dust motes from the surrounding air). This is the essence of the scientific method.

Clearly, such a controlled experiment would be impossible if our scientist were required to entertain the possibility that some factor exists that can affect the color in the test tubes but which can never be controlled in these ways—a factor that cannot be held constant, cannot be measured by any physical means, and cannot be said to act randomly. But that is exactly what the religious, supernaturalist worldview *does* require. Untestable, unmeasurable, and nonrandom occurrences are commonplace in all supernatural religions and pseudosciences.

Fundamental Incompatibilities

This fundamental incompatibility between the supernaturalism of traditional religion and the experimental method of science has been, nevertheless, remarkably easy to dismiss. The *findings* of science over the past three centuries have been eagerly welcomed for their practical value. The *method*, however, has been treated with suspicion, even scorn. It has been perceived as being responsible for revealing the material workings of ever more of the mysteries of life which used to inspire religious awe. From the point of view of the religious believer, it has seemed as though the goal of science has been to push belief in the supernatural to ever more remote redoubts until it might disappear entirely.

This is not, and cannot be, the goal of science. Rather, a nonmysterious, understandable, material universe is the basic *assumption* behind all of science. Scientists do not chart their progress with ghost-busting in mind. Naturalism, or materialist monism, is not so much the product of scientific research as it is its starting point. In order for science to work, scientists must assume that the universe they are investigating is playing fair, that it is not capable of conscious deceit, that is does not play favorites, that miracles do not happen, and that there is no arcane or spiritual knowledge open only to a few. Only by making the assumption of materialist monism will the scientist be able to *trust* the universe, to assume that although its workings are blind and random it is for this very reason that they can be depended upon, and that what is learned in science can, to some degree, be depended upon to reflect reality.

The Unifying Theory

As evolution is the unifying theory for biology, so naturalism is the unifying theory for all of science. In his book, *Chance and Necessity*, biochemist Jacques Monod called this basic assumption "the postulate of objectivity," since it assumes that the universe as a whole is dispassionate of, indifferent to, and unswayed by human concerns and beliefs about its nature. Its inverse—in which the universe is passionately involved in, partial to, and swayed by human concerns and beliefs about its nature—is the basic assumption that underlies the supernatural, religious worldview. We call it the "postulate of design."

The postulate of a purposefully designed universe, as we have seen, destroys any meaning we might hope to find in the experimental *method* of science. But in doing, it also ensures that it will never be incompatible with any of the *findings* of science.

This ability of the supernatural view to adjust itself to any finite set of facts has, ironically, made it seem easy to accept both the findings of science and the consolations of spiritualism. Scientists, as human beings, are susceptible to the temptation of these comforts. Some believe that the world of the supernatural lies just beyond where they are performing their controlled experiments, although they usually feel that it is even more evident in fields other than their own. However, we need not reject their results. As long as they are honest—reporting not only their conclusions but also their methods and reasoning—such nonmaterialist scientists can still contribute to the progress of science in their own fields of study.

Scientific Integrity

The issue at stake here is whether or not our worldview is to possess consistency and integrity. Science has worked so well and has been so successful that it is difficult, if not impossible, to live in the modern world while rejecting its findings. But by accepting those findings as a free bounty—while rejecting the hard assumptions and hard work that made them possible—the supernaturalist embraces a lie.

The Flagrant Lie

For the first time in history a civilization is trying to shape itself while clinging desperately to the animist tradition to justify its values, and at the same time abandoning it as the source of knowledge, of *truth*. For their moral bases the "liberal" societies of the West still teach—or pay lip-service to—a disgusting farrago of Judeo-Christian religiosity, scientistic progressism, belief in the "natural" rights of man, and utilitarian pragmatism. . . . All these systems rooted in animism exist at odds with objective knowledge, face away from truth, and are strangers and fundamentally *hostile* to science, which they are pleased to make use of but for which they do not otherwise care. The divorce is so great, the lie so flagrant, that it afflicts and rends the conscience of anyone provided with some element of culture, a little intelligence, and spurred by that moral questioning which is the source of all creativity.

Jacques Monod, *Chance and Necessity*, 1971.

It is often claimed that science can say nothing about values and ethics because it can only tell us what *is*—not what ought to be. But once again this is a case of attempting to divorce the findings from the method of science. Properly understood, science tells us not only what is but also *how we must behave if we are to understand what is*. Science has succeeded as a cooperative human effort by asserting the belief that the universe can only be understood through the values of integrity and truth-telling. In the process it has *become* a system of values, and it has provided humankind with a language which transcends cultural boundaries and connects us in a highly satisfying way to all the observable universe. It also has the potential to be used as the basis for a workable and profoundly satisfying system of ethics. Indeed, it *must* be so used if we are to accept its findings without self-deceit.

Overcoming Ignorance

A naturalistic system of ethics is not likely to be popular, however, until science can overcome the currently evident public attitude of ignorance and hostility. In response to a recent *San Diego Union* story outlining new developments in cosmological theory, a reader pointed out that "God is in control of the universe, and the sooner these so-called scientists realize this, they will not need to invent hocus-pocus 'dark or unseen matter' as a man-made explanation instead of acknowledging the true source of all things, the all-powerful, omnipotent, omnipresent God, the creator."

He's right, of course. Accept the supernatural and the hard work of making and testing theories becomes a pointless enterprise, along with all human-made explanations and meaning. But if we allow such myths to limit the scope and uses of science, we will do so to our own peril and shame.

What Started the Clock

In an article in the October 4, 1985, issue of *Science*, cosmologist Steven Weinberg said that, even if science manages to trace the materialist explanation back to the first ten-billionth of a second of the existence of the universe, we still don't know what started the clock. "It may be that we shall never know," he wrote, "just as we may never learn the ultimate laws of nature. But I wouldn't bet on it."

Thank you, Professor Weinberg. We needed that.

"Christianity is scientifically unsupported and probably unsupportable, philosophically suspect at best and disreputable at worst, and historically fraudulent."

Science Should Replace Religion

Delos B. McKown

Over the past century many scholars have disputed religion's relevance to modern life. The following viewpoint is by Delos B. McKown, a philosophy professor at Auburn University. McKown argues that science has disproved many religious claims and made religious faith outmoded. Traditionally religious Americans are torn between religion and science, McKown believes. This conflict has led to fundamentalist backlash against science, he contends, because science has proven to be the new truth.

As you read, consider the following questions:

1. What contrast does McKown see between the religion believed by most people and the religion that some scholars believe can be reconciled with science?
2. What two religious principles has science destroyed, according to the author?
3. Why does McKown believe that Christianity is historically fraudulent?

Delos B. McKown, "Science vs. Religion in Future Constitutional Conflicts," *Free Inquiry*, Summer 1984. Reprinted with permission.

The Founding Fathers gave us an utterly secular Constitution, yet one that protects the free exercise of religion more surely than the free exercise of science. Thomas Jefferson and James Madison, though they were cool toward much in religion, were fervent on the behalf of freedom, including the freedom to be or not to be religious. Cognizant of past and present threats to religion from government, they were also aware of past and present threats to government from religion. The religion clauses of the First Amendment took shape accordingly.

Although Jefferson and Madison were aware of the sectarian strife that would simmer, if not boil over, in a free society, they were content that it would be so, hoping only that it would nullify itself politically. It never occurred to them that progress in "science and useful arts" (i.e., technology) would, one day, so provoke and dismay religion as to be endangered by it. As deists, they believed the study of nature to be the surest way to the creator's mind. Thus, the major premise of religion, God's existence, seemed inviolable by science. Moreover, perceiving no danger to science from religion, our forefathers took no preventive measures. The unforeseen result is that religion is constitutionally favored over science. . . .

Religion's Threat to Science

Even as our forefathers foresaw no threat of science versus religion worth precluding, so multitudes today perceive none either, believing that science and religion, properly understood, do not conflict. No less a scientist than Stephen Jay Gould has endorsed this mistake. Although he did not show how a true religion (presumably compatible with science) can be extracted from the swarming mass of false religions, one can guess what it would involve—namely, a creator who made the world as it is because of his purpose(s) for it. But, this is no more than deism.

Deism, however, is not a proper paradigm for most existing religions. It is too spare, ideal, and rarefied to resemble very much the garden varieties in which people actually believe. The price Gould pays in supplying a religion that does not conflict with science is the price of extreme attenuation, of draining religion of its blood and guts, as it were.

Viewed from a religion with guts, a religion whose blood is boiling at present, i.e., from the standpoint of American fundamentalism, there is no conflict between science and religion either. Of course the price science would have to pay in making good on this absurd claim is nothing less than its own dismemberment. An astronomer recently estimated that if creationist claims were true, about 50 percent of his introductory course in astronomy would have to be deleted, a disaster approximating that with which creationism threatens biology. Geology would also be gutted, and archaeology and anthropology would suffer substantially, as would much, if not most, of the study of prehistory. Any aspect of science relying on radiometric dating techniques would be emasculated, and not even linguistics would go unscathed.

Real Religion

People often have trouble comprehending that, for many believers, real religion, if not true religion (whatever that might be), involves some form or another of scriptural literalism. For multitudes of Christians, belief in the inerrancy of the Bible is, religiously, on a par with belief in the existence of God and the redemption of Christ. There are, of course, ways in which science and religion cannot conflict that involve unrelated functions. For example, science does not address itself to saving souls or to performing rites of passage, and religion does not attempt to elucidate electromagnetics or to release the atom's energy. But, given scriptures that make unsupported pronouncements on the nature of the universe, the earth, life, and humankind; given people whose religion includes, as a major doctrine, belief in scriptural inerrancy; and given constitutional guarantees for the free exercise of any real, heartfelt religion, conflict between science and religion is inevitable. Given its inevitability, one wonders how intense and extensive the conflict will become. It is important to notice that the conflict is already intense and extensive and that it will almost certainly get worse in the foreseeable future. . . .

Christianity is scientifically unsupported and probably unsupportable, philosophically suspect at best and disreputable at worst, and historically fraudulent.

False Stories

Religious faith, in the hundred thousand forms it has taken, is almost always linked to imaginary scenarios and false mythology, false stories. It's a part of the predisposition to make *complete* stories about the universe and about the tribe. But they are almost always false; they are arguments of convenience to achieve another ultimate purpose. Science tends to wipe them out, one after the other.

E.O. Wilson in *The Omni Interviews*, 1984.

To say that Christianity is scientifically unsupportable is not to say that scientists must be atheists or hostile to religion, nor that teleology is logically incompatible with every cosmology. What it says has been well put by Ralph A. Alpher: "Surely if a necessity for a god-concept in the universe ever turns up, that necessity will become evident to the scientist." Scientific investigation as such does not begin with this concept; it leads to no such concept and is not ever likely to do so.

Sheer indifference to theology, however, is not the only characteristic of modern science. At times it is hostile, as the Medawars have shown:

> [T]he physicists were in the main very well disposed towards God, the geneticists are not.
>
> It is upon the notion of *randomness* that geneticists have based their case against a benevolent or malevolent deity and against there being any overall purpose or design in nature.

Sensing the coming dark night for Western religion, Freud wrote:

> Humanity has in the course of time had to endure from the hands of science two great outrages upon its naive self-love. The first was when it realized that our earth was not the center of the universe. . . . The second was when biological research robbed man of his particular privilege of having been specially created, and relegated him to a descent from the animal world.

How long can it go unnoticed that Christianity is unsupported (and is probably unsupportable) by the dominant mode of modern knowledge? At present the religious right does not see science as its true nemesis but rather as a tiny band of secular humanists, satanically inspired of course. Perhaps the scales will fall from their eyes one day and they will see perspicuously. Perhaps some, or even many, liberal Jews and Christians will join them in perspicuous viewing. What will happen to science and science education then?

No Support from Philosophy

When the empirical rug is pulled from under a person, the most likely landing is philosophy—for sophisticates at least. But, nowadays, philosophy is not a welcome place to land. No longer the handmaiden of theology, it probes theology's major premise with impunity. Put epigrammatically, the invisible and nonexistent look much alike, so much so that when intending to speak of the invisible, the theologian may be speaking of the nonexistent. How shall we know? What referent, if any, does "God" name univocally? Unless and until theologians show us that they are speaking of more than their own concepts, it is pointless to continue, even though they go on and on endlessly.

When one is denied logical proofs for the existence of God and thus forced to depend upon faith alone, the next lower landing is so-called religious experience. Since all the religions of the world are validated in at least part by the experiences of their devotees, what is the evidentiary nature of these experiences relative to the truth of a religion in general or to any of its separable doctrines? We in the West who have lately learned more of Islam can scarcely doubt that this great faith is often supported by vital, if not fanatic, feelings. Yet this faith denies the Trinity, the virgin birth, and the death of Jesus by crucifixion—doctrines that are powerfully validated by the religious experiences of Christians. Experiences that validate contradictory doctrines cannot but be suspect. Concerning theism in general and Christianity in particular, one must conclude that they are philosophically suspect at best, disreputable at worst.

A Historical Fraud

The last and perhaps most distressing part of the litany of modern knowledge is that Christianity is historically fraudulent. The fraud at issue, of course, is pious fraud nonetheless. Morton Smith observes tartly that, whenever "a theologian talks of a 'higher truth,' he is usually trying to conceal a lower falsehood." Three examples of pious fraud must suffice here.

A Total Break

Modern societies accepted the treasures and the power that science laid in their laps. But they have not accepted—they have scarcely even heard—its profounder message: the defining of a new and unique source of truth. . . . Armed with all the powers, enjoying all the riches they owe to science, our societies are still trying to live by and to teach systems of values already blasted at the root by science itself.

Jacques Monod, *Chance and Necessity*, 1971.

First, it can no longer be maintained that the church is founded on the New Testament; rather the church compiled the New Testament, and out of intensely partisan documents written by churchmen with theological axes to grind. Moreover, orthodox Christianity preserved only those documents that furthered its theological and hierarchical ends, suppressing those it took to be inimical. No wonder we know so little of the historical Jesus! But, then, if we knew him better, we might admire him less.

Second, much in the Gospels concerning Jesus is suspect. Neither history nor biography, they were written that their recipients might believe in him (John 20:31). Intent on convincing Jews of Jesus' messiahship, the Gospel (and other New Testament) writers wrenched passages and prophecies out of the Jews' own scriptures and made them apply willy-nilly to Jesus. This massive misuse of the Old Testament amounts to outright fraud. Taking scriptural license into account plus fabricated birth stories, suspiciously different resurrection tales, and many inconsistencies, Albert Schweitzer concluded, "The Jesus of Nazareth who came forward publicly as the Messiah, preached the ethic of the Kingdom of God, who founded the Kingdom of Heaven on earth, and died to give his work its final consecration, never had any existence."

69

Third, the church has always represented Christianity as the religion of and from Jesus, but it is not the religion of Jesus. That religion was Judaism, the religion he shared with the original Jerusalem church (Acts 21:17-31). Nor is orthodox Christianity the religion from Jesus. It is the religion about Jesus emanating from St. Paul's paranormal experiences, unmitigated gall, and desire to dominate the movement (Gal. 1:11, 2:11-16; 2 Cor. 11-12). So different is the contrivance of Paul from Jesus' religion that we can say (paraphrasing Jeremy Bentham) that, with respect to Jesus, Paul was at the beginning of his Christianity what Judah was at the end of his. One could go on and on, but enough is enough.

To get the point, simply let the litany ring out again: Christianity is scientifically unsupported and probably unsupportable, at best, disreputable at worst, and historically fraudulent. . . .

The schools cannot teach modern science without adopting the rational empiricism that underlies it, nor can they teach scientific method without aiding and abetting the secularism that follows in its wake. The contents and attitudes of public school curricula that so aggrieve religious rightists have not been caused by a handful of secular humanists but by the general secularism that has followed science as surely as have its technological applications. Religious rightists, incapable of recognizing this and casting about for something else to blame, have seized on what they like to call "the godless religion of secular humanism.". . . How absurd! Nevertheless, that is the dilemma in which the public schools are caught, particularly now, as new emphasis is being placed on improved science education. . . .

The impossible dream is that scientific inquiry and the acquisition and diffusion of knowledge in general, and in the public schools in particular, might have constitutional guarantees equivalent to those enjoyed by religion. It is very hard, however, to foresee an amendment that says Congress shall not subordinate scientific information to religious information or prohibit the free dissemination of the former, or one that says Congress must promote scientific knowledge even at the expense of religious sensibilities.

Better Science Education

Without waiting for such a guarantee, we should (1) work to improve and expand science education across the board in the public schools; (2) seek ways, including the possible use of professional sanctions, to help safeguard the integrity of science instruction in public schools and to shield science teachers against uninformed public opinion or other political pressures; (3) explore with various scientific organizations the possibility of the nonprofit production and publication of science textbooks for the public schools as an economic weapon against unprincipled commercial publishers; (4) attempt to involve scientists and their professional organizations, as never before, in curriculum development and improvement in the public schools; (5) attempt, formally and informally, through education, to increase Americans' appreciation of science and to heighten their awareness of its advantages to the nation and its citizens; (6) join or support organizations committed to the separation of church and state; and (7) work through education to help wean Americans from their traditional religion, especially in its fundamentalistic, literalistic, and authoritarian manifestations.

Weaning Americans from their traditional religion will, of course, be most difficult. A recent article in *U.S. News & World Report* began as follows: "Sensing a gnawing disillusionment with science and secularism as the driving forces in U.S. society, churches are growing more aggressive in proclaiming spirituality that is the root of their very existence," and went on to say that there "is a newfound determination by those of religious faith to 'search out the sacred' in a society that has increasingly moved away from its religious underpinnings." Thus, while some of us press ahead, welcoming more science and secularity, others work to reestablish the reign of religion.

A Total Break Is Needed

Jacques Monod deserves the final word for the compassionate acuteness of his diagnosis of current Western culture. He wrote:

> Modern societies accepted the treasures and the power that science laid in their laps. But they have not accepted—they have scarcely even heard—its profounder message: the defining of a new and unique source of truth, and the demand for a thorough revision of ethical premises, for a total break with the animist tradition, the definitive abandonment of the "old covenant," the necessity of forging a new one. Armed with all the powers, enjoying all the riches they owe to science, our societies are still trying to live by and to teach systems of values already blasted at the root by science itself.
>
> No society before ours was ever rent by contradictions so agonizing.

"The Judeo-Christian tradition is not undermined by science; rather, it is confirmed as the most comprehensive, coherent, and compelling view."

Science Cannot Replace Religion

Charles P. Henderson Jr.

In the following viewpoint, Charles P. Henderson Jr. disputes the arguments of scientific atheists who believe science is a new truth and religion an outdated superstition. Henderson believes that scientific logic is of little use when faced with the irrational elements that are part of human life. Just as good theology incorporates the findings of science into its worldview, so good science must respect the role of spirituality in scientific discovery. Henderson is the senior minister at Central Presbyterian Church in New York City and a member of Union Theological Seminary's board of directors.

As you read, consider the following questions:

1. What point does the author make by contrasting the time he spends in New York City with the time he spends in Vermont?
2. According to the author, what have the scientific theories of Freud, Marx, Darwin, and Einstein revealed about spirituality?
3. How does Henderson believe his view of God corresponds with science's view of nature?

Charles P. Henderson Jr., *God and Science: The Death and Rebirth of Theism.* Atlanta, GA: John Knox Press, 1986. Reprinted with permission.

In New York, where I serve as minister of Central Presbyterian Church, I am constantly aware of how profoundly this civilization is shaped by science and technology. As I walk the streets and avenues of this great city, it often strikes me that I am not treading upon mother earth; rather, I am traversing a maze of concrete and steel. In New York one walks over a labyrinth of wires and pipes—telephone wires and sewage pipes, power lines and steam conveying pipes. Beneath all this plumbing and electrical equipment, there is the vault of the subway system. In New York we are surrounded on all sides by the products of human inventiveness: giant buildings soaring upwards, jet aircraft circling overhead in intricate patterns, satellites in orbit around the earth itself. Here we live in a cocoon of science and technology.

In Vermont

Traveling north toward Vermont one gradually peels away layer after layer from this crust of civilization. Cities are replaced by towns and towns by villages, and gradually the fields and mountains prevail. On the hillside where I sit down to write I am surrounded by trees and flowers; my writing companions are field mice and a beautiful pair of cedar waxwings, creatures of yellow and black, brown and gray that feed upon the mulberries and blueberries growing in front of my cabin. Here it is possible to enter into a direct relationship with the land, with clouds and sun, with nature, and with nature's God. In Vermont, I am aware there is an infinite, qualitative difference between living in a world which is generally believed to be the direct creation of God and living in a culture shaped by human hands, and it is the city which prefigures the future. Even in Vermont the forests are invaded by snowmobiles and chain saws, and acid rain slowly wreaks havoc among the trees. More importantly, even in this remote location people have come to see the world through the lens of science, and technology provides the tools and instruments which are mediators in our relationship to the natural world. Here television and radio interpret changes in the weather to be the result of shifts in the direction of the jet steam, cold fronts, or high pressure zones which trace their path across the surface of our planet. Photographs of the weather maps are received directly from satellites through a giant disk antenna located in a neighbor's wheat field. It sits here in eloquent testimony to the all-persuasive presence of technology.

In this civilization of science and technology it is no longer necessary to label every natural phenomenon as an act of God. In fact, just the opposite is true. We tend to consider every other explanation for the significant events of life. Wars are the result of geopolitical conflicts among nations and empires; crime rates reflect underlying societal pressures; the rate of unemployment is tied to policies of giant bureaucracies; the innermost feelings

73

of the individual are understood in scientific perspective as events in the chemical and electrical circuitry of the brain. Increasingly we see our lives as being shaped by forces that are entirely within the sphere of science. . . .

As almost everyone from the President to a ward politician would affirm, we face a spiritual crisis, but the severity of the crisis is not to be measured in statistics on church attendance, changes in conventional morality, or opinion polls measuring the popularity of God. The problem is basically a failure of religious imagination. The present situation requires a new way of thinking about God commensurate to the challenge presented by a culture of science and technology.

The Modern View of God

Perhaps the greatest single obstacle to this task of reconstruction is the widely perceived conflict between science and religion. For several generations of Americans, the ideas and intellectual movements associated with science have been seen to be antithetical to faith. At the same time, the impression has been created

ROTHCO
BOROTHE PHOENIX GAZ '87

TEXTBOOK VIEW OF WORLD WITH ALL REFERENCE TO RELIGION REMOVED

© Boro/Rothco

that religion is fighting a rearguard action against the advancing armies of human knowledge. As we learn more and more about the great mysteries of life, there seems to be less and less justification for belief in God. Whole generations of college students in the period since World War II have been introduced to the idea that God is merely an intellectual crutch. God belongs to the old world of myth and superstition, soon to be replaced by the new world of high technology. Of course, God still scores high in the opinion polls, but for many of the college graduates who have now become the shapers of secular culture God is seen as a philosophical dinosaur whose time of extinction is near. God's only remaining purpose is to fill the remaining gaps in human knowledge and answer the yet unanswered questions. . . .

A Case for Theism in Atheism

The major criticisms of religion which have been put forward in the past two hundred years, largely in the name and under the banner of modern science, must be taken with utmost seriousness. One must pursue all the reasonable arguments of contemporary atheism, for behind them all may be found the resources for the building of a greater and deeper faith. When one pursues the precise logic of skepticism, one discovers nothing less than a new case for theism. When one carries the new scientific theories to their logical conclusions, more often than not, one discovers surprising confirmation for the most ancient insights of religion. In fact, all the arguments that are used today in defiance of God may be turned inside out to be used in God's defense. . . .

In the age of dualistic thinking it was commonly asserted that, while reason could lead us to the point of acknowledgment that God exists, only revelation could lead to any knowledge of God's true nature. While we might rely upon logic to lead us toward the fact of God's existence, only religious experiences could make clear God's identity and character. This is the same thinking that lies at the root of [Immanuel] Kant's declaration, "I have therefore found it necessary to deny *knowledge*, in order to make room for *faith.*" In the two hundred years since Kant it has become increasingly apparent that knowledge and faith cannot be so clearly separated, for there is a residue of faith which remains even after the most rigorous attempt to purge away all emotional or subjective factors so as to arrive at something called "pure reason." There are also elements of reason which remain even in the realm of "pure emotion": music, poetry, personal relationships. In fact, the scientific theories of Marx, Darwin, Freud, and Einstein have revealed the futility of trying to separate scientific knowledge from its roots in the rich soil of the human spirit. As Freud demonstrated so clearly, we are constantly and continually influenced by subconscious factors that can never be subjected to the sovereignty of the conscious mind.

75

In this context the irrational elements that lie at the heart of science become all the more apparent. For by its own initiative and within its own reach reason cannot grasp what is most real. As Einstein and [Scottish theologian Thomas F.] Torrance both recognized, the order of the universe is revealed to us as much through faith as through any process of rational analysis. Faith does not begin where logic ends; rather, faith is required from the very beginning to the very end of the arduous search for life's deepest secrets. As the work of science and theology proceed apace, there comes a point when one must make what is essentially a character judgment of the cosmos. In the very attempt to integrate various experimental data with experiential fact, one eventually begins to wonder whether the universe is hospitable or alien to life. Either one sees the highest aspirations of our species as being rooted and grounded in reality or one concludes that our deepest aspirations are illusory.

Profound Insights

Science and religion attract one another, and this very attraction breeds the bolts they exchange. To switch metaphors, science and religion jostle for position on a common ground. Far from separate, they are linked in an inevitable tension that will never be resolved.

However, understanding lies in that tension. The hold that science and religion have exercised on the human mind over the centuries demonstrates that both offer profound insights into the mystery of what is. The religious community can learn by allowing scientific thinking to penetrate its worldview. . . . The scientific community can let some fresh air into rooms stale with rationalism and cluttered with inert facts.

David M. Byers, *America*, January 14, 1984.

It is the central affirmation of the Judeo-Christian faith that this cosmos is the creation of a just and loving God. There is a fundamental compatibility between the creation and the Creator. Though it is not easy to reconcile all the contradictory circumstances that we observe with this symbol of an all-loving God, still it is possible, reasonable, and profoundly desirable that we do so. For, if we do not see this cosmos to be a place which opens itself to our adoration, then it is unlikely that we will continue in the struggle to be the faithful stewards of the world.

Using the Widest Sources of Information

Does the creation contain within it convincing evidence of a creator? Does the universe offer reliable clues pertaining to the reality of a just and loving God? To make such judgments one must draw upon the widest, broadest, and deepest sources of information. To ignore the findings of science is theologically irresponsible, and to ignore the deepest impulses of the human spirit is scientifically suicidal. To understand the universe we must understand it, in so far as it is possible, in its totality.

Scientific atheism consistently makes the mistake of trying to reduce the cosmos to its smallest, discrete components, whereas the religious or theological enterprise is to discern the cosmos as the sum of its varied parts. There is a strong consensus within the community of science, as well as within the community of faith, that the whole is greater, even far greater, than the sum of all its parts. Therefore, models of the universe which reduce reality to a mechanical process or an abstraction of the mind are defeated by the principle of consistency as well as by the principle of coherence.

The symbol of a personal God allows for the same crosscurrents of order and spontaneity, predictability and chance, regularity and novelty that science sees in nature. In this sense all the old arguments, which move from reason, order, and design in nature, must be combined with a complementary appeal to spontaneity, unpredictability, and mystery. When this is done and when the arguments are seen as finding a focal point in the symbol of the just and loving God, then it becomes clear that the Judeo-Christian tradition is not undermined by science; rather, it is confirmed as the most comprehensive, coherent, and compelling view available within western culture. In fact, from this perspective it can be seen that both agnostic humanism and atheistic science are essentially truncated versions of the Judeo-Christian faith.

God's Existence

Moreover, belief in a just and loving God is a stance that can be tested in the same way that scientific theories can. There are particular events and experiences that count for or against this faith. For example, the very existence of a scientific, technological culture is perhaps the most powerful confirmation of this faith, for it is the hope of this religion that civilization can be made compatible with the deepest aspirations of the human spirit. We can, with the aid of science and technology and with the guidance of religion, move this society toward closer realization of the justice and love of God. . . .

Modern theologians have surrendered to scientific atheism just at the moment this opponent was about to self-destruct. In the new age of God, as science and theology enter into new forms of partnership and as we see transformation and convergence taking place all along the horizons of consciousness, it is time to regain the confidence and creativity expressed in the old proofs for God.

"The warfare between science and Christian theology . . . is nearly ended, and I think most Christians would admit that their religion is the better for it."

Science Improves Religion

Bertrand Russell

At the age of 23, Bertrand Russell became a fellow of Trinity College at Cambridge University. A philosopher and mathematician, Russell won the Nobel Prize for literature in 1950. The following viewpoint is an excerpt from his book, *Religion and Science*. Russell views science as a rational tool that has improved the lives of millions. Rigid religious dogma stifles human freedom, he argues. Russell concludes that science has won the war between the two disciplines, and that religion has improved under science's influence.

As you read, consider the following questions:

1. Why do science and religion conflict, according to the author?
2. In Russell's opinion, why were medieval theologians threatened by scientific advances?
3. What aspect of religious life does the author find desirable?

Reprinted from *Religion and Science* by Bertrand Russell (1935) by permission of Oxford University Press.

Religion and Science are two aspects of social life, of which the former has been important as far back as we know anything of man's mental history, while the latter, after a fitful flickering existence among the Greeks and Arabs, suddenly sprang into importance in the sixteenth century, and has ever since increasingly moulded both the ideas and the institutions among which we live. Between religion and science there has been a prolonged conflict, in which, until the last few years, science has invariably proved victorious. . . .

Science is the attempt to discover, by means of observation, and reasoning based upon it, first, particular facts about the world, and then laws connecting facts with one another and (in fortunate cases) making it possible to predict future occurrences. Connected with this theoretical aspect of science there is scientific technique, which utilizes scientific knowledge to produce comforts and luxuries that were impossible, or at least much more expensive, in a pre-scientific era. It is this latter aspect that gives such great importance to science even for those who are not scientists.

Three Elements of Religion

Religion, considered socially, is a more complex phenomenon than science. Each of the great historical religions has three aspects: (1) a Church, (2) a creed, and (3) a code of personal morals. The relative importance of these three elements has varied greatly in different times and places. The ancient religions of Greece and Rome, until they were made ethical by the Stoics, had not very much to say about personal morals; in Islam the Church has been unimportant in comparison with the temporal monarch; in modern Protestantism there is a tendency to relax the rigors of the creed. Nevertheless, all three elements, though in varying proportions, are essential to religion as a social phenomenon, which is what is chiefly concerned in the conflict with science. A purely personal religion, so long as it is content to avoid assertions which science can disprove, may survive undisturbed in the most scientific age.

Creeds are the intellectual source of the conflict between religion and science, but the bitterness of the opposition has been due to the connection of creeds with Churches and with moral codes. Those who questioned creeds weakened the authority, and might diminish the incomes, of churchmen; moreover, they were thought to be undermining morality, since moral duties were deduced by Churchmen from creeds. Secular rulers, therefore, as well as Churchmen, felt that they had good reason to fear the revolutionary teaching of the men of science.

In what follows, we shall not be concerned with science in general, nor yet with religion in general, but with those points where they have come into conflict in the past, or still do so at the present time. So far as Christendom is concerned, these conflicts have been of two kinds. Sometimes there happens to be a text in the Bible making some assertion as to a matter of fact, for example, that the hare chews the cud. Such assertions, when they are refuted by scientific observation, cause difficulties for those who believe, as most Christians did until science forced them to think otherwise, that every word of the Bible is divinely inspired. But when the Biblical assertions concerned have no inherent religious importance, it is not difficult to explain them away, or to avoid controversy by deciding that the Bible is only authoritative on matters of religion and morals. There is, however, a deeper conflict when science controverts some important Christian dogma, or some philosophical doctrine which theologians believe essential to orthodoxy. Broadly speaking, the disagreements between religion and science were, at first, of the former sort, but have gradually become more and more concerned with matters which are, or were, considered a vital part of Christian teaching.

Authority vs. Observation

The conflict between theology and science was quite as much a conflict between authority and observation. The men of science did not ask that propositions should be believed because some important authority had said they were true; on the contrary, they appealed to the evidence of the senses, and maintained only such doctrines as they believed to be based upon facts which were patent to all who chose to make the necessary observations. The new method achieved such immense successes, both theoretical and practical, that theology was gradually forced to accommodate itself to science.

Bertrand Russell, *Religion and Science*, 1961.

Religious men and women, in the present day, have come to feel that most of the creed of Christendom, as it existed in the Middle Ages, is unnecessary, and indeed a mere hindrance to the religious life. But if we are to understand the opposition which science encountered, we must enter imaginatively into the system of ideas which made such opposition seem reasonable. Suppose a man were to ask a priest why he should not commit murder. The answer "because you would be hanged" was felt to be inadequate, both because the hanging would need justification, and because police methods were so uncertain that a large proportion of murderers escaped. There was, however, an answer which, before the rise of science, appeared satisfactory to almost everyone, namely, that murder is forbidden by the Ten Commandments, which were revealed by God to Moses on Mount Sinai. The criminal who eluded earthly justice could not escape from the Divine wrath, which had decreed for impenitent murderers a punishment infinitely more terrible than hanging. This argument, however, rests upon the authority of the Bible, which can only be maintained intact if the Bible is accepted as a whole. When the Bible seems to say that the earth does not move, we must adhere to this statement in spite of the arguments of Galileo, since otherwise we shall be giving encouragement to murderers and all other kinds of malefactors. Although few would now accept this argument, it cannot be regarded as absurd, nor should those who acted upon it be viewed with moral reprobation. . . .

Science's Method

The way in which science arrives at its beliefs is quite different from that of mediaeval theology. Experience has shown that it is dangerous to start from general principles and proceed deductively, both because the principles may be untrue and because the reasoning based upon them may be fallacious. Science starts, not from large assumptions, but from particular facts discovered by observation or experiment. From a number of such facts a general rule is arrived at, of which, if it is true, the facts in question are instances. This rule is not positively asserted, but is accepted, to begin with, as a working hypothesis. If it is correct, certain hitherto unobserved phenomena will take place in certain circumstances. If it is found that they do take place, that so far confirms the hypothesis; if they do not, the hypothesis must be discarded and a new one must be invented. However many facts are found to fit the hypothesis, that does not make it certain, although in the end it may come to be thought in a high degree probable; in that case, it is called a theory rather than a hypothesis. A number of different theories, each built directly upon facts, may become the basis for a new and more general hypothesis from which, if true, they all follow; and to this process of generalization no limit can be set. But whereas, in mediaeval thinking, the most general principles were the starting point, in science they are the final conclusion—final, that is to say, at a given moment, though liable to become instances of some still wider law at a later stage.

Absolute Truth

A religious creed differs from a scientific theory in claiming to embody eternal and absolutely certain truth, whereas science is always tentative, expecting that modifications in its present theories will sooner or later be found necessary, and aware that its method is one which is logically incapable of arriving at a complete and final demonstration. But in an advanced science the changes needed are generally only such as serve to give slightly greater accuracy; the old theories remain serviceable where only rough approximations are concerned, but are found to fail when some new minuteness of observation becomes possible. Moreover, the technical inventions suggested by the old theories remain as evidence that they had a kind of practical truth up to a point. Science thus encourages abandonment of the search for absolute truth, and the substitution of what may be called "technical" truth, which belongs to any theory that can be successfully employed in inventions or in predicting the future. "Technical" truth is a matter of degree: a theory from which more successful inventions and predictions spring is truer than one which gives rise to fewer. "Knowledge" ceases to be a mental mirror of the universe, and becomes merely a practical tool in the manipulation of matter. But these implications of scientific method were not visible to the pioneers of science, who, though they practiced a new method of pursuing truth, still conceived truth itself as absolutely as did their theological opponents. . . .

Reason and Morals

The price in blood and tears that mankind generally has had to pay for the comfort and spiritual refreshment that religion has brought to a few has been too great to justify our entrusting moral accountancy to religious belief. By "moral accountancy" I mean the judgment that such and such an action is right or wrong, or such a man good and such another evil.

I am a rationalist—something of a period piece nowadays, I admit—but I am usually reluctant to declare myself to be so because of the widespread misunderstanding or neglect of the distinction that must always be drawn in philosophic discussion between the *sufficient* and the *necessary*. I do not believe—indeed, I deem it a comic blunder to believe—that the exercise of reason is *sufficient* to explain our condition and where necessary to remedy it, but I do believe that the exercise of reason is at all times unconditionally *necessary* and that we disregard it at our peril. I and my kind believe that the world can be made a better place to live in—believe, indeed, that it has already been made so by an endeavor in which, in spite of shortcomings which I do not conceal, natural science has played an important part, of which my fellow scientists and I are immensely proud.

Peter B. Medawar, *The Limits of Science*, 1984.

There is, however, one aspect of the religious life, and that perhaps the most desirable, which is independent of the discoveries of science, and may survive whatever we may come to believe as to the nature of the universe. Religion has been associated, not only with creeds and churches, but with the personal life of those who felt its importance. In the best of the saints and mystics, there existed in combination the belief in certain dogmas and a certain way of feeling about the purposes of human life. The man who feels deeply the problems of human destiny, the desire to diminish the sufferings of mankind, and the hope that the future will realize the best possibilities of our species, is nowadays often said to have a religious outlook, however little he may accept of traditional Christianity. Insofar as religion consists in a way of feeling, rather than in a set of beliefs, science cannot touch it. Perhaps the decay of dogma may, psychologically, make such a way of feeling temporarily more difficult, because it has been so intimately associated with theological belief. But this difficulty need not endure forever; in fact, many free thinkers have shown in their lives that this way of feeling has no essential connection with a creed. No real excellence can be inextricably bound up with unfounded beliefs; and if theological beliefs are unfounded, they cannot be necessary for the preservation of what is good in the religious outlook. To think otherwise is to be filled with fears as to what we may discover, which will interfere with our attempts to understand the world; but it is only in the measure in which we achieve such understanding that true wisdom becomes possible. . . .

Victorious Science

In the period since Copernicus, whenever science and theology have disagreed, science has proved victorious. . . . Where practical issues were involved, as in witchcraft and medicine, science has stood for the diminution of suffering, while theology has encouraged man's natural savagery. The spread of the scientific outlook, as opposed to the theological, has indisputably made, hitherto, for happiness.

The issue is now, however, entering upon a wholly new phase, and this for two reasons: first, that scientific technique is becoming more important in its effects than the scientific temper of mind; secondly, that newer religions are taking the place of Christianity, and repeating the errors of which Christianity has repented. . . .

The War Is Almost Over

The warfare between science and Christian theology, in spite of an occasional skirmish on the outposts, is nearly ended, and I think most Christians would admit that their religion is the better for it. Christianity has been purified of inessentials inherited from a barbarous age, and nearly cured of the desire to persecute. There remains, among the more liberal Christians, an ethical doctrine which is valuable: acceptance of Christ's teaching that we should love our neighbours, and a belief that in each individual there is something deserving of respect, even if it is no longer to be called a soul.

"If a mystical sense of reverence is . . . the right response to the vast and incomprehensible universe, then science itself requires it."

Religion Improves Science

Mary Midgley

A traditional argument concerning science and religion has been that because science depends on reason while religion depends on faith, the two inevitably conflict. In the following viewpoint, Mary Midgley argues that this dichotomy is too simplistic and too rigid. Subjective, mystical factors are inevitably involved in science, she expains. Midgley, the author of several books, was formerly senior lecturer in philosophy at the University of Newcastle upon Tyne in Great Britain.

As you read, consider the following questions:

1. How does Midgley believe modern physics has affected the relationship between science and religion?
2. What arguments does the author use to support her contention that the motives behind science are emotional and mystical?
3. Why do many scientific hypotheses often require faith from laypersons, according to Midgley?

Mary Midgley, *Evolution as a Religion*. London: Methuen & Company, 1985. Reprinted with permission.

Something I owe to the soil that grew—
　　More to the life that fed—
But most to Allah Who gave me two
　　Separate sides to my head.

I would go without shirt or shoes
　　Friends, tobacco or bread
Sooner than for an instant lose
　　Either side of my head.

Rudyard Kipling, Kim, Chapter VIII

The constrast between science and religion is unluckily not as plain, nor the relation between them as simple, as is often supposed. . . . Thoughtful scientists have often mentioned this problem, but a great many of their colleagues, and of the public generally, cling to the reassuringly simple opposition. What often seems to happen is that a great number of different antitheses are mixed up here, and used rather indiscriminately, as each happens to be convenient, to give colour to the idea of a general crusade of light against darkness. We could group them roughly like this:

1. science	v.	superstition partiality error magic wish-fulfilment dogmatism blind conformism childishness
2. common sense science rationalism logic	v.	intuition mysticism faith
materialism	v.	idealism animism vitalism mind-body dualism commonsense agnosticism
3. hard	v.	soft
progress	v.	tradition
determination	v.	free will
mechanism	v.	teleology
empiricism	v.	rationalism metaphysics
scepticism	v.	credulity
reason	v.	feeling or emotion
objective	v.	subjective
quantity	v.	quality

physical science	v.	the humanities
realism	v.	reverence
specialism	v.	holism
prose	v.	poetry
male	v.	female
clarity	v.	mystery

Seeking Intelligible Patterns

The *raison d'être* of science is not the generation of data but the attainment of intelligibility. Scientists look for patterns that relate one bit of sensory data to another, and it is these patterns of intelligibility which constitute reality, not the data themselves. Most of modern physics, for example, points toward a structure of reality that cannot be visualized, or described in standard language. But the insights of physics are "true" or "real" because with them the behavior of matter becomes intelligible.

Understanding science as the search for the intelligible is significant, because it suggests that science and religion share the same ultimate goal—to give intelligibility to the world and human experience.

William H. King, *The Christian Century*, July 2-9, 1986.

A mental map based on this strange group of antitheses, a map which showed them all as roughly equivalent and was marked only with the general direction 'keep to the left', has for the last century usually been issued to English-speaking scientists with their first test-tube and has often gone with them to the grave. In spite of its wild incoherence, it still has great influence, though at least two recent developments within science itself have lately shaken it, and more are to be expected. The first shock is the series of changes whereby modern physics now shows indeterminacy as lying near the centre of causation, and solid matter as dissolving, on inspection, into non-solid energy. This is a severe upset to the crucial notions of mechanism and determinism. What perhaps cuts deepest, however, is something symbolic which looks more superficial and which would not matter at all if people were really only interested in facts and not in drama. It is the disturbance to the notion of 'hardness', a metaphor whose application is entirely mysterious, but which has somehow served to keep the whole left-hand column together.

At present, this change results in a flow of popular books such as *The Tao of Physics* by Fritjof Capra and *The Dancing Wu Li Masters* by Gary Zukav, which suggest that energy is spirit, and that what modern physics teaches is, give or take a mantra or two, very much what Zen masters and Hindu sages have been saying for centuries, or possibly millennia. Whatever else may be thought about this, it does at least point to the need to look again at our list of antitheses. On the face of things, these books do draw attention to the arbitrary narrow-mindedness which has been imposed on scientists, and call for science to look outward, though at times they also seem to convey the opposite message: science, especially physics, is already far more spiritual, and therefore more all-sufficient, than we have so far supposed. At least, however, the traditional set of antitheses is broken up. Serious physicists seem at present more aware than many biologists of its confusions and inadequacies. . . .

Left Brain vs. Right Brain

The second shock was delivered by recent discoveries about the functions of brain hemispheres. In its early days, this was often read, in a way which is itself a notable indicator of the underlying dramas expected, as a story about the 'dominance' of one hemisphere, namely of course the calculating, articulate, scientific one, over the other, which was intuitive, humble and not really very distinctively human. Further research, however, has steadily shown more and more serious functions for the right-hand hemisphere, and has led increasingly to the acceptance of Kipling's picture expressed at the beginning of this [viewpoint], where it is utterly vital to have, and to keep in balance, the two separate sides of one's head. . . .

Brain evolution, in short, is not a simple success story establishing the right of all left-hand members in our antitheses to subdue their partners. Since the members of the two sets are in any case such a mixed lot as to make this wholesale arrangement impossible, we had better look at them separately on their merits.

Science and Superstition

Which among these antitheses are really the ones we need, which of them give clear ground for a crusade? The ones in the first group seem the most promising for crusaders. In them science stands opposed to something undoubtedly bad. But in these cases it is certainly not the only opponent of the evils in question. Superstition and the rest find their opposites in clear thinking generally, and a particular superstition is as likely to be corrected by history or logic or common sense as by one of the physical sciences. The second group deals in ideas which are more ambitious, more interesting, but also much more puzzling, because we at once need definitions of the terms involved, and cannot easily give them without falling into confusion. The odd tendency of both rationalism and common sense to jump the central barrier is only one indication of the difficulties. In the third group, we have contrasts which are a good deal clearer. But they do not seem to provide material at all suitable for a crusade. They describe pairs of complementary elements in life and thought, both members of which are equally necessary, and indeed could scarcely be identified except in relation to each other as parts of a whole. We no longer want that truculent little 'v.' to divide them. They go very well together, and crusaders must avoid trying to set them at loggerheads. Thus it does not matter here that 'reason' appears on both sides; we no longer want to reduce all these contrasts to a single underlying shape. The lines of division cross each other. Different distinctions are needed for different purposes.

Creating a Context

Science is more dependent on creative imagination and metaphor than we might think. A number of philosophers have suggested that science cannot be concerned only with "bare facts," for all data come to the observer within a context of assumptions which are not provable by the immediate data. . . .

Most of the data cited in the theory of evolution were available long before Darwin's time. Scientific progress was made only when he created a context, a theory, around the notion of natural selection. This was as much a creative act as the writing of a symphony or the painting of a picture. The really significant moment for the scientist, as for the poet, is when he or she finds a new way to speak of what is familiar, creating a new context for understanding.

William H. King, *The Christian Century*, July 2-9, 1986.

How hard it is to relate these various antitheses clearly can be seen in Bertrand Russell's very interesting and influential paper 'Mysticism and logic'. Russell's main enterprise here is an admirable attempt to move the whole debate into our group 3, to show apparently warring elements as both necessary and complementary:

Metaphysics, or the attempt to conceive the world as a whole by means of thought, has been developed, from the first, by the union and conflict of two very different human impulses, the one urging men towards mysticism, the other urging them towards science. . . . In Hume, for instance, the scientific impulse reigns quite unchecked, while in Blake a strong hostility to science co-exists with profound mystic insight. But the greatest men who have been philosophers have felt the need both of science and of mysticism; the attempt to harmonize the two was what make their life, and what always must, for all its arduous uncertainty, make philosophy, to some minds, a greater thing than either science or religion. . . . Mysticism, is, in essence, little more than a certain intensity and depth of feeling in regard to what is believed about the universe. . . . Mysticism is to be com-

88

mended as an attitude towards life, not as a creed about the world. The metaphysical creed, I shall maintain, is a mistaken outcome of the emotion, although this emotion, as colouring all other thoughts and feelings, is the inspirer of whatever is best in Man. Even the cautious and patient investigation of truth by science, which seems the very antithesis of the mystic's swift certainty, may be fostered and nourished by that very spirit of reverence in which mysticism lives and moves.

Russell has got a lot of things right here. He has 'got in', as they say, many items from the right-hand column of our antitheses in legitimate relation to science. He has got in emotion and poetry, indeed he has got in Blake, with his criticisms of Newton. He sees that emotion is so far from being an opponent of science, or a menace to it, that emotion of a suitable kind is necessary for science, and that part of that emotion can quite properly be called 'reverence'. He sees that something of the sort is necessary for metaphysics too. . . .

Russell, who had the advantage of having started his philosophical life as a disciple of Hegel, was not tempted, as Hume and his disciples were, to suppose that good metaphysics merely meant cutting down one's thoughts on such topics to a minimum. He knew that, far from that, even highly constructive metaphysicians like Plato and Heraclitus, Leibnitz and Hegel often had something very important to say, especially about mathematics. Yet he was now a convert to empiricism, and he wanted to set limits on the thought-architecture of these bold rationalists. His solution was, on the whole, to concentrate on the emotional function of this large-scale, constructive metaphysics, and on the intellectual function of science and of more sceptical philosophy. Thus mystical, constructive metaphysics was to supply the heart of the world-grasping enterprise, while science supplied the head.

The Motives of Science

This is a bold and ingenious idea, but something has gone wrong with it. He has fitted the head of one kind of enquiry on to the heart of another. Constructive metaphysics has its own thoughts, and science its own motives. If the word *science* means what it seems to mean here—primarily the search for particular facts— then it is powered emotionally by the familiar motive of detailed curiosity. If it means the building of those facts into a harmonious, satisfying system, then it draws upon a different motive, the desire for intellectual order; which is also the motive for metaphysical endeavour. Without this unifying urge, science would be nothing but mindless, meaningless collecting. At the quite ordinary scientific level, before any question of mystically contemplating the whole comes in, the system-building tendency, with its aesthetic criteria of elegance and order, is an essential part of every science, continually shaping the scrappy data into usable patterns. Scientific hypotheses are not generated by randomizers, nor do they grow on trees, but on the branches of these ever-expanding thought systems.

This is why the sciences continually go beyond everybody's direct experience, and do so in directions that quickly diverge from that of common sense, which has more modest systems of its own. And because isolated systems are always incomplete and can conflict with each other, inevitably in the end they require metaphysics, 'the attempt to conceive the world as a whole', to harmonize them.

Science Requires Faith

To what are interestingly called *lay* people, however, these intellectual constructions present problems of belief which are often quite as difficult as those of religion, and which can call for equally strenuous efforts of faith. This happens at present over relativity, over the size and expansion of the universe, over quantum mechanics, over evolution and many other matters. Believers are—perhaps quite properly—expected to bow to the mystery, admit the inadequacy of their faculties, and accept paradoxes. If a mystical sense of reverence is, as Russell suggested, the right response to the vast and incomprehensible universe, then science itself requires it, since it leads us on directly to this situation. It cannot therefore be right to call mysticism and science, as Russell does, two distinct, co-ordinate 'human impulses'. Mysticism is a range of human faculties; physical science, a range of enquiries which can, at times, call these faculties into action. But long before it does so, it has passed the limits of common sense, transcended experience and begun to ask for faith.

"Science without religion is lame, religion without science is blind."

Science and Religion Are Interdependent

Albert Einstein

Albert Einstein's theory of relativity revolutionized physics and earned him the Nobel Prize in 1921. Einstein renounced his German citizenship in 1933, when Adolf Hitler gained power. That year he accepted a position at the Institute for Advanced Study in Princeton, New Jersey and lived there until his death in 1955. The following viewpoint is an essay Einstein wrote in 1941 in which he contends that science and religion depend upon each other. While disagreeing with the idea of a personal God who controls the universe, he maintains that great scientists are inspired by a religious faith that the universe is rational.

As you read, consider the following questions:

1. Why does Einstein argue that ideally, there should be no conflicts between religion and science?
2. How does religion influence and benefit scientists, according to the author?
3. What harmful consequences does Einstein believe result from belief in a personal God?

It would not be difficult to come to an agreement as to what we understand by science. Science is the century-old endeavor to bring together by means of systematic thought the perceptible phenomena of this world into as thorough-going an association as possible. To put it boldly, it is the attempt at the posterior reconstruction of existence by the process of conceptualization. But when asking myself what religion is I cannot think of the answer so easily. And even after finding an answer which may satisfy me at this particular moment I still remain convinced that I can never under any circumstances bring together, even to a slight extent, all those who have given this question serious consideration.

The Definition of Religion

At first, then, instead of asking what religion is I should prefer to ask what characterizes the aspirations of a person who gives me the impression of being religious: A person who is religiously enlightened appears to me to be one who has, to the best of his ability, liberated himself from the fetters of his selfish desires and is preoccupied with thoughts, feelings, and aspirations to which he clings because of their super-personal value. It seems to me that what is important is the force of this super-personal content and the depth of the conviction concerning its overpowering mean-ingfulness, regardless of whether any attempt is made to unite this content with a divine Being, for otherwise it would not be possible to count Buddha and Spinoza as religious personalities. Accordingly, a religious person is devout in the sense that he has no doubt of the significance and loftiness of those super-personal objects and goals which neither require nor are capable of rational foundation. They exist with the same necessity and matter-of-factness as he himself. In this sense religion is the age-old endeavor of mankind to become clearly and completely conscious of these values and goals and constantly to strengthen and extend their effect. If one conceives of religion and science according to these definitions then a conflict between them appears impossible. For science can only ascertain what *is*, but not what *should be*, and outside of its domain value judgments of all kinds remain necessary. Religion, on the other hand, deals only with evalua-tions of human thought and action: it cannot justifiably speak of facts and relationships between facts. According to this interpreta-tion the well-known conflicts between religion and science in the past must all be ascribed to a misapprehension of the situation which has been described.

For example, a conflict arises when a religious community in-sists on the absolute truthfulness of all statements recorded in the Bible. This means an intervention on the part of religion into the sphere of science; this is where the stuggle of the Church against the doctrines of Galileo and Darwin belongs. On the other hand, representatives of science have often made an attempt to arrive at fundamental judgments with respect to values and ends on the basis of scientific method, and in this way have set themselves in opposition to religion. These conflicts have all sprung from fatal errors.

Now, even though the realms of religion and science in themselves are clearly marked off from each other, nevertheless there exist between the two strong reciprocal relationships and dependencies. Though religion may be that which determines the goal, it has, nevertheless, learned from science, in the broadest sense, what means will contribute to the attainment of the goals it has set up. But science can only be created by those who are thoroughly imbued with the aspiration towards truth and understanding. This source of feeling, however, springs from the sphere of religion. To this there also belongs the faith in the possibility that the regulations valid for the world of existence are rational, that is, comprehensible to reason. I cannot conceive of a genuine scientist without that profound faith. The situation may be expressed by an image: Science without religion is lame, religion without science is blind.

A Strong and Noble Force

The ethical behavior of man is better based on sympathy, education and social relationships, and requires no support from religion. Man's plight would, indeed, be sad if he had to be kept in order through fear of punishment and hope of rewards after death.

It is, therefore, quite natural that the churches have always fought against science and have persecuted its supporters. But, on the other hand, I assert that the cosmic religious experience is the strongest and the noblest driving force behind scientific research. No one who does not appreciate the terrific exertions, and, above all, the devotion without which pioneer creations in scientific thought cannot come into being, can judge the strength of the feeling out of which alone such work, turned away as it is from immediate practical life, can grow. What a deep faith in the rationality of the structure of the world and what a longing to understand even a small glimpse of the reason revealed in the world there must have been in Kepler and Newton to enable them to unravel the mechanism of the heavens in long years of lonely work!

Albert Einstein, *The New York Times Magazine*, November 9, 1930.

Though I have asserted above that in truth a legitimate conflict between religion and science cannot exist I must nevertheless qualify this assertion once again on an essential point, with reference to the actual content of historical religions. This qualification has to do with the concept of God. During the youthful period of mankind's spiritual evolution human fantasy created gods in man's own image, who, by the operations of their will were supposed to determine, or at any rate to influence the phenomenal world. Man sought to alter the disposition of these gods in his own favor by means of magic and prayer. The idea of God in the religions taught at present is a sublimation of that old conception of the gods. Its anthropomorphic character is shown, for instance, by the fact that men appeal to the Divine Being in prayers and plead for the fulfillment of their wishes.

Nobody, certainly, will deny that the idea of the existence of an omnipotent, just and omnibeneficent personal God is able to accord man solace, help, and guidance; also, by virtue of its simplicity it is accessible to the most undeveloped mind. But, on the other hand, there are decisive weaknesses attached to this idea in itself, which have been painfully felt since the beginning of history. That is, if this being is omnipotent then every occurrence, including every human action, every human thought, and every human feeling and aspiration is also His work; how is it possible to think of holding men responsible for their deeds and thoughts before such an almighty Being? In giving out punishment and rewards He would to a certain extent be passing judgment on Himself. How can this be combined with the goodness and righteousness ascribed to Him?

The Source of Conflicts

The main source of the present-day conflicts between the spheres of religion and of science lies in this concept of a personal God. It is the aim of science to establish general rules which determine the reciprocal connection of objects and events in time and space. For these rules, or laws of nature, absolutely general validity is required—not proven. It is mainly a program, and faith in the possibility of its accomplishment in principle is only founded on partial successes. But hardly anyone could be found who would deny these partial successes and ascribe them to human self-deception. The fact that on the basis of such laws we are able to predict the temporal behavior of phenomena in certain domains with great precision and certainty is deeply embedded in the consciousness of the modern man, even though he may have grasped very little of the contents of those laws. He need only consider that the planetary courses within the solar system may be calculated in advance with great exactitude on the basis of a limited number of simple laws. In a similar way, though not with the same precision, it is possible to calculate in advance the mode of operation of an electric motor, a transmission system, or of a wireless apparatus, even when dealing with a novel development.

To be sure, when the number of factors coming into play in a phenomenological complex is too large, scientific method in most cases fails us. One need only think of the weather, in which case prediction even for a few days ahead is impossible. Nevertheless no one doubts that we are confronted with a causal connection whose causal components are in the main known to us. Occurrences in this domain are beyond the reach of exact prediction because of the variety of factors in operation, not because of any lack of order in nature.

Rapt in Awe

The most beautiful thing we can experience is the mysterious. It is the source of all true art and science. He to whom this emotion is a stranger, who can no longer pause to wonder and stand rapt in awe, is as good as dead: his eyes are closed. This insight into the mystery of life, coupled though it be with fear, has also given rise to religion. To know that what is impenetrable to us really exists, manifesting itself as the highest wisdom and the most radiant beauty which our dull faculties can comprehend only in their most primitive forms—this knowledge, this feeling, is at the center of true religiousness. In this sense, and in this sense only, I belong in the ranks of devoutly religious men.

Albert Einstein, in *Living Philosophies*, 1985.

We have penetrated far less deeply into the regularities obtaining within the realm of living things, but deeply enough nevertheless to sense at least the rule of fixed necessity. One need only think of the systematic order in heredity, and in the effect of poisons, as for instance alcohol, on the behavior of organic beings. What is still lacking here is a grasp of connections of profound generality, but not a knowledge of order in itself.

An Ordered, Regular Universe

The more a man is imbued with the ordered regularity of all events the firmer becomes his conviction that there is no room left by the side of this ordered regularity for causes of a different nature. For him neither the rule of human or the rule of divine will exists as an independent cause of natural events. To be sure, the doctine of a personal God interfering with natural events could never be *refuted*, in the real sense, by science, for this doctrine can always take refuge in those domains in which scientific knowledge has not yet been able to set foot.

But I am persuaded that such behavior on the part of the representatives of religion would not only be unworthy but also fatal. For a doctrine which is able to maintain itself not in clear light but only in the dark, will of necessity lose its effect on mankind, with incalculable harm to human progress. In their struggle for the ethical good, teachers of religion must have the stature to give up the doctrine of a personal God, that is, give up that source of fear and hope which in the past placed such vast power in the hands of priests. In their labors they will have to avail themselves of those forces which are capable of cultivating the Good, the True, and the Beautiful in humanity itself. This is, to be sure, a more difficult but an incomparably more worthy task. After religious teachers accomplish the refining process indicated they will surely recognize with joy that true religion has been ennobled and made more profound by scientific knowledge.

Spirituality's Role in Science

If it is one of the goals of religion to liberate mankind as far as possible from the bondage of egocentric cravings, desires, and fears, scientific reasoning can aid religion in yet another sense. Although it is true that it is the goal of science to discover rules which permit the association and foretelling of facts, this is not its only aim. It also seeks to reduce the connections discovered to the smallest possible number of mutually independent conceptual elements. It is in this striving after the rational unification of the manifold that it encounters its greatest successes, even though it is precisely this attempt which causes it to run the greatest risk of falling a prey to illusions. But whoever has undergone the intense experience of successful advances made in this domain, is moved by profound reverence for the rationality made manifest in existence. By way of the understanding he achieves a far-reaching emancipation from the shackles of personal hopes and desires, and thereby attains that humble attitude of mind towards the grandeur of reason incarnate in existence, and which, in its profoundest depths, is inaccessible to man. This attitude, however, appears to me to be religious, in the highest sense of the word. And so it seems to me that science not only purifies the religious impulse of the dross of its anthropomorphism but also contributes to a religous spiritualization of our understanding of life.

Rational Knowledge

The further the spiritual evolution of mankind advances the more certain it seems to me that the path to genuine religiosity does not lie through the fear of life, and the fear of death, and blind faith, but through striving after rational knowledge. In this sense I believe that the priest must become a teacher if he wishes to do justice to his lofty educational mission.

Recognizing Statements That Are Provable

From various sources of information we are constantly confronted with statements and generalizations about social and moral problems. In order to think clearly about these problems, it is useful if one can make a basic distinction between statements for which evidence can be found and other statements which cannot be verified or proved because evidence is not available, or the issue is so controversial that it cannot be definitely proved.

Readers should be aware that magazines, newspapers, and other sources often contain statements of a controversial nature. The following activity is designed to allow experimentation with statements that are provable and those that are not.

The following statements are taken from the viewpoints in this chapter. Consider each statement carefully. *Mark P for any statement you believe is provable. Mark U for any statement you feel is unprovable because of the lack of evidence. Mark C for any statements you think are too controversial to be proved to everyone's satisfaction.*

If you are doing this activity as a member of a class or group, compare your answers with those of other class or group members. Be able to defend your answers. You may discover that others will come to different conclusions than you. Listening to the reasons others present for their answers may give you valuable insights in recognizing statements that are provable.

P = *provable*
U = *unprovable*
C = *too controversial*

1. While the argument that science and religion need not conflict may appear open-minded and comforting to many, this view is nonsense.

2. Science is the attempt to discover, by observation and reasoning based on observation, particular facts about the world and laws connecting facts with one another.

3. Physical science requires mysticism and faith.

4. The path to true religiosity does not lie through the fear of death or blind faith, but through striving after rational knowledge.

5. We know that the evolution of the cosmos during the past 20 billion years has been a continuous process—new structures have been created and old ones have died.

6. In New York City, one is surrounded on all sides by products of human science: skyscrapers, subways, and telephone wires.

7. Metaphysics is the attempt to conceive the world as a whole by means of thought.

8. Given the fabricated birth stories and suspiciously different resurrection tales in the New Testament, obviously, Jesus never actually existed.

9. Some Christian doctrines are the Trinity, the virgin birth, and the death of Jesus by crucifixion.

10. Schools cannot teach modern science without aiding the secularism that naturally follows in its wake.

11. The scientific method involves creating appropriate concepts to describe natural phenomena and then making connections between these phenomena.

12. It is evident that the public is currently hostile and ignorant toward science.

13. What modern physics teaches us, give or take a mantra or two, is very much what Zen masters and Hindu sages have been saying for centuries.

14. Hinduism has thousands of gods, all of them considered embodiments of the divine unity of the cosmos.

15. Science can only ascertain what *is*, but not what *should be*—it cannot make value judgments.

How Did the Universe Originate?

SCIENCE&
RELIGION

Chapter Preface

Does the universe, as Albert Einstein believed, reflect the "presence of a superior reasoning power," an all-encompassing order that should make scientists and religionists alike stand in awe of an unseen, guiding hand? Or is it a chaotic jumble, the result of elements accidentally commingling in a vast primordial soup?

This is one of the most controversial debates over the origin of the universe. Many scientists and religious believers argue that the careful detail and balance found in the physical world are proof of God's creation and plan. While many disagree over how the universe began, they do agree that mathematically and spiritually the universe seems to reflect, in William Blake's words, "a fearful symmetry" shaped by an "immortal hand."

Other scientists disagree, believing that to look for proof of God in the physical realm of the universe is misguided and inappropriate. If scientists attempt to mix research with spiritual goals, their efforts to prove the existence of God may cause them to ignore important clues to the origin and workings of the universe. They argue that, far from mirroring God's firm and careful hand, scientific evidence suggests the universe was born of chaos and fire. They go further still and say that unpredictable, chaotic, chemical reactions continue to foil scientists who search for order.

The authors in the following chapter disagree not only on how the universe was created and its age, but they also debate a more practical question: whether science can be used to prove faith.

"The signs say the universe is young."

The Universe Is Young

Harold S. Slusher

Harold S. Slusher holds a Ph.D. from Columbia Pacific University and an honorary Doctor of Science degree from Indiana Christian University in recognition of his work on the time scale for the cosmos. In the following viewpoint, Slusher questions the scientific evidence that places the universe at 15-20 billion years old. He presents evidence that he believes proves the universe is much younger—5000 to 6000 years old—and coincides with the Biblical account of Genesis.

As you read, consider the following questions:

1. Why does the author believe that galaxies are not very old?
2. Why does Slusher believe that stars and star clusters are young? What evidence does he present?
3. What is the author's opinion of the Big Bang theory?

Harold S. Slusher, *The Origin of the Universe: An Examination of the Big Bang and Steady State Cosmogonics*. El Cajon, CA: Institute for Creation Research, 1980. Reprinted with the author's permission.

The age of the universe has been the object of intense study and wide speculation. There are certain fundamental unknowns in the problem that seem impossible of determination though definite upper limits may be assessed on the age of the universe. The inability of scientists to describe the origin of things, the explaining of all things in an evolutionary framework, and the feeling that the uniformitarian geologist is right about the age of the earth has led astronomers to push the age of the universe further and further back in time, hiding all the unsolvable problems of the naturalistic cosmogonies behind a veil of time. The beginning of the universe, if one follows the big bang model, would be at 10 to 20 billion years ago. If one believes the continuous-creation model, though it is in rather ill repute today, he would say the universe is infinitely old, having no real beginning and, supposedly, no end. The opposing position to these naturalistic views is that the universe was created a short time ago with all the celestial bodies that make up the universe coming into existence simultaneously. This position maintains that there is a Creator, which is basic and original, which exists on its own. *This Creator has caused all the other things (the universe) and this universe will cease to exist if the Creator ceases to maintain it.* The very long time scale is extremely important in the naturalistic nature-myths since a young universe would be the death of the big bang and steady state concepts.

The age of the universe is hard to come by, but it is very easy to approach the problem with ready-made answers. However, it is possible to pick up some clues which will tell us whether it is young or old. If the universe is very old (on the order of billions of years), it should show certain signs of age. Let us assume for this discussion the big bang model of the origin of the universe, since this version holds the center stage of cosmogony today. From this model we should expect the universe to show its age by certain appearances. Let us see if this old age for the steller system is really the case, or if a youthfulness is more the appearance of the stars, galaxies, clusters of galaxies, and dust and gas in space. . . .

An Age Index for the Big Bang Model

The big bang concept starts with all the matter in the universe concentrated in a superdense core with a density of 10^{25} g/cm³ and a temperature in excess of 10^{16} °K. The alleged initial superdense, hot cosmic fluid was a mix of the strongly interacting elementary particles composed of mesons, protons, neutrons, etc., and a smaller proportion of photons and the lighter-weight muons, electrons, neutrinos, etc. Supposedly there was an equal amount of antimatter present also. At the near instantaneous origin of time by this scheme, there was the annihilation of heavier elementary particles into gamma radiation resulting in a huge fireball. The fireball stage ends as radiation decouples from matter. Quasars and clusters of proto-galaxies condense. And, finally, galaxies and stars form and, it is said, they are still forming today. There you have it—the big bang—tremendously exciting but not a shred of evidence to prove it and much to disprove the notion in the first place!

A Young Solar System

Evolution requires an old earth and an old solar system. Without billions of years, virtually all informed evolutionists will admit that their theory is dead. But by hiding the "origins question" behind the veil of vast periods of time, the unsolvable problems become difficult for scientists to see and laymen to imagine. Our media and text books have implied for over a century that this almost unimaginable age is correct, but practically never do they or the professors examine the shaky assumptions and growing body of contrary evidence. Therefore, most people instinctively believe that things are old, and it is disturbing (at least initially) to hear evidence that our origins are relatively recent.

Actually most dating techniques show that the earth and solar system are young, usually less than 10,000 years old.

Institute for Creation Research, *Evidence for Creation Series*, March 1981.

Using the conventional model of star formation based on the above described big bang, as matter expanded outward from the explosion, stars were formed by gravitational collapse of huge, turbulent clouds of hydrogen. The cloud temperature was raised as gravitational potential energy was given up when the cloud presumably collapsed. At some stage thermonuclear reactions became possible because of the high temperatures supposedly generated in the cloud, and hydrogen was converted to energy and helium according to processes involving the proton-proton cycle, the C-N-O cycle, etc. With the passage of time the various heavier chemical elements should be formed in the stars. As time elapses the chemical composition of the stars and, of course, the interstellar medium (material between the stars) should change considerably, says this model. After 15 to 20 billion years there should be rather tremendous chemical evolution of the universe. This, then, would be one of the signs of aging for the universe in this big bang concept. What do we see?

Chemical Composition of Stars

The spectra of a wide variety of stars show atmospheric compositions for them very similar to that of the sun. The similarity in abundance for stars of as widely differing ages as a Bo star, which, according to the evolutionary scheme, formed only a few million years ago, and a red giant or the planetary nebulae, which by the evolutionary scheme, should be among the oldest objects in the galaxy and, hence, seven or more billion years old, indicate that the interstellar medium has hardly changed at all. There is this serious lack of evidence for so-called chemical evolution. In other words, the sun; a very "young" Bo star; Tau Scorpii; planetary nebulae; and many other normal stars all have the same chemical composition, within the limits of observational error. This is significant because the alleged ages of these objects cover the whole supposed lifetime of the Milky Way.

These analyses show that throughout this supposed lifetime of the galaxy the interstellar matter has had an almost unchanged composition. There are a small number of exceptional stars, however, that do show a quite different chemical makeup than the other stellar bodies. But the stars that are suspected of being the "oldest" in the evolution scheme show abundances of the elements from carbon to barium that are two magnitudes smaller than the "younger" stars like the sun when they should be much larger. This evidence would seem to indicate that the universe is nothing near its alleged age since it shows practically no change, or that the energy generation processes in the stars and their exchange with the interstellar medium are not remotely understood, or both!

Age of Galaxies

The formation of galaxies in the first place seems to be an insurmountable difficulty for all the various naturalistic cosmogonies. There are some observations that would lead one to believe that galaxies are of recent origin and, thus, do not fit the time scheme of the naturalistic cosmogonies:

1. Galaxies never appear to occur singly. They are only found in pairs or in larger aggregates.

2. In general, the masses of the galaxies that are members of a physically well-isolated group or cluster seem to be smaller than the mass that would be required to bind the galaxies gravitationally. Thus, the groups or clusters of galaxies must be of recent origin or they would have long ago disintegrated the groupings by their tremendous velocities exceeding the escape speeds for the clusters.

3. Some pairs of or multiple galaxies are joined by bridges of luminous matter. In a few cases it has been noted that the speeds of the galaxies along the radial direction alone are of the order of several thousand kilometers per second so that these galaxies cannot be gravitationally bound and would separate quite rapidly. They, therefore, must have originated recently, and it would seem as completely formed galaxies!

4. Further, a galaxy is an assemblage of stars that cannot rotate as a rigid body; the inner parts revolve in shorter times than the

outer. An enormous difficulty which all theories that propose a large age for the universe encounter is that any spiral-arm galaxy structure will be wound up into a near circle in a fraction of one to a few revolutions of the galaxy—10 million to, say, 500 million years. Optical observations of rotations of galaxies indicate for most galaxies the spiral arms turn in the rotational direction or they "trail."

There are a number of explanations for the arms in a spiral galaxy. One hypothesis is that the material in the disk of the galaxy is concentrated into separate lanes or avenues having a high density of gas and dust and many stars. These avenues radiate from the center of the galaxy and are curved into the spiral form by the spin of the galaxy. . . .

Proof that Science Is Wrong

Because of hard research by scientists who are creationists, many are taking a second look at the idea that 4.5 billion years could be the age of the earth, or that the universe started with a "Big Bang," or that space is curved because of possible relativity relationships. Some of these space concepts are accepted because God has been ruled out of space science. . . .

Just because distance might be 40 billion light-years does not mean that the universe is 40 billion years old. With God and His special creation in the picture, God could easily have made all of this, by a Word, only 6,000 years ago. If these immense years were true, all the dust in the solar system should have been swept into the sun by now, but we still find it in space. The spiral galaxies should no longer be spiral if there were these immense ages. If the moon is even only 3.5 billion years old, there ought to be at least 50 feet of dust on the moon, and we have found almost none.

Bible-Science Association, "The Heavens Declare the Glory of God."

A spiral galaxy with an open structure would have a lifetime vastly shorter than the evolutionist's time scale. As Robert Jastrow puts it: "There are far too many Sc galaxies in the sky to be consistent with such a short lifetime as this: "If this system of differential rotation, with varying rotation speeds at different distances from the center, has persisted since the origin of the galaxy, from the evolutionist viewpoint based on their huge time scale, one may wonder why there are still spiral arms in our galaxy and in other galaxies we observe. In the evolutionist time scale the sun could have made fifty revolutions during the alleged lifetime of the galaxy, but matter closer to the center would have made many more revolutions. Thus, the obvious question is: why haven't the arms wound up very tightly? Perhaps not a single revolution has occurred. This writer thinks the galaxies just recently came to be and this unique spiral structure, though tending to disperse, has not had time to do so since a short time scale is involved. . . .

Time Scale for Generation of Stellar Energy

Another problem regarding the ages of the stars comes from the Eddington mass-luminosity law that has to do with the rate at which stars burn up their energy. Very massive stars burn up their energy so much faster than less massive stars that they cannot last nearly as long. The Eddington mass-luminosity law says that the power radiated by a star is given by the expression: $L = kM^{3.4}$. It is argued that the very bright and hot stars (O and B) must be of recent origin since, if they were born at the alleged beginning (10 to 20 billion years ago by the evolutionist scheme) of things with their present very large masses, they should have burned out long ago. However, it should be pointed out that many astronomers do not agree that new stars are constantly being formed. The late C.F. von Weizsacker argued that all stars in the Milky Way galaxy must have condensed at about the same time from the original gas and dust, and that present bright stars got their luminosity by accretion of matter from interstellar matter. This view is based on the accretion theory proposed by Fred Hoyle, R.A. Lyttleton, and Herman Bondi.

It used to be thought that all the stars were the same age. There is the co-existence of giants (20 x sun's mass) and dwarfs (1 x sun's mass) in the same clusters. If the members of the clusters had the same origin from the same source at the same time, how could they differ in age? If we imagine time to run backward from the present instant, it is found by R.A. Lyttleton that a star's mass will build up to infinity in a small fraction of the time that it would take for the hydrogen content of the star to diminish by one-half with time running the ordinary way. . . .

Conclusions About Time

These clues do not exactly determine the actual age of the universe but do put upper limits on the age. These upper limits deny the huge time span necessary for the evolutionist's case. The signs say the universe is young.

The myth that unlimited time is available in which the evolutionists may frame their schemes to explain things has been around for quite a while now. However, the scientific evidence continues to accumulate labelling the huge ages of the universe, the solar system, and the earth as a fable, not a conclusion reached by an adherence to scientific proof.

Was there really a big bang? *I believe that the answer clearly must be no!* When we come to the universe in total and the large number of complex objects in it, the big bang is able to explain nothing. Further, the age of the universe appears to be young, not old as is demanded by the big bang and steady state hypotheses.

To repeat (in order to emphasize the incredibility of the big bang as an explanation), the big bang supposedly is chaos leading to diversity and order. This hypothesis begins with strange and incredible ideas regarding a so-called primeval atom and its original state. If this "physical monstrosity" were not in equilibrium, it must have been unstable in the beginning, which is a contradiction in terms to say the least; if it were in equilibrium, some external force would be necessary to start it in motion. Henry Brinton points out that this hypothesis proposes "a state of equilibrium which spontaneously unbalances after an infinite time." In other words, starting with an initial chaotic and homogeneous mixture of the three elements: radiation, hydrogen, and helium, we are supposed to believe that this would end with, for example, our solar system, the earth, and life on it. The big bang cosmology starts off with a very compact and heavy body comprising all energy and matter in the universe which disperses at very high speeds, and then, for reasons no one has been able to explain, some parts of the cloud stop expanding and condense to form the galaxies and these bodies within each galaxy, stars, and then as if by magic, start moving apart. Or, taking a later view, that all these highly complex bodies somehow formed by gravitational condensation while all the matter was moving apart at tremendously high speed and was in such a state that the density was 10^{-25} to 10^{-24} gm/cm^3. Disorganized, randomly oriented gas clouds are supposed eventually to produce highly organized compact bodies, such as complex stars and planets. Stars supposedly are recycled many times to account for the cosmic abundances of the elements since the big bang could not account for them. The preceding discussions have shown the futility of such fanciful speculations, but Professor F.M. Johnson's little verse comes to mind as the big bang hypothesis is considered:

> What power man has to believe
> With blindness or selective sieve;
> The universe must fit his mind
> Put facts and figures far behind.

Perhaps what Professor R. Benton said regarding black holes could be applied to the followers of the big bang cosmogony:

> Theoretical astrophysicists—some of the more renowned ones—are staring into a black box from which any number of assumptions can be made on the existence of things they envision from the nothingness they see.

Truly we have suffered too long and too disastrously under serfdom to barren naturalistic nature-myths regarding the cosmology and the cosmogony of this actual universe. The evolutionist lives in a dream world in which any resemblance to the real world is lacking.

Hans Alfven has remarked that the evidence for the big bang

. . . is totally obliterated but the less there is of scientific support, the more fanatical is the belief in it. As you know this cosmology is utterly absurd—it claims that the whole of the universe was created at a certain instant as an exploding atomic bomb with a size much less than the head of a pin. It seems that in the present intellectual climate it is a great asset of the big bang cosmology that it offends common sense: (I believe because it it absurd!)

Otto Struve regarded cosmogonical theories as "bubbles of pure thought." Herman Bondi remarked recently: "As one erstwhile cosmologist, I speak with feelings of the fact that the theories of the origin of the Universe have been disproved by present day empirical evidence, as have various theories of the origin of the Solar System."

In the light of the data about our universe and the laws of physics and chemistry, the actual universe must be the result of intelligent design and intelligently ordered creation of space, matter, energy, time, motion and the initiation of intelligently ordered energy transformation by the infinite, omniscient, omnipotent Creator.

"I am content to do my science by building a coherent picture of a multibillion-year-old creation."

The Universe Is Ancient

Owen Gingerich

Owen Gingerich is a professor of astronomy and of the history of science at Harvard University. He is a member of the American Academy of Arts and Sciences and the American Philosophical Society. In the following viewpoint, Gingerich presents his evidence for the age of the universe and argues that it is billions of years old. He takes issue with creation-scientists' attempts to date the universe to make it coincide with a biblical interpretation.

As you read, consider the following questions:

1. What "clues" does the author give the reader to support his interpretation that the universe is ancient?
2. Gingerich gives three ways to determine the age of objects in the universe. How do these methods conflict with the methods of the author in the opposing view?
3. What does the author believe is wrong with the creation-scientists' views?

Owen Gingerich, "Let There Be Light: Modern Cosmogony and Biblical Creation," in *Is God a Creationist?: The Religious Case Against Creation-Science*. New York: Charles Scribner's Sons, 1983.

In the microscopic world of the atom there are marvels to stagger the imagination. Physicists have become modern alchemists, transforming gold to mercury and uranium to strontium. Submicroscopic particles can annihilate antiparticles, transforming matter into a burst of energy, or, in reverse, pure energy can give birth to matter with exotic, newly described properties of charm, color, and strangeness as well as mass and electrical charge. At the other end of the scale, astronomers plumb the world of the large, delineating our Milky Way as a giant pinwheel galaxy containing over 200 billion stars, about fifty for every man, woman, and child on earth. And beyond our own stellar system, countless other galaxies are scattered out to the fringes of the universe, some 10 billion light years away.

These are all discoveries of our own century, most of them scarcely half a century old. Yet none of them is quite as astonishing as the scientific scenario that has now been outlined for the first moments of creation. During this past decade knowledge of the world of the smallest possible sizes, the domain of particle physics, has been combined with astronomy to describe the universe in its opening stages. The physics ultimately fails as the nucleo-cosmologists push their calculations back to Time Zero, but they get pretty close to the beginning, to 10 (-43) second. At that point, at a second split so fine that no clock could measure it, the entire observable universe is compressed within the wavelike blur described by the uncertainty principle, so tiny and compact that it could pass through the eye of a needle. Not just this room, or the earth, or the solar system, but *the entire universe* squeezed into a dense dot of pure energy. And then comes the explosion. "There is no way to express that explosion," writes the poet Robinson Jeffers.

> . . . All that exists
> Roars into flame, the tortured fragments rush away from
>   Each other into all the sky, new universes
> Jewel the black breast of night; and far off the outer nebulae
>   like charging spearmen again
> Invade emptiness. . . .

Evidence for the Big Bang

But, you may well ask, what evidence do we have that this wondrous tale is true? Or is it some kind of strange fiction? "Where wast thou when I laid the foundations of the earth?" the Lord asked Job from the whirlwind (Job 38:4) and, to be sure, none of us was there. So, I must admit, what the scientists in my detective story have devised is an intricate reconstruction, assembled just as the detective in a whodunit thriller systematically reconstructs the crime. That metaphor is not bad, for a great deal of modern science rests on conjecture, albeit rational conjecture. Yet it is not quite adequate to convey the grandeur and extent of

110

modern science. Personally, I believe there is a better metaphor in likening science to a beautiful, panoramic tapestry. It is beautiful in the way the contrasting patterns and themes are organized into a unified, coherent whole. It is panoramic in its scope, the majestic sweep that covers all of nature from the minutest subatomic particle to the vast outer reaches of space and time. Like a tapestry, it is a human artifact, ingeniously and seamlessly woven together. It is not easy to unravel one small part without affecting the whole.

I cannot, in my short compass here, lay in place all the threads of this vast tapestry whose pattern includes the first moments of creation. Nevertheless, let me try to weave several skeins into place. . . .

A Universe Billions of Years Old

The universe still took billions of years to form. The average person may think of an explosion as occurring in one instant of time—perhaps as quickly as you can say "Let there be." But, of course, this is not true with respect to the type of explosion described in the Big Bang theory. According to that theory the explosion started about ten billion years ago and is still continuing today. This, it is said, accounts for the presently expanding universe.

Ralph B. Shirley, *American Atheist*, December 1980.

The problem of ages is closely akin to that of the distances. Around 1917, V.M. Slipher, working at the Lowell Observatory, found that key features in the spectra of the spiral nebulae were shifted toward the red end of the spectral rainbow compared to similar laboratory measurements. When interpreted as a Doppler shift (similar to the change in pitch of a siren as it passes and recedes from us), these red shifts indicated surprisingly high recessional velocities, some exceeding a thousand kilometers per second. Such speeds are high by any terrestrial standard, but slow compared to the speed of light. After Edwin Hubble had determined the distances to some of these spirals, it became apparent that the farther the galaxy, the faster it was rushing away from us.

These data arrived on the scene just as the cosmologists had begun to speculate on the large-scale properties of the universe, and out of this confluence of theory and observation arose the concept of the expansion of the universe. It was a concept of quite awesome beauty: from a super-dense state, "All that exists/Roars into flame, the tortured fragments rush away from/Each other into all the sky." What is more, given the rate of expansion and the distances of the galaxies, we can calculate backwards to the time when they were back together, "crushed in one harbor," in Robinson Jeffers' phrase. And the time comes out about 10 to 20 billion

111

years ago, a time that can be interpreted as the age of the universe itself.

There are two quite independent ways to get the ages of some very old things in the universe. I have before me a fragment of the Allende meteorite, a ton of which fell in northern Mexico in 1969. It is probably the oldest object I'll ever touch, dated at 4.6 billion years. How is that age determined? The meteorite contains trace amounts of several radioactive isotopes such as palladium-107, which very gradually changes to silver. In the early stages of the solar system, certain minerals crystallized out as the meteorite formed and cooled, and these crystals contained specific but different amounts of the isotopes, depending on the mineral. Once the atoms were locked up in the crystal structure, they couldn't move, but the radioactive palladium would slowly disintegrate at a known rate, increasing the silver-107. But the original amount of the other silver isotopes remain unchanged, so careful analyses of the isotope ratios in several of the minerals can give the time of crystallization. According to this analysis, the minerals in the small white nodules within the Allende meteorite crystallized 4.6 billion years ago.

Determining the Age of Objects

Not only has it been possible to determine the age of a specific object such as the Allende meteorite, but even the elements themselves can be dated. If the atoms were infinitely old, then radioactive uranium and thorium would have turned to lead. Their very existence tells us that they were formed at a finite time past. Long ago a supernova may have gone off in our neighborhood of the Milky Way, spewing forth within its nuclear ashes a wide variety of elements. We are all recycled star stuff. The iron in our blood is a typical sample of reused cosmic wastes. Included among that stellar ejecta were a variety of radioactive atoms, and the nuclear physicists can calculate the original ratios of these isotopes. Then, from the currently observed ratios, they can calculate back to the time of the supernova explosion. Careful modeling of the pattern of multiple supernova explosions and the examination of isotopes such as iodine-129 and plutonium-244 yields an age of about 10 billion years. These radioactive dating methods do not give a highly precise answer, but what seems to me very impressive is that the results fall in the same ballpark as the expansion age, that is, roughly 10 billion years. It would really be embarrassing if the ages of the atoms came out, say, 50 billion years, that is, several times older than the universe, but fortunately that hasn't happened.

The third way to arrive at a truly ancient age is to calculate the evolution of stars in a globular star cluster, one of those immense and fundamental units Shapley used for inferring the vastness of our Milky Way system. The globular clusters are gravitationally

Great Scientific Papers of the Ages

very stable, and therefore they can hang together for a long time. The brightest stars in these clusters are yellow and orange. That means they're a lot cooler than, for example, the profligate blue stars that make up most of the constellation Orion. We can calculate how fast those blue Orion stars use up their nuclear fuel; the most luminous will spend their energy in a few million years. If the dinosaurs were smart enough to have looked up to the stars, they wouldn't have seen the constellation Orion—if it had been there then, it wouldn't be here now, for its stars would have long since burned out. (I don't think the dinosaurs were smart enough to notice the stars, but on the other hand some birds, who might be considered descendants of the dinosaurs, do use the stars to navigate in their long migrational flights!)

In the globular clusters the brightest blue stars have long since burned out, and our calculations show that the cluster stars somewhat fainter have now evolved into the yellow giants that bejewel these celestial brooches. The calculations of a star's evolving structure are complex, and could scarcely be made without high-speed electronic computers, but they do show that the globulars are very ancient objects: at least 10 billion, but probably not over 15 billion years. . . .

A Superdense Beginning

The evidence that the universe had a definite, superdense beginning is somewhat different in nature, and we must approach it more circuitously. Suppose we run time backward in our calculations, to see what the universe is like as its density increases. The total mass and energy will remain the same, but the temperature will rise as the matter-energy is compressed. Finally the temperature becomes so high, and the mean energy of the components so great, that the presently-known laws of physics no longer apply. This happens when we are a split second from squashing the universe into nothingness.

Now let us run the clock forward again, and let me briefly describe the action. In the first few minutes things happen much faster than we can possibly describe them. In the first microseconds the high-energy photons vastly outnumber particles of matter, but there is a continual interchange between the photons and heavy particles of matter and antimatter. Einstein's famous $E=mc^2$ equation helps describe this situation in which the energy of the photons is converted into mass and vice versa. By the end of the first millisecond, the creation of protons and antiprotons is essentially finished, and the vast majority of them have already been annihilated back into photons. As the universe loses its incredible compression, the average energy per photon drops, and during this first second electrons and antielectrons (called positrons) are repeatedly formed and annihilated, finally leaving about 100 million photons of light for every atom, a ratio that still remains.

The thermonuclear detonation of the universe is now on its way, and in the next minute fusion reactions take place that build up deuterium and helium nuclei. After the first few minutes the explosive nuclear fireworks are over, but the headlong expansion continues, and the cosmic egg gradually cools. Still, the temperature remains so high for the next 300,000 years that whenever an electron and proton combine into a neutral hydrogen atom, it is almost immediately split apart by one of the abundant, omnipresent photons. Gradually, however, the average energy of the photons drops, and they lose their potency for ionizing the hydrogen. This detail I would have omitted from my sketch, except for its interesting observational consequence. At that moment when the photons lose their potency, the universe becomes transparent. This happens because the photons no longer interact so intensively with the atoms; the photons fly across space unimpeded, although their color is redshifted by the expansion of the universe. They are ours to observe, and they have been observed by looking out every direction into space, the fossil evidence of the primeval fireball of the Big Bang. This observed background radiation is one piece of evidence supporting the contemporary scientific picture of creation, and the other is the observed abundance of helium and of deuterium, which match well the predicted amounts that would be formed in that cosmic explosion.

The Big Bang and Genesis

This is indeed a thrilling scenario of all that exists roaring into flame and charging forth into emptiness. And its essential framework, of everything springing forth from that blinding flash, bears a striking resonance with those succinct words of Genesis 1:3: "And God said, 'Let there be light.'" Who could have guessed even a hundred years ago, not to mention two or three thousand years ago, that a scientific picture would emerge with electromagnetic radiation as the starting point of creation! According to the NASA astrophysicist Robert Jastrow, the agnostic scientists should sit up and take notice, and even be a little worried. But let us look a little more carefully at the extent of the convergence. Both the contemporary scientific account and the age-old biblical account assume a beginning. The scientific account concerns only the transformation of everything that now is. It does not go beyond that, to the singularity when there was nothing and then suddenly the inconceivably energetic seed for the universe abruptly came into being. . . .

The band of theologians has an answer: God did it!

But for either a self-professed agnostic like Jastrow or for a believer, such an answer is unrevealing and even superficial, for it cloaks our ignorance beneath a name and tells us nothing further about God beyond the concept of an omnipotent Creator. Perhaps for that reason even the book of Genesis tacitly ignores that mind-boggling step when something came from nothing. What the Bible has to say concerns what happened next and, in fact, both the scientific and the biblical accounts portray the latent creativity as the universe begins to unfold, beginning with the grand and simple, and leading to the immediate and complex. The scientific picture sketches the creation of atoms, of galaxies, of stars, of life, even of man. Likewise, Genesis speaks of the sun and moon, of plants and animals, and of man.

Science vs. Religion

But there is a truly fundamental difference in their viewpoints. The great tapestry of science is woven together in a grand and awesome design with the question "How?" How can the universe end up with a preponderance of positively charged nuclei? How can fluctuations arise to give birth to galaxies? How can the presence of iron atoms be explained? How can hemoglobin come about? The scientific account starts with our present, everyday universe. Detailed observations of the natural world provide the warp of our tapestry, and the theoretical explanations provide the "how," the weft that holds the picture together. . . .

I know, just as the Catholic Church in Galileo's day knew, that there can be alternate explanations for certain observations. For example, I accept as a working hypothesis the Big Bang model of the universe, but I know that the evidence I have cited concerning the background radiation and the abundances of the elements might have any number of other explanations. But what I am not willing to accept—and this is very important—is some special explanation that does not fit the rest of the picture. All of science is in a sense hypothetical. But the tapestry is of a piece, and it cannot by shredded easily. That is why I am uninterested in the ad hoc and particular claims made here or there by the advocates of "creation science." Perhaps the ultimate truth is that the world was created only 6,000 years ago, but since the Creator has filled it with wonderful clues pointing back 10 or 20 billion years, I am content to do my science by building a coherent picture of a multibillion-year-old creation, even though that may be only a grand hypothesis. Because it is the coherency of the picture and the systematic procedures for getting there—not the final truth—that science is all about.

"Order occurs by chance all the time."

The Universe Was Created by Accident

Victor Stenger

A near-constant battle between scientists and theologians over the origins of the universe centers on whether or not the universe was created by a "Grand Designer." Theologians argue that the many factors that resulted in the creation of an Earth inhabited by man did not happen by coincidence, but required the hand of God. In the following viewpoint, Victor Stenger, a professor of physics at the University of Hawaii, takes issue with the theologians' view. He argues that physicists see order created out of chaos all the time.

As you read, consider the following questions:

1. Does the author believe that there is any evidence for the premise that the universe was created? Why or why not?
2. What point does Stenger make when he compares the creation of the universe with that of a raindrop freezing?
3. Does the author believe that everything must have a cause? Why or why not?

Victor Stenger, "Was the Universe Created?" *Free Inquiry*, Summer 1987. Reprinted with permission.

Physicists are now claiming that the hundreds of billions of stars and galaxies, including the earth and humanity, are not conscious creations but an accident. There is no Creator, because *there was no creation.*

This is not a new idea. It first appeared in modern scientific literature in a short article in *Nature* (Tryon 1973) that received little notice. Suggestive as it was, it nonetheless failed to examine all the evidence adequately or to develop its hypothesis. Since 1980, however, there has been a tremendous upsurge in theoretical work on the early universe; hundreds of papers have appeared describing conditions during the first tiny fraction of a second after time began. Only a few of these papers directly touch on the question of whether the universe's origin was accidental or designed. Yet these studies are rapidly converging on the conclusion that the universe spontaneously formed out of a void. It would be too strong to say that we have final "proof"—if there is such a thing as proof in science—against the creation of the universe or the existence of a Grand Design. But it is fair to say that *there is not a single shred of evidence that demands that we hypothesize that the universe was created,* and we can now at least provisionally understand how all we are and all we know could have come about by *chance.*

The Inflationary Universe

Evidence that the universe is now expanding from a Big Bang that occurred ten to twenty billion years ago is overwhelming. Not only has the remnant of that explosion—the 3 degrees Kelvin microwave background—been discovered, but detailed calculations on the synthesis of helium and other light elements extant during the explosion agree exactly with observations. Nevertheless, the pre-1980 Big Bang model was incomplete, and it usually assumed certain *initial conditions.* In scientific terms, this is what the debate over planned versus chance creation comes down to: Is it necessary to invoke a set of initial conditions from which the universe evolved—the Grand Design—or can we show that the structure of the universe naturally evolved from nothing?

Note that it is not sufficient merely to say, "You can't get something from nothing." While our everyday experience and common sense seem to support this principle, if there is anything that we have learned from twentieth-century physics, it is this: Common sense is often wrong, and our normal experiences are but a tiny fraction of reality. We should not be surprised when science jars our picture of the cosmos.

The scientific revolution, still in progress after four hundred years, is not so much the result of people getting smarter as it is both the cause and effect of the advance of technology. Increasingly sensitive instruments bring us data about the very large and

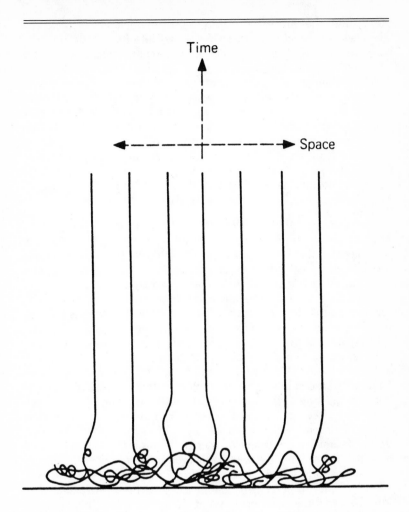

The universe begins in a chaotic state. Imagine, as in this illustration, a large number of strings hanging vertically. At floor level the strings are coiled, tangled, and knotted together in a dense layer. In this analogy each string is a worldline along which intervals of time are measured. High above the floor there is an orderly arrangement, as in ordinary space-time, where events occur sequentially and affect each other in a deterministic manner; but close to the floor the worldlines are jumbled into closed and open loops and there is no common sequential property that we can identify with time. Everything has become irrational and indeterministic.

very small that are inaccessible to our unaided senses. And the theories we develop to describe these data feed back into the development of yet more precise and innovative instruments; and thus the cycle continues. . . .

The universe very likely went through a period of exponential inflation during which it increased in size by fifty orders of magnitude in 10^{-30} seconds or less. Much has been written on the "inflationary universe," so I will not linger on this point. Rather, I will attempt to show how inflation probably was triggered by accident from an initial state of total chaos and, more generally, confront the question of whether the evidence of an orderly universe around us requires that there was, at the beginning, or now, any Grand Design. Let me start with the latter.

Entropy and the Grand Design

The universe presented to our senses is obviously not a random jumble of data. There is order, though less than most people believe. This order is frequently cited as evidence for a Grand Design: How could it all have happened by chance?

Physicists well understand, however, that order occurs by chance all the time. Crystals grow into intricate patterns that are not predictable—and *predictability* is what we mean by order. The old saying that no two snowflakes are alike is profound: each intricate, unique, and beautiful pattern is accidental.

The measure of disorder or unpredictability is *entropy*. Order can be produced in some local region, with a *decrease* in the local entropy, as long as the total entropy of the universe remains constant or increases. That is, the rest of the universe must become more disorderly when a smaller system becomes ordered. This is the famous second law of thermodynamics.

When the second law was discovered in the nineteenth century by Nicolas Carnot and others, people were led to a depressing conclusion: The universe must be proceeding inexorably to a state of ultimate total disorder, to what has been called "heat death." Small pockets of order like the earth may occasionally form, but eventually everything must collapse into chaos. There was, however, a glimmer of hope in this idea: The universe must have begun in a state of very high order. Many concluded that only a divine creator could have produced that order.

Order and Disorder

Several fundamental developments in this century turn that conclusion on its head. Nineteenth-century science viewed the universe as a place of more or less fixed stars in a *firmament*. In 1932 the concept of such a firmament of stars was disproved and replaced by the model of an expanding universe when Edwin Hubble discovered the galaxies and found them to be rapidly receding from one another. This, coupled with the observation of the microwave background in 1964 by Penzias and Wilson, made it possible to conceive of the universe as having irrupted from utter amorphousness—that is, from entropy—and still being able to produce orderly systems like galaxies and DNA.

This appears paradoxical, but it is not too hard to see how it could happen. First, most of the universe's entropy is carried in the microwave background (or in a background of "dark matter" that is believed to be present but has not yet been detected by scientific instruments; its existence affects the details but not the general conclusions reported here). For every atom in the galaxies there are a billion photons in the background. In fact, the galaxies—including the Milky Way, which contains the earth and our sun—are really no more than minor residue left over from the Big Bang. They would not be there except for a slight asymmetry between matter and antimatter that resulted when the particles and forces formed.

During the Big Bang most matter and antimatter annihilated into the photons that have since cooled to 3 degrees Kelvin and formed the current background. But the burning was imperfect; and the billions of galaxies in the observable cosmos comprise the tiny bit of unburned remnant that has remained. This asymmetry between matter and antimatter is not just a guess; it is a fundamental part of modern particle physics and was first serendipitously glimpsed by Cronin and Fitch in 1964 in an accelerator experiment involving K-mesons.

Who Made the Universe?

When you get the question "Who made all this?" I answer "Gravity and Chaos made all this. Gravity was born north of the north pole and Chaos was born south of the south pole. They both grew up, fell in love, and the sparks of their love making can be seen in a clear sky every night."

G. Stanley Brown, *American Atheist*, March 1983.

Second, as the universe expands, the maximum entropy that can be contained in its volume increases. A larger volume has more room for disorderly behavior. So, in an expanding universe little pockets of order can easily form in which most of the particles are part of a uniform background; the local entropy decrease is easily compensated for by an entropy *increase* in the remaining part of the universe. Since the orderly part of the universe—the galaxies—includes only a minute fraction of the total particle count, there is plenty of room—and more than adequate energy—for minor, little-ordered structures like the earth and life to appear. . . .

Now, as we extrapolate this variable maximum entropy back in time, it decreases; and, if we go back far enough, we find a remarkable thing. At a very special instant, when the universe was only 10^{-43} second old, the *Planck time*, when the maximum entropy was exactly equal to that of a black hole 10^{-33} centimeter in diameter—a distance known as the *Planck length*. (A particle traveling at the speed of light will travel 10^{-33} centimeter in 10^{-43} second.)

No Grand Design

The entropy of a black hole of any size is the maximum entropy any system of that size can have. This follows from the fact that no light or other carrier of information can escape a black hole. Because we can have no information about what goes on inside one, we can infer that black holes are filled by total chaos, or maximum entropy. In the trade, the fact that a black hole is completely featureless is wittily expressed by the phrase "Black holes have no hair." If the universe had the entropy of a black hole at some time, then it had to be in a state of complete disorder at that time. So we conclude: *There could not have been any Grand Design at the Planck time.*

If the universe had the entropy of a 10^{-33} centimeter black hole at 10^{-43} second, then it was, for all practical purposes, a black hole. Order formed in the universe after this black hole disintegrated into radiation that then cooled to form the universe. That order appeared as a random crystallizing process similar to the formation of a snowflake from a raindrop in an expanding container of water vapor. . . .

There is no point in asking what happened *before* the Planck time; there was no before, because there was not time. It is impossible operationally to define zero absolute time. Further, we have seen that the entropy of the universe at that time was maximal—the universe was as disorderly as it possibly could have been. So if the universe was created, it was placed in a state of complete and utter chaos without even the space, time, and forces needed to produce the ultimate order, which then was generated by chance. I doubt whether that is what most people would regard as a "creation." . . .

When Einstein developed his general theory of relativity he found it necessary to add a new repulsive force, the "cosmological constant," to balance the attraction of gravity and keep the universe a firmament. Later, when Hubble discovered that the universe was expanding, Einstein dropped the constant, calling it his "biggest blunder."

While the cosmological term is of little value in describing gravity dominated by matter, it does allow for an intriguing possibility: A universe empty of matter and radiation can still have a space-time curvature proportional to this cosmological constant. Einstein's equations admit any value or sign for this curvature. He assumed a sign that gave a repulsion to balance the attraction of gravity formed by matter. But the same sign in the absence of matter results in an exponential expansion, far faster than the linear Hubble expansion observed in the red-shifts of galaxies.

So what had to happen to start the universe was the formation of an empty bubble of highly curved space-time. How did this bubble form? What *caused it?* Not everything requires a cause. It could have just happened spontaneously as one of the many linear combinations of universes that has the quantum numbers of the void. Formed with the random values of the cosmological constant and maximum entropy, this bubble expanded exponentially, increasing the maximum entropy, opening up all kinds of room for order to form. This order, the elementary particles and the laws they obeyed in forming the universe, then "froze out," breaking the highly symmetric state of the universe the way an iceberg breaks the planar symmetry of a polar sea. . . .

So we now have order, but the particular order of our universe was a chance happening. Other universes could have formed as well, with other chance orientations of their field vectors and with characteristics totally different from ours. Some may have quickly deflated instead of inflating, being born with an attractive cosmological term. Just as the characteristics of each of us result from a chance encounter between a sperm and an egg, the characteristics of our universe are just those that it happened to get, and they were conducive to forming our kind of life. Our universe is a very unlikely one, but it is the only one we have. And this unlikeliness of our universe is no argument for its having been planned.

No Evidence for Creation

Undoubtedly, in the course of future study we will find many changes in the picture reported here, and even more in the detailed theories that are being developed to describe the events of the early universe. Much is still in the speculative stage, and I must admit that there are yet no known empirical or observational tests that can be used to test the idea of an accidental origin. I believe these will come, as the theories become more specific in their details. The scientific method demands excessive conservatism, and it in fact is just that conservatism that leads us to our current conclusion: There is no evidence for a creation, so one must not presume it. The burden of proof that there was and is a Grand Design rests with those seeking to demonstrate it. It is they who must slide down Occam's razor.

The need for initial conditions at the beginning of time may some day be demonstrated—although I will be surprised if it is. But, if so, it will be by the work of future scientists with bigger telescopes and accelerators, more powerful computers and mathematical methods. And, when that happens, I doubt very much that this new picture of the creation will resemble the primitive mythological image of the Creation that has been carried down by the Judeo-Christian tradition.

"The odds against a universe like ours coming out of something like the Big Bang are enormous. I think there are clearly religious implications."

The Universe Was Created by Design

Holmes Rolston III

Holmes Rolston III is a professor of philosophy at Colorado State University. In the following viewpoint, Rolston quotes many prominent physicists and scientists on the origin of the universe. He concludes that scientific theory is swinging back to the 19th century belief that the universe was created by design.

As you read, consider the following questions:

1. Rolston believes that it is economical to believe that the universe was created by design. Why?
2. What part should the development of mankind play in theories about the universe, according to the author?

Holmes Rolston III, "Shaken Atheism: A Look at the Fine-Tuned Universe." Copyright 1986 Christian Century Foundation. Reprinted by permission from the December 3, 1986 issue of *The Christian Century*.

125

Both astrophysicists and microphysicists have lately been discovering that the series of events that produced our universe had to happen in a rather precise way—at least, they had to happen that way if they were to produce life as we know it. Some might find this fact unremarkable. After all, we are here, and it is hardly surprising that the universe is of such kind as to have produced us. It is simply a tautology to say that people who find themselves in a universe live in a universe where human life is possible. Nevertheless, given the innumerable other things that could have happened, we have reason to be impressed by the astonishing fact of our existence. Like the man who survives execution by a 1,000-gun firing squad, we are entitled to suspect that there is some reason we are here, that perhaps there is a Friend behind the blast.

When we consider the first seconds of the big bang that created the universe, writes Bernard Lovell, an astronomer, "it is an astonishing reflection that at this critical early moment in the history of the universe, all of the hydrogen would have turned into helium if the force of attraction between protons—that is, the nuclei of the hydrogen atoms—had been only a few percent stronger. . . . No galaxies, no stars, no life would have emerged. It would have been a universe forever unknowable by living creatures. A remarkable and intimate relationship between man, the fundamental constants of nature and the initial moments of space and time seems to be an inescapable condition of our existence."

Astronomer Fred Hoyle reports that his atheism was shaken by his own discovery that in the stars, carbon just manages to form and then just avoids complete conversion into oxygen. If one atomic level had varied half a percent, life would have been impossible. "Would you not say to yourself . . . 'Some super-calculating intellect must have designed the properties of the carbon atom, otherwise the chance of my finding such an atom through the blind forces of nature would be utterly minuscule'? Of course you would. . . . The carbon atom is a fix. . . . A common sense interpretation of the facts suggests that a superintellect has monkeyed with the physics. . . . The numbers one calculates from the facts seem to me so overwhelming as to put this conclusion almost beyond question."

Religious Implications

"Somebody had to tune [the universe] very precisely," concludes Marek Demianski, a Polish cosmologist. Stephen Hawking, the Einstein of our time, agrees: "The odds against a universe like ours coming out of something like the Big Bang are enormous. I think there are clearly religious implications." How the various physical processes are "fine-tuned to such stunning accuracy is surely one of the great mysteries of cosmology," remarks P.C.W. Davies, a physicist. "Had this exceedingly delicate tuning of values been even slightly upset, the subsequent structure of the universe would have been totally different." "Extraordinary physical coincidences and apparently accidental cooperation ... offer compelling evidence that something is 'going on.' ... A hidden principle seems to be at work."

B.J. Carr and M.J. Rees, cosmologists, conclude, "Many interrelations between different scales that at first sight seem surprising are straightforward consequences of simple physical arguments. But several aspects of our Universe—some of which seem to be prerequisites for the evolution of any form of life—depend rather delicately on apparent 'coincidences' among the physical constants. ... The Universe must be as big and diffuse as it is to last long enough to give rise to life."

The Universe Was No Accident

If there was no Creator, how did the universe come into being? I don't believe, I could simply not get myself to think that it all happened by accident. ...

God made two creations: one of the world and one of the laws of nature. He presented the laws of nature through Noah after the Flood, as you read in the fourth chapter of Genesis. Henceforth there should be seed-time and harvest, summer and winter, day and night, and so forth, and I promise by the rainbow that I shall keep this promise.

Henry Margenau, *The World & I*, April 1987.

No universe can provide several billion years of stellar cooking time unless it is several billion light years across. If the size of the universe were reduced from 10^{22} to 10^{11} stars, that smaller but still galaxy-sized universe might seem roomy enough, but it would run through its entire cycle of expansion and recontraction in about one year. And if the matter of the universe were not as homogeneous as it is, then large portions of it would have been so dense that they would already have undergone gravitational collapse. Other portions would have been so thin that they could not have given birth to galaxies and stars. On the other hand, if it were entirely homogeneous, then the chunks of matter that make development possible could not have assembled.

Physicists have made some other, quite striking thought experiments. If the universe were not expanding, then it would be too hot to support life. If the expansion rate of the universe had been a little faster or slower, then the universe would already have recollapsed or else the galaxies and stars could not have formed. The extent and age of the universe are not obviously an outlandish extravagance. Indeed, ours may be the most economical universe in which life and mind can exist—so far as we can cast that question into a testable form.

Change slightly the strengths of any of the four forces that hold the world together (the strong nuclear force, the weak nuclear force, electromagnetism, gravitation—forces ranging over 40 orders of magnitude), or change various particle masses and charges, and the stars would burn too quickly or too slowly, or atoms and molecules, including water, carbon and oxygen, would not form or would not remain stable.

Small Changes

It is not that we cannot imagine another world in which intelligence or life might exist. It is rather that, in this world, any of a hundred small shifts this way or that would render everything blank. Astrophysicists John D. Barrow and Joseph Silk calculate that "small changes in the electric charge of the electron would block any kind of chemistry." A fractional difference, and there would have been nothing. It would be so easy to miss, and there are no hits in the revised universes we can imagine; and yet this universe is a delicate, intricate hit.

One can still explain the universe by randomness—this universe is one of a run of universes and big bangs, and ours happened to have the right characteristics for life. Or one can invoke the many-worlds theory: the universe is constantly splitting into many worlds, some of which will be right for life. But to invent myriads of other worlds in order to explain how this one came to be seems to show an addiction to randomness in one's explanatory scheme. It seems more economical (and remember that science often recommends simplicity in explanations) to posit that there were some constraints on the only universe we know that made it right for life.

The human world stands about midway between the infinitesimal and the immense. The size of our planet is near the geometric mean of the size of the known universe and the size of the atom. The mass of a human being is the geometric mean of the mass of the earth and the mass of a proton. A person contains about 10^{28} atoms, more atoms than there are stars in the universe. Such considerations yield perhaps only a relative location. Still, questions of place and proportion arise.

Nebulae and stars exist at low structural ranges. A galaxy is mostly nothing, as is an atom. Fine-tuned though the system is, at both ends of the spectrum of size nature lacks the complexity found at the meso levels in Earth's ecosystem. Humans do not live at the range of the infinitely small, nor at that of the infinitely large, but they may well live within the range of the infinitely complex, a range generated and supported by the simpler but stunning microphysics and astrophysics. In our 150 pounds of protoplasm, in our three pounds of brain, there may be more operational organization than there is in the whole of the Andromeda Galaxy. The number of associations possible among our 10 billion neurons, and hence the number of thoughts humans can think, may exceed the number of atoms in the universe. Humans, too, are stars in the show.

The Universe and Humans

The point is not that the whole universe is necessary to produce Earth and *Homo sapiens*. To so conclude would demonstrate myopic pride. The issue is richness of potential, not anthropocentrism. There is no need to insist that everything in the universe has some relevance to our being here. God may have overdone the creation in pure exuberance, but why should the parts irrelevant to us trouble us? We might even be a bit sorry if the entire sublime universe turned out to be needed simply for our arrival, or even for the scattering of life and mind here and there within the universe. But certainly we cannot leave ourselves out of the account, either.

In the Mind of God

The principle of simplicity, not to mention the virtue of humility, may again resolve the issue as it did for the founders of science: by recognizing that the order we perceive subsists in the mind of an active God rather than the "choices of nature" or the perception of man; by understanding that the startling design of the cosmos and of life is contingent upon the will of the Lord rather than our existence or upon matter having a soul; by returning to the point where, as astronomer Allan Sandage puts it, "Scientists can believe in order to understand."

A renewed metaphysics may finally allow science to come to terms with its origins after decades of official agnosticism. The "new science" may finally reveal a closer relationship between the Creator and his creation than mere mechanism had assumed. As T.S. Eliot prayed in the twentieth century: "We praise Thee, O God . . . For all things exist only as seen by Thee, only as known by Thee, all things exist/only in Thy light."

Bill Durbin Jr., *Christianity Today*, April 3, 1987.

Since Copernicus, physics has made us wary of claiming a privileged location for Earth. Since Darwin, humans have seemed the result of selection operating over blind variation. Since Newton, the world has seemed only matter in motion. Since Einstein, our location in space and time has seemed a function of our reference frame as observers. Humans have been dwarfed from above, celestially; deflated from below, atomically; and shown to be nothing but electronic particles. In a universe 20 billion years old and 20 billion light years across, humans, the result of 5 billion years of evolution, have felt lost in the stars and in the agelong struggle for life.

But physics has been busy painting a new picture. Christians caught up in the debate over creation in biology may not have noticed how congenial physics and theology have become. The physical world is looking like a fine-tuned watch again, and this time many quantitative calculations support the argument. The forms that matter and energy take seem strangely suited to their destiny.

"[The scientist] has scaled the mountains of ignorance . . . as he pulls himself over the final rock, he is greeted by a band of theologians who have been sitting there for centuries."

God May Be the Creator

Robert Jastrow

Robert Jastrow is an American scientist who has become widely known through his writing on subjects related to science and nuclear arms. He received his Ph.D. from Columbia University in New York. He has researched in the fields of nuclear physics, planetary science, and atmospheric physics, and he received the NASA Medal for Exceptional Scientific Achievement. In spite of his achievements, Jastrow invited the scorn of many fellow scientists with the publication of his timeless book, *God and the Astronomers*. In that book, excerpted in the following viewpoint, Jastrow suggests that God may be the cause of the Big Bang which brought the universe into being.

As you read, consider the following questions:

1. What discovery did Arno Penzias and Robert Wilson make at the Bell Laboratories in 1965?
2. According to Jastrow, why are astronomers upset over the prospect of the universe having a beginning?
3. What does Jastrow say about the state of the universe before the Big Bang?

When an astronomer writes about God, his colleagues assume he is either over the hill or going bonkers. In my case it should be understood from the start that I am an agnostic in religious matters. However, I am fascinated by some strange developments going on in astronomy—partly because of their religious implications and partly because of the peculiar reactions of my colleagues.

In the Beginning

The essence of the strange developments is that the Universe had, in some sense, a beginning—that it began at a certain moment in time, and under circumstances that seem to make it impossible—not just now, but *ever*—to find out what force or forces brought the world into being at that moment. Was it, as the Bible says, that

"Thou, Lord, in the beginning hast laid the foundations of the earth, and the heavens are the work of thine hands"?

No scientist can answer that question; we can never tell whether the Prime Mover willed the world into being, or the creative agent was one of the familiar forces of physics; for the astronomical evidence proves that the Universe was created twenty billion years ago in a fiery explosion, and in the searing heat of that first moment, all the evidence needed for a scientific study of the cause of the great explosion was melted down and destroyed.

This is the crux of the new story of Genesis. It has been familiar for years as the "Big Bang" theory, and has shared the limelight with other theories, especially the Steady State cosmology; but adverse evidence has led to the abandonment of the Steady State theory by nearly everyone, leaving the Big Bang theory exposed as the only adequate explanation of the facts.

An Expanding Universe

The general scientific picture that leads to the Big Bang theory is well known. We have been aware for fifty years that we live in an expanding Universe, in which all the galaxies around us are moving apart from us and one another at enormous speeds. The Universe is blowing up before our eyes, as if we are witnessing the aftermath of a gigantic explosion. If we retrace the motions of the outward-moving galaxies backward in time, we find that they all come together, so to speak, fifteen or twenty billion years ago.

At that time all the matter in the Universe was packed into a dense mass, at temperatures of many trillions of degrees. The dazzling brilliance of the radiation in this dense, hot Universe must have been beyond description. The picture suggests the explosion of a cosmic hydrogen bomb. The instant in which the cosmic bomb exploded marked the birth of the Universe.

Now we see how the astronomical evidence leads to a biblical view of the origin of the world. The details differ, but the essential elements in the astronomical and biblical accounts of Genesis are the same: the chain of events leading to man commenced suddenly and sharply at a definite moment in time, in a flash of light and energy.

Penzias and Wilson

Some scientists are unhappy with the idea that the world began in this way. Until recently many of my colleagues preferred the Steady State theory, which holds that the Universe had no beginning and is eternal. Evidence makes it almost certain that the Big Bang really did occur many millions of years ago. In 1965 Arno Penzias and Robert Wilson of the Bell Laboratories discovered that the earth is bathed in a faint glow of radiation coming from every direction in the heavens. The measurements showed that the earth itself could not be the origin of this radiation, nor could the radiation come from the direction of the moon, the sun, or any other particular object in the sky. The entire Universe seemed to be the source.

God Must Exist

There was too much logic, too much purpose—it was just too beautiful to have happened by accident. It doesn't matter how you choose to worship God, or by whatever name you call him, but he has to exist to have created what I was privileged to see.

Eugene Cernan, astronaut, quoted in *St. Paul Pioneer Press*, April 9, 1985.

The two physicists were puzzled by their discovery. They were not thinking about the origin of the Universe, and they did not realize they had stumbled upon the answer to one of the cosmic mysteries. Scientists who believed in the theory of the Big Bang had long asserted that the Universe must have resembled a white-hot fireball in the very first moments after the Big Bang occurred. Gradually, as the Universe expanded and cooled, the fireball would have become less brilliant, but its radiation would have never disappeared entirely. It was the diffuse glow of this ancient radiation, dating back to the birth of the Universe, that Penzias and Wilson apparently discovered.

A Puzzling Conflict

No explanation other than the Big Bang has been found for the fireball radiation. The clincher, which has convinced almost the last doubting Thomas, is that the radiation discovered by Penzias and Wilson has exactly the pattern of wavelengths expected for the light and heat produced in a great explosion. Supporters of the Steady State theory have tried desperately to find an alternative explanation, but they have failed. At the present time, the Big Bang theory has no competitors.

Theologians generally are delighted with the proof that the Universe had a beginning, but astronomers are curiously upset. Their reactions provide an interesting demonstration of the response of the scientific mind—supposedly a very objective mind—when evidence uncovered by science itself leads to a conflict with the articles of faith in our profession. It turns out that the scientist behaves the way the rest of us do when our beliefs are in conflict with the evidence. We become irritated, we pretend the conflict does not exist, or we paper it over with meaningless phrases. . . .

Violation of Scientific Faith

Scientists cannot bear the thought of a natural phenomenon which cannot be explained, even with unlimited time and money. There is a kind of religion in science; it is the religion of a person who believes there is order and harmony in the Universe, and every event can be explained in a rational way as the product of some previous event; every effect must have its cause; there is no First Cause. Einstein wrote, "The scientist is possessed by the sense of universal causation." This religious faith of the scientist is violated by the discovery that the world had a beginning under conditions in which the known laws of physics are not valid, and as a product of forces or circumstances we cannot discover. When that happens, the scientist has lost control. If he really examined the implications, he would be traumatized. As usual when faced with trauma, the mind reacts by ignoring the implications—in science this is known as "refusing to speculate"—or trivializing the origin of the world by calling it the Big Bang, as if the Universe were a firecracker.

An Unanswerable Question

Consider the enormity of the problem. Science has proven that the Universe exploded into being at a certain moment. It asks, What cause produced this effect? Who or what put the matter and energy into the Universe? Was the Universe created out of nothing, or was it gathered together out of pre-existing materials? And science cannot answer these questions, because, according to the astronomers, in the first moments of its existence the Universe was compressed to an extraordinary degree, and consumed by the heat of a fire beyond human imagination. The shock of that instant must have destroyed every particle of evidence that could have yielded a clue to the cause of the great explosion. An entire world, rich in structure and history, may have existed before our Universe appeared, but if it did, science cannot tell what kind of world it was. A sound explanation may exist for the explosive birth of our Universe; but if it does, science cannot find out what the explanation is. The scientist's pursuit of the past ends in the moment of creation.

This is an exceedingly strange development, unexpected by all but the theologians. They have always accepted the word of the Bible: In the beginning God created heaven and earth. To which St. Augustine added, "Who can understand this mystery or explain it to others?" It is unexpected because science has had such extraordinary success in tracing the chain of cause and effect backward in time. We have been able to connect the appearance of man on this planet to the crossing of the threshold of life, the manufacture of the chemical ingredients of life within stars that have long since expired, the formation of those stars out of the primal mists, and the expansion and cooling of the parent cloud of gases out of the cosmic fireball.

A Purpose to the Universe

As biochemists discover more and more about the awesome complexity of life, it is apparent that the chances of it originating by accident are so minute that they can be completely ruled out. Life cannot have arisen by chance.

Fred Hoyle, *The Intelligent Universe*, 1983.

Now we would like to pursue that inquiry farther back in time, but the barrier to further progress seems insurmountable. It is not a matter of another year, another decade of work, another measurement, or another theory; at this moment it seems as though science will never be able to raise the curtain on the mystery of creation. For the scientist who has lived by his faith in the power of reason, the story ends like a bad dream. He has scaled the mountains of ignorance; he is about to conquer the highest peak; as he pulls himself over the final rock, he is greeted by a band of theologians who have been sitting there for centuries.

"Any real comparison between what the Bible says and what the astronomer thinks shows us instantly that the two have virtually nothing in common."

God Is Not
the Creator

Isaac Asimov

Isaac Asimov is a prolific science writer. He has written countless books and articles, both scientific and science fiction, for young and adult readers. In the following viewpoint, Asimov responds to Robert Jastrow's book, excerpted in the opposing viewpoint. Asimov argues that the Bible and astronomy have nothing in common.

As you read, consider the following questions:

1. List some of the comparisons between the Bible and astronomical research outlined by Asimov.
2. According to the author, what three things might be happening to the universe?
3. Do you think that Asimov's criticism of Jastrow is valid? Why or why not?

Isaac Asimov, "Do Scientists Believe in God?" *Gallery*, June 1979. By permission of the author and of Gallery Magazine. Copyright © 1979 by Montcalm Publishing Corp.

Some scientists are making their peace with theology. If we listen to them, they will tell us that science has only managed to find out, with a great deal of pain, suffering, storm, and strife, exactly what theologians knew all along.

A case in point is Robert Jastrow, an authentic professor of astronomy who has written a book called *God and the Astronomers*. In it he explains that astronomers have discovered that the Universe began very suddenly and catastrophically in what is called a big bang and that they're upset about it.

The theologians, however, Jastrow says, are happy about it, because the Bible says that the Universe began very suddenly when god said, *Let there be light!*

Or, to put it in Jastrow's very own words: "For the scientist who has lived by his faith in the power of reason, the story ends like a bad dream. He has scaled the mountains of ignorance; he is about to conquer the highest peak; as he pulls himself over the final rock, he is greeted by a band of theologians who have been sitting there for centuries."

If I can read the English language, Jastrow is saying that astronomers were sure, to begin with, that the Bible was all wrong; that if the Bible said the Universe had a beginning, astronomers were sure the Universe had *no* beginning; that when they began to discover that the Universe *did* have a beginning, they were so unhappy at the Bible being right that they grew all downcast about their own discoveries.

Nothing in Common

Furthermore, if I can continue to read the English language, Jastrow is implying that since the Bible has all the answers—after all, the theologians have been sitting on the mountain peak for centuries—it has been a waste of time, money, and effort for astronomers to have been peering through their little spyglasses all this time.

Perhaps Jastrow, abandoning his "faith in the power of reason" (assuming he ever had it), will now abandon his science and pore over the Bible until he finds out what a quasar is, and whether the Universe is open or closed, and where black holes might exist—questions astronomers are working with now. Why should he waste his time in observatories?

But I don't think Jastrow will, because I don't really think he believes that all the answers are in the Bible—or that he takes his own book very seriously.

In the first place, any real comparison between what the Bible says and what the astronomer thinks shows us instantly that the two have virtually nothing in common. And here are some real comparisons:

1. The Bible says that the Earth was created at the same time as the Universe was (*In the beginning god created the heavens and*

the earth), with the whole process taking six days. In fact, whereas the Earth was created at the very beginning of creation, the Sun, Moon, and stars were not created until the fourth day.

The astronomer, on the other hand, thinks the Universe was created 15 billion years ago and the Earth (together with the Sun and the Moon) was not created until a little less than five billion years ago. In other words, for ten billion years the Universe existed, full of stars, but without the Earth (or the Sun or the Moon).

The Age of the Universe

2. The Bible says that in the six days of creation, the whole job was finished. (*Thus the heavens and the earth were finished, and all the host of them. And on the seventh day god ended his work which he had made.*)

The astronomer, on the other hand, thinks stars were being formed all through the 15 billion years since the Universe was created. In fact, stars are still being formed now, and planets and satellites along with them; and stars will continue being formed for billions of years to come.

Accidental Details

Genesis is not a book of science. It is accidental if some things agree in detail. I believe the heavens declare the glory of God only to people who've made a religious commitment.

Owen Gingerich, Historian-Astronomer, Harvard University.

---

3. The Bible says that human beings were created on the sixth day of creation, so that the Earth was empty of human intelligence for five days only.

The biologist, on the other hand, thinks (and the astronomer does not disagree) the earliest beings that were even vaguely human didn't appear on the Earth until well over 4 ½ billion years after its creation.

4. The Bible doesn't say when the creation took place, but the most popular view among the theologians on that mountain peak is that creation took place in 4004 B.C.

As I've said, the astronomer thinks creation took place 15 billion years ago.

5. The Bible says the Universe was created through the word of god.

The astronomer, on the other hand, thinks the Universe was created through the operation of the blind, unchanging laws of nature—the same laws that are in operation today.

(Notice, by the way, that in these comparisons I say, "The Bible says. . . . " but "The astronomer thinks. . . . " That is because theologians are always certain in their conclusions and scientists are always tentative in theirs. That, too, is an important distinction.)

Theologians on Their Backs

There are enormous differences, and it would be a very unusual astronomer who could imagine finding any theologians on *his* mountain peak. Where are the theologians who said that creation took place 15 billion years ago? That the Earth was formed ten billion years later? That human beings appeared 4½ billion years later still?

Some theologians may be willing to believe this *now*, but that would only be because scientists showed them the mountain peak and carried them up there.

So what the devil is Jastrow talking about? Where is the similarity between the book of Genesis and astronomical conclusions?

One thing. One thing only.

The Bible says the Universe had a beginning. The astronomer thinks the Universe had a beginning.

That's all.

But even this similarity is not significant, because it represents a *conclusion*, and conclusions are cheap. *Anyone* can reach a conclusion—the theologian, the astronomer, the shoeshine boy down the street.

Anyone can reach a conclusion in any way—by guessing it, by experiencing a gut feeling about it, by dreaming it, by copying it, by tossing a coin over it.

And no matter who reaches a conclusion, and no matter how he manages to do it, he may be right, provided there are a sharply limited number of possible conclusions. If eight horses are running a race, you might bet on a particular horse because the jockey is wearing your favorite colors or because the horse looks like your Aunt Hortense—and you may win just the same.

If two men are boxing for the championship and you toss a coin to pick your bet, you have one chance in two of being right—even if the fight is rigged.

Three Choices

How does this apply to the astronomical and theological view of the Universe? Well, we're dealing with something in which there are a sharply limited number of conclusions—more than a two-man prizefight, but fewer than an eight-animal horserace. There are, after all, just three things that might be happening to the Universe in the long run:

A. The Universe may be unchanging, on the whole, and therefore have neither a beginning nor an end—like a fountain, which, although individual water drops rise and fall, maintains its overall shape indefinitely.

B. The Universe may be changing progressively; that is, in one direction only, and may therefore have a distinct beginning and a different end—like a person, who is born, grows older (never younger), and eventually dies.

C. The Universe may be changing cyclicly, back and forth, and therefore have an end that is at the beginning, so that the process starts over endlessly—like the seasons, which progress from spring, through summer, fall, and winter, but then return to spring again, so that the process starts over. . . .

Questions No Theologian Can Answer

What counts is *not* that astronomers are currently of the opinion that there was once a big bang, in which an enormously concentrated "cosmic egg" that contained all the matter there is exploded with unimaginably catastrophic intensity to form the Universe. What counts is the long chain of investigation that led to the observation of the isotropic radio wave background (shortwave radio waves that reach Earth faintly, and equally, from all directions) that supports that opinion.

Many Theories But God Didn't Do It

The speculation concerning the beginning of the Universe has been right at the top of the list of things for man to understand for as long as there has been recorded history. It is not hard for me to imagine that the same was true long before recorded history as well. . . .

It stands to reason that whatever was "before" must have been the same as "now." It may have been total energy, or it may have been very dense matter, or it may have been just as it is now.

The only thing of which I feel certain: god didn't do it.

Thomas W. Gurley, *American Atheist*, October 1980.

So when the astronomer climbs the mountain, it is irrelevant whether theologians are sitting at the peak or not, if they have not *climbed* the mountain.

As a matter of fact, the mountain *peak* is no mountain peak; it is merely another crossroad. The astronomer will continue to climb. Jastrow seems to think the search has come to an end and there is nothing more for astronomers to find. There occasionally have been scientists who thought the search was all over. They are frequently quoted today, because scientists like a good laugh.

What was the cosmic egg and how did it come to explode at a particular moment in time? How did it form? Was there something before the big bang? Will the results of the explosion make themselves felt forever, or will the exploding fragments at some time begin to come together again? Will the cosmic egg form again and will there be another big bang? Is it alternative C that is the true explanation of the Universe?—these are only some of the infinite number of questions that those astronomers who are not convinced it is all over are interested in. In their search they may eventually reach new and better conclusions, find new and higher mountain peaks, and no doubt, find on each peak guessers and dreamers who have been sitting there for ages and will continue to sit there. And the scientists will pass by on a road that, it seems possible, will never reach an end, but will provide such interesting scenery *en route* that this, by itself, gives meaning to life and mind and thought.

Distinguishing Between Fact and Opinion

This activity is designed to help develop the basic reading and thinking skill of distinguishing between fact and opinion. Consider the following statement: "The big bang theory holds that an enormously concentrated cosmic egg containing all the matter there is exploded with unimaginably catastrophic intensity to form the Universe." This is a fact—the statement decribes a theory about the origins of the universe. The reader could check the accuracy of the description by reading other explanations of the big bang theory in a science textbook. Now consider this statement: "It is absurd to think there is a Creator who made the Universe when we know that random forces joined together to form the Universe." This is clearly an opinion—it is probably impossible to prove or disprove as a fact whether God exists. And the idea that the Universe was formed by random forces in one theory about its origins—many would disagree with this theory.

When investigating controversial issues it is important that one be able to distinguish between statements of fact and statements of opinion. It is also important to recognize that not all statements of fact are true. They may appear to be true, but some are based on inaccurate or false information. For this activity, however, we are concerned with understanding the difference between those statements which appear to be factual and those which appear to be based primarily on opinion.

The following statements are taken from the viewpoints in this chapter. Consider each statement carefully. *Mark O for any statement you believe is an opinion or interpretation of facts. Mark F for any statement you believe is a fact.*

If you are doing this activity as a member of a class or group, compare your answers with those of other class or group members. Be able to defend your answers. You may discover that others will come to different conclusions than you. Listening to the reasons others present for their answers may give you valuable insights in distinguishing between fact and opinion.

O = opinion
F = fact

1. A ton of the Allende meteorite fell in northern Mexico in 1969.

2. The astronomical evidence proves that the Universe was created twenty billion years ago in a fiery explosion.

3. The actual universe must be the result of intelligent design and intelligently ordered creation of space, time, matter, and energy.

4. Crystals grow into intricate patterns that are not predictable—and *predictability* is what we mean by order. *Entropy* is the measure of disorder or unpredictability.

5. The Bible says the Universe was created through the word of God.

6. Science is, by its very nature, godless.

7. There is a kind of religion in science; it is the religion of a person who believes there is order and harmony in the Universe and every event can be explained in a rational way.

8. Theologians are always certain in their conclusions and scientists are always tentative in theirs.

9. In the stars, carbon just manages to form and then just avoids complete conversion into oxygen. If one atomic level had varied half a percent, life would have been impossible.

10. The Milky Way is a giant pinwheel galaxy containing over 200 billion stars.

11. C.F. von Weizsacker argued that all stars in the Milky Way must have condensed at about the same time from the original gas and dust.

12. Christians caught up in the debate over creation in biology may not have noticed how congenial physics and theology have become.

13. The big bang is tremendously exciting but there is not a shred of evidence to prove it and much to disprove the notion.

14. Most astronomers think the Universe was created 15 billion years ago and the Earth was not created until a little less than 5 billion years ago.

How Did
Life Originate?

Chapter Preface

Since Charles Darwin first proposed his theory of biological evolution in the nineteenth century, it has been a continual source of conflict between science and religion.

Evolutionary biologists argue that humans evolved from lower life forms. "Descent with modification" was a phrase Darwin used to explain the process by which creatures alive now descended from previous life forms. Natural factors explained why animals with the same ancestor have different features. As the environment around an animal changed, its form adapted to help it survive in its habitat. Furthermore, the animals most likely to successfully reproduce were ones whose features helped them avoid danger. As the readings in the following chapter make clear, many of the nation's most respected scientists and leading scientific organizations defend evolution as a firmly proven fact.

Despite this strong conviction among many scientists, a 1982 Gallup poll found skeptics among the general public. Only nine percent of those surveyed thought evolution occurred solely by natural processes, as Darwin proposed. Forty-four percent believed in creationism. Creationists argue that God created human life, exactly as explained in the Genesis chapter in the Old Testament. Creation scientists studying the same fossil records as evolutionists come to completely opposite conclusions. They argue that what evolutionists call "gaps" in the fossil record are actually proof that each species was separately created. Dozens of species have remained unchanged over centuries and some species reproduce despite having impractical features. Hence the creationists conclude that evolution must be wrong.

Many religious believers do not support creationism, however. Thirty-eight percent of the respondents to the polls said they agreed that human life had evolved, but they thought that God had started and aided evolution. Unlike creationists, they do believe that evolution occurred. They disagree with creationists' using the Bible in so literal a sense: they view it as a book of spiritual inspiration, not science. Their belief that God started and aided evolution is not in agreement with Darwin, however, who proposed natural causes to explain evolution.

The sharp disagreements between the authors in this chapter suggest that the debate about the origins of human life will long remain a fundamental source of conflict between science and religion.

"There is no significant scientific doubt about the close evolutionary relationships among all primates or between apes and humans."

Evolution Best Explains the Origin of Life

National Academy of Sciences

The following viewpoint is an excerpt from a book by the National Academy of Sciences, an honorary organization of scientists that advises the federal government on scientific issues. The Academy argues that creationism is not scientific, because creationists first conclude that a supernatural being created life and then try to make science conform with their religious belief. Evolution, on the other hand, has been subjected to rigorous scientific testing. The Academy concludes that evolution has proven to be the best explanation of the origin of life and the universe.

As you read, consider the following questions:

1. What is wrong with the creationists' approach to the scientific method, according to the Academy?
2. In the authors' opinion, how do fossils support the theory that species descended from a common ancestor?
3. Why does the Academy argue that evidence of human evolution disproves the creationist belief that the earth is only 10,000 years old?

Reprinted from "Science and Creationism: A View from the National Academy of Sciences," 1984, with permission of the National Academy Press, Washington, DC.

It is important to clarify the nature of science and to explain why creationism cannot be regarded as a scientific pursuit. The claim that equity demands balanced treatment of the two in the same classroom reflects misunderstanding of what science is and how it is conducted. Scientific investigators seek to understand natural phenomena by direct observation and experimentation. Scientific interpretations of facts are always provisional and must be testable. Statements made by any authority, revelation, or appeal to the supernatural are not germane to this process in the absence of supporting evidence. In creationism, however, both authority and revelation take precedence over evidence. The conclusions of creationism do not change, nor can they be validated when subjected to test by the methods of science. Thus, there are profound differences between the religious belief in special creation and the scientific explanations embodied in evolutionary theory. Neither benefits from the confusion that results when the two are presented as equivalent approaches in the same classroom.

What Science Is

In broadest terms, scientists seek a systematic organization of knowledge about the universe and its parts. This knowledge is based on explanatory principles whose verifiable consequences can be tested by independent observers. Science encompasses a large body of evidence collected by repeated observations and experiments. Although its goal is to approach true explanations as closely as possible, its investigators claim no final or permanent explanatory truths. Science changes. It evolves. Verifiable facts always take precedence. . . .

Scientists operate within a system designed for continuous testing, where corrections and new findings are announced in refereed scientific publications. The task of systematizing and extending the understanding of the universe is advanced by eliminating disproved ideas and by formulating new tests of others until one emerges as the most probable explanation for any given observed phenomenon. This is called the scientific method. . . .

The Acceptance of Scientific Theories

Scientific theories are accepted only provisionally. It is always possible that a theory that has withstood previous testing may eventually be disproved. But as theories survive more tests, they are regarded with higher levels of confidence. A theory that has withstood as many severe tests as, for example, that of biological evolution by means of natural selection is held with a very high degree of confidence.

In science, then, facts are determined by observation or measurement of natural or experimental phenomena. A hypothesis is a proposed explanation of those facts. A theory is a hypothesis that has gained wide acceptance because it has survived rigorous investigation of its predictions. . . .

By the standards described above, special creation is neither a successful theory nor a testable hypothesis for the origin of the universe, the earth, or of life thereon. Creationism reverses the scientific process. It accepts as authoritative a conclusion seen as unalterable and then seeks to support that conclusion by whatever means possible.

In contrast, science accommodates, indeed welcomes, new discoveries: its theories change and its activities broaden as new facts come to light or new potentials are recognized. Examples of events changing scientific thought are legion. . . .

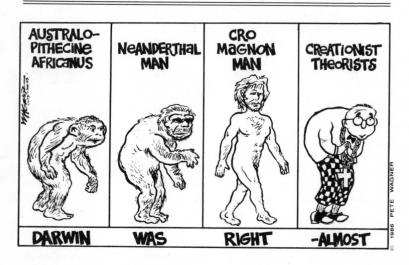

Pete Wagner, reprinted with permission.

Prior acceptance of the fixed *ad hoc* hypotheses of creationism—ideas that are certified as untestable by their most ardent advocates—would have blocked . . . important advances that have led to the great scientific achievements of recent years. Truly scientific understanding cannot be attained or even pursued effectively when explanations not derived from or tested by the scientific method are accepted. . . .

The Origins of Evolution

Evolution was first used as a biological term in 1670 to describe the changes observed in the maturation of insects. However, it was not until the 1873 edition of *The Origin of Species* that Darwin first applied the term. Before that he used the expression *descent with modification*, which is still as good a brief definition of biological evolution as any. In later editions of the book, Darwin paid tribute to the earlier views of Jean Baptiste de Lamarck (1802, 1809) and others about the subject we now call biological evolution or simply evolution. . . .

Relation by Common Descent

Evidence for relation by common descent has been provided by paleontology, comparative anatomy, biogeography, embryology, biochemistry, molecular genetics, and other biological disciplines. The idea first emerged from observations of systematic changes in the succession of fossil remains found in a sequence of layered rocks. Such layers are now known to have a cumulative thickness of many scores of kilometers and to represent at least 2.7 billion years of geological time. The first observation that the final sequence changes systematically upward in an undeformed succession of stratified rocks (and thus with time) was announced in 1799 by a practical engineer named William Smith. His findings were confirmed and extended by a number of paleontologists and geologists who used the fossils not as proof of evolution but as a basis for working out the original sequences of structurally disturbed rock strata.

The general sequence of fossils had thus already been recognized when Darwin perceived that the observed progression of biological forms strongly implied common descent. The farther back into the past one looked, the less the fossils resembled recent forms, the more the various lineages merged, and the broader the implications of a common ancestry appeared. . . .

The fossil record thus provides compelling evidence of systematic change through time—of descent with modification. From this consistent body of evidence it can be predicted that no reversals will be found in future paleontological studies. That is, amphibians will not appear before fishes nor mammals before reptiles, and no complex life will occur in the geological record before the oldest eucaryotic cells. That prediction has been upheld by the evidence that has accumulated thus far: no reversals have been found. . . .

Molecular Biology

Very recent studies in molecular biology have independently confirmed the judgments of paleontologists and classical biologists about relationships among lineages and the order in which species appeared within lineages. They have also provided detailed information about the mechanisms of biological evolution.

DNA (deoxyribonucleic acid), the hereditary material within all cells, and the proteins encoded by genes in the DNA both offer extensive information about the ancestry of organisms. Analysis of such information has made it possible to reconstruct evolutionary events that were previously unknown and to confirm and date events already surmised but not precisely dated. The precision whereby evolutionary events can be thus reconstructed is one reason why the evidence from molecular biology is so compelling.

In unveiling the universality of the chemical basis of heredity, molecular biology has profoundly affirmed common ancestry. In all organisms—bacteria, plants, and animals, including humans—the hereditary information is encoded in DNA, which is in all instances made up of the same four subunits called nucleotides. The genetic code by which the information contained in the nuclear DNA is used to form proteins is essentially the same in all organisms. Proteins in all organisms are invariably composed of the same 20 amino acids, all having a "left-handed" configuration, although there are amino acids in nature with both "right-" and "left-handed" configurations. The metabolic pathways through which the most diversified organisms produce energy and manufacture cell components are also essentially the same.

This unity reveals the genetic continuity of living organisms, thereby giving independent confirmation of descent from a common ancestry. There is no other way consistent with the laws of nature and probability to account for such uniformity. . . .

Outside the Realm of Science

The claim that the universe, the earth, and life were made by an undetectable Creator using supernatural powers falls outside of science. It makes no predictions that can be tested. It cannot be negated by science. If it had any real possibility of negation, it would lose many of the advantages that it offers to its adherents. . . .

Evolution passes as science; creation science, by its own admission, does not.

Robert Shapiro, *Origins: A Skeptic's Guide to the Creation of Life on Earth*, 1986.

Studies in evolutionary biology have led to the conclusion that mankind arose from ancestral primates. This association was hotly debated among scientists in Darwin's day, before molecular biology and the discovery of the now abundant connecting links. Today, however, there is no significant scientific doubt about the close evolutionary relationships among all primates or between apes and humans. The "missing links" that troubled Darwin and his followers are no longer missing. Today, not one but many such connecting links, intermediate between various branches of the primate family tree, have been found as fossils. These linking fossils are intermediate in form and occur in geological deposits of intermediate age. They thus document the time and rate at which primate and human evolution occurred.

150

The possibility of error in determining ages has been reduced by new methods based on measurements of reversals in the earth's magnetic field in ancient rocks. Furthermore, fossils continue to be found with great frequency. The combination of information from stratigraphy, fossils, and dating techniques and findings from studies in molecular biology has enabled scientists to develop the following scheme of human evolution. The human line separated from that of the apes approximately 5 million years ago. About 4 million years ago, our ancestors were already bipedal but had brains no larger than those of the contemporary apes. Within 2 million years after that, these small-brained bipeds were making stone tools. In the next half million years, the brain doubled in size and the stone tools became much more complex. Change was very slow until people anatomically similar to ourselves had evolved. Then in a few thousand years, humans reached Australia, the Arctic, and the New World. This revolution was accompanied by the development of agriculture and, shortly thereafter, from an evolutionary point of view, the complex social and industrial world we know today.

Intermediate Species

From the time of our earliest ancestors onward, there were successive and regular increases in average brain volume and body size, coupled in later stages with a progressive reduction in the thickness of the brain case, the protrusion of brow ridges, and the size of cheek teeth. These changes occurred through a succession of well-documented intermediate forms or species. Finally, approximately 50,000 years ago, *Homo sapiens sapiens*—the oldest human being of morphologically modern character—appeared. This appearance of fully developed modern man close to 50,000 years ago is, of course, inconsistent with the creationist view that the earth is perhaps only 10,000 years old or less.

These conclusions from comparative anatomy, stratigraphy, dating techniques, and paleoanthropology are backed up by findings from studies in molecular biology. A 99 percent similarity is found between the DNA of human beings and the DNA of chimpanzees. Such studies link humans, the chimpanzee, and the gorilla together in the same biological family. . . .

Science's Understanding of Nature

Scientists, like many others, are touched with awe at the order and complexity of nature. Religion provides one way for human beings to be comfortable with these marvels. However, the goal of science is to seek naturalistic explanations for phenomena— and the origins of life, the earth, and the universe are, to scientists, such phenomena—within the framework of natural laws and principles and the operational rule of testability.

No body of beliefs that has its origin in doctrinal material rather than scientific observation should be admissible as science in any science course. Incorporating the teaching of such doctrines into a science curriculum stifles the development of critical thinking patterns in the developing mind and seriously compromises the best interests of public education. This could eventually hamper the advancement of science and technology as students take their places as leaders of future generations.

The Evidence Supports Evolution

Our confidence that evolution occurred centers upon three general arguments. First, we have abundant, direct, observational evidence of evolution in action, from both field and laboratory. This evidence ranges from countless experiments on change in nearly everything about fruit flies subjected to artificial selection in the laboratory to the famous populations of British moths that became black when industrial soot darkened the trees upon which the moths rest. (Moths gain protection from sharp-sighted bird predators by blending into the background.) . . .

The second and third arguments for evolution—the case for major changes—do not involve direct observation of evolution in action. They rest upon inference, but are no less secure for that reason. Major evolutionary change requires too much time for direct observation on the scale of recorded human history. All historical sciences rest upon inference, and evolution is no different from geology, cosmology, or human history in this respect.

Stephen Jay Gould, *Hen's Teeth and Horse's Toes*, 1983.

It is, therefore, our unequivocal conclusion that creationism, with its accounts of the origin of life by supernatural means, is not science. It subordinates evidence to statements based on authority and revelation. Its documentation is almost entirely limited to the special publications of its advocates. And its central hypothesis is not subject to change in light of new data or demonstration of error. Moreover, when the evidence for creationism has been subjected to the tests of the scientific method, it has been found invalid.

"The evidence simply does not support slow gradual change."

Creation Best Explains the Origin of Life

Donald E. Chittick

Creation scientists have argued that the evidence for evolution is too weak and contradictory for evolution to be true. Donald E. Chittick begins the following viewpoint by examining gaps in the fossil record. Fossil evidence is far too sketchy to prove that life has evolved over centuries, Chittick argues. He then contends that creation science, by accepting the truth of God's word, is the best way to understand life and nature. Chittick has a doctorate degree in physical chemistry from Oregon State University and has taught and lectured on creation science for the past two decades.

As you read, consider the following questions:

1. What does the author believe was wrong about the way Charles Darwin formulated his theory of evolution?
2. Why was Chittick drawn to the creationist position?
3. How is creation science's view broader than that of evolutionary science, according to the author?

Darwin suggested that all of the various forms of life we see on earth today descended from more primitive ancestors by slow gradual change over millions of years of time. Only natural processes were involved. . . .

If the Darwinian process really took place, remains of plants and animals (fossils) should show a gradual and continual change from one type of animal or plant into another. One of the things that worried Darwin in his day, as well as modern evolutionists, was that the fossil record did not supply these intermediate life forms.

Darwin's Belief System

Darwin did not base his ideas on observation of scientific data. He did not begin with data. He began with a belief system and then looked for data to support his beliefs. Not only did he *not* see evidence of a slow, gradual change from his observation of the fossil record of the past, but he believed change of one species into another in living forms could not even be observed within the single lifetime of a scientist. In other words, evolution could not be observed in the present. Actual observation of evolutionary change was therefore not possible. . . .

How did Darwin get around the obvious discrepancy between his theory and factual observation? He did it by inventing additional postulates in an attempt to prop up his theory to fit the actual evidence. He postulated that the fossil record was incomplete. Rather than admit his theory was wrong, he blamed the fossil record for being imperfect.

No In-Between Fossils

For more than one hundred years since Darwin's day scientists have continued to study the fossil record intensely. How has the situation changed? Of all the countless fossil remains which have been discovered and studied, in-between forms are still missing from the record. Even today, scientists still use the same excuse that Darwin used: the fossil record is incomplete; we just haven't found the in-between species yet. . . .

A direct look at the fossil record would lead one to conclude that animals reproduced after their kind as Genesis states. They did not change from one kind into another. The evidence now, as in Darwin's day, is in agreement with the Genesis record of direct creation. Animals and plants continue to reproduce after their kind. In fact, the conflict between paleontology (study of fossils) and Darwinism is so strong that some scientists are beginning to believe that the in-between forms will never be found. One scientist observes, "It is not even possible to make a caricature of evolution out of paleobiological facts. The fossil material is now so complete that the lack of transitional series cannot be explained by the scarcity of the material. The deficiencies are real, they will never be filled [from *Why Scientists Accept Evolution* by Robert T. Clark and James D. Bales]."

The evidence simply does not support slow gradual change. To believe and advocate a theory in spite of evidence is an abuse of scientific theory known as subjectivism. It is a serious abuse and a block on the path toward finding truth. . . .

The Genetic Code

Genetics poses an additional problem for the evolutionary hypothesis. How did the genetic code arise in the first place? The genetic code is associated with complex molecules known as DNA and RNA (deoxyribonucleic acid and ribonucleic acid). To function, these molecules need a living cell. However, a living cell, to function, needs the DNA and RNA genetic apparatus. It's sort of like the chicken and the egg question ("Which came first, the chicken or the egg?"). Evolutionists admit this is a real problem for their hypothesis, yet they will not concede to creation. . . .

"Creation? Let's not start dragging religion into this. The way I feel is, 'Darwin said it, I believe it, and that settles it for me'!"

Wayne Stayskal. Reprinted by permission: Tribune Media Services.

In addition to all this evidence against evolution, there is much positive observational evidence that strongly points to design and purpose in nature. Evidence of design and purpose point to creation. Even Darwin recognized this. He admits that it caused him much mental distress. . . .

With new discoveries since Darwin's day, evidence for design is even stronger now than it was then. The eye remains a prime example. If one were to come across an optical instrument such as a telescope or a camera, one would immediately conclude that it had been designed. Evolutionists, however, in looking at an eye, which has many of the same features and even more perfection than most cameras, conclude that there is no designer.

> But most scientists today do not share Darwin's doubts; they are convinced that his theory of evolution removes the need for a guiding hand in the Universe. The great evolutionist George Gaylord Simpson expressed a nearly universal opinion among scientists when he wrote that evolution "achieves the aspect of purpose without the intervention of a purposer, and has produced a vast plan without the action of a planner."
>
> —Niles Eldredge

To reject evidence of design when it is so clearly evident is again an example of the abuse of scientific theory known as subjectivism. The evidence is clear; there is no excuse for missing it. As Romans 1:20 explains, "For since the creation of the world God's invisible qualities—his eternal power and divine nature—have been clearly seen, being understood from what has been made, so that men are without excuse."

Competing Philosophies

Science is not studied in a vacuum. It is always carried out in a philosophical framework. Evolution and creation are two such competing frameworks. Although many people today hold to an evolutionary philosophical framework and study science in that context, in my opinion it provides an inferior and limited view of reality. Evolution is not adequate for the big questions. It is not in agreement with the universe as we find it. It is not in agreement with facts and reality.

If evolution is not true, what do we put in its place? It is one thing to throw stones at a theory or world view, but it is another to offer something better. Creation science does offer a fully acceptable and satisfying alternative. Creation science begins with wholly biblical presuppositions and interprets data from all of reality, including science, within that framework. . . .

The creation position seemed to me to have the ring of truth. At last, here was a position with which I as a Christian and as a scientist could relax. No longer need I always be on guard to explain away either theological truth or scientific truth. Truth could be a unified whole. Furthermore, I could read the Bible using the standard rules of communication. I could read it in a normal, straightforward manner; I did not always have to be on guard for some special or obscure interpretation.

The creation position began from an absolute reference point, the truth of God's Word. That was an exciting discovery for me. Truth could objectively and absolutely exist. . . .

If science is a search for truth about the natural world, and if the Bible makes statements about the natural world, then the Bible can be a starting point for truth in the study of science. "The fear of the LORD is the beginning of knowledge, But fools despise wisdom and instruction" (Proverbs 1:7). Using the Bible and the presuppositions it suggests about the natural world, we can then develop a sufficient theology of science.

Creation Ex Nihilo

A theology of science begins where the Bible does: "In the beginning God created the heavens and the earth." This and other supportive biblical passages form the basis of the doctrine of creation *ex nihilo*, the doctrine of creation out of nothing but pure spiritual power. According to the Bible, God did not start with energy, matter, and a set of natural laws and then order them into

---

Pre-Existing Intelligence

Not only is there a complete lack of fossil evidence to indicate how the first life originated, but no one has yet shown how the enormous amount of genetic intelligence in a single-celled organism could have come spontaneously from non-living chemicals. . . .

The scientific evidence shows that whenever any basically different type of life first appeared on Earth, all the way from single-celled protozoa to man, it was complete and its organs and structures were complete and fully fuctional. The inescapable deduction to be drawn from this fact is that there was some sort of pre-existing intelligence before life first appeared on Earth.

Luther D. Sunderland, *Darwin's Enigma*, 1984.

---

the present universe. God created out of nothing. He did not require pre-existing materials. He alone is infinite. Philosophically, one has a choice of either starting with matter as eternal or with Mind (God) as eternal. The material universe is finite; it was created. Only God is infinite and eternal. He existed before the beginning; he existed before time began. He is the self-existent one. . . .

Laws of Science

What do we mean when we use the term *scientific law?* Let's take a moment here to review and discuss this term. Science is a study of the present universe. Scientists observe the material universe in its present state and describe what they see. From a large number of observations of some object or phenomenon, scientists observe that the universe behaves in a certain orderly way. Scientific laws or laws of "nature" are simply scientists' descriptions of this orderly behavior. . . .

It is well to note that science did not invent the way nature behaves; it simply describes it. Scientific laws are man's formulations of his observations about the way the material universe behaves. Laws did not come into existence because science exists; science exists rather because nature behaves in a predictable way. Science, then, is a description of the way nature behaves. We express these descriptions in generalizations known as scientific laws and these laws are understandable and can be communicated by rational minds. . . .

A basic question arises: Why are the laws of science as they are? Why, for example, does the speed of light have its particular value? Why isn't it three times this value or half or some other multiple? Out of the limitless possible values for the speed of light, why is it what it is? . . .

The Profound Answer

Creation *ex nihilo* answers this question. The laws of science are as they are because God willed them to be that way. This is not a simplistic answer, but a most profound one. An act of the will, a choice, implies intelligence. It implies intelligence or mind behind the universe. As [E.H. Andrews] succinctly puts it,

> Without intelligence there is no true choosing but only a response to the rules of chance. But before even *those* rules existed, a choice or distinction was made as to what they should be! The unavoidable conclusion is, therefore, that intelligence pre-existed the natural universe and the laws by which it functions. The only escape from this argument lies in a total agnosticism concerning the fundamental nature of scientific law.

That God willed the laws to be as they are is a big answer to an important question. . . .

Big Answers to Big Questions

Creation science is science carried on within a different philosophical framework. It begins with the assumption that the material universe (nature) is dependent on God. Creation science takes a broader view and is capable of giving big answers to big questions.

However, science carried on within an evolutionary framework can only give limited answers since it only admits to a limited reality. Evolutionary science thus has a severe built-in limitation.

We have seen that the conflict between creation and evolution is one between differing belief systems. It is a philosophical conflict. Science is concerned with making observations of the present universe, and these observations are formulated into what are known as natural laws. Yet science is studied within a philosophical framework or belief system. That philosophical framework can be evolutionary, which begins by assuming that the material universe is autonomous and follows an infinite regression of cause and effect. However, this philosophical system gives only a partial view of reality. It does not answer the question of why there should be laws of science or why the laws of science are as they are. It does not answer questions about the inward universe, the nature of man, nor does it give an answer to the question of mind.

"The fact of evolution is as well established as anything in science."

Evolution Is a Scientific Fact

Stephen Jay Gould

Stephen Jay Gould is a well-known paleontologist and prolific science writer who has won a National Book Award in Science and an Award for General Nonfiction from the National Book Critics Circle. He teaches biology, geology, and the history of science at Harvard University. In the following viewpoint, Gould argues that scientists dispute how evolution occurred but do not dispute that it did in fact occur. The scientific evidence is overwhelming, he contends, and evolution is the most logical explanation of the origin of human life.

As you read, consider the following questions:

1. What distinction does Gould make between fact and theory? How then does he argue that evolution is a fact?
2. What three types of data prove evolution, according to the author?
3. How does Gould's definition of science's purpose differ from that of the pattern cladists' definition?

Stephen Jay Gould, "Darwinism Defined: The Difference Between Fact and Theory," *Discover*, January 1987. Copyright © 1987.

Charles Darwin, who was, perhaps, the most incisive thinker among the great minds of history, clearly divided his life's work into two claims of different character: establishing the fact of evolution, and proposing a theory (natural selection) for the mechanism of evolutionary change. He also expressed, and with equal clarity, his judgment about their different status: confidence in the facts of transmutation and genealogical connection among all organisms, and appropriate caution about his unproved theory of natural selection. He stated in the *Descent of Man:* "I had two distinct objects in view; firstly, to show that species had not been separately created, and secondly, that natural selection had been the chief agent of change . . . If I have erred in . . . having exaggerated its [natural selection's] power . . . I have at least, as I hope, done good service in aiding to overthrow the dogma of separate creations."

Fact and Theory

Darwin wrote those words more than a century ago. Evolutionary biologists have honored his fundamental distinction between fact and theory ever since. Facts are the world's data; theories are explanations proposed to interpret and coordinate facts. The fact of evolution is as well established as anything in science (as secure as the revolution of the earth about the sun), though absolute certainty has no place in our lexicon. Theories, or statements about the causes of documented evolutionary change, are now in a period of intense debate—a good mark of science in its healthiest state. Facts don't disappear while scientists debate theories. As I [has previously written]. . . , "Einstein's theory of gravitation replaced Newton's but apples did not suspend themselves in mid-air pending the outcome.". . .
outcome." . . .

In this period of vigorous pluralism and intense debate among evolutionary biologists, I am greatly saddened to note that some distinguished commentators among non-scientists, in particular Irving Kristol in a *New York Times* Op Ed piece of Sept. 30, 1986 ("Room for Darwin and the Bible"), so egregiously misunderstand the character of our discipline and continue to confuse this central distinction between secure fact and healthy debate about theory. . . .

Direct Evidence of Evolutionary Change

Our confidence in the fact of evolution rests upon copious data that fall, roughly, into three great classes. First, we have the direct evidence of small-scale changes in controlled laboratory experiments of the past hundred years (on bacteria, on almost every measurable property of the fruit fly *Drosophila*), or observed in nature (color changes in moth wings, development of metal tolerance in plants growing near industrial waste heaps), or produced during a few thousand years of human breeding and agriculture. Creationists can scarcely ignore this evidence, so they respond by arguing that God permits limited modification within created types, but that you can never change a cat into a dog (who ever said that you could, or that nature did?).

The Fossil Record

Second, we have direct evidence for large-scale changes, based upon sequences in the fossil record. The nature of this evidence is often misunderstood by non-professionals who view evolution as a simple ladder of progress, and therefore expect a linear array of "missing links." But evolution is a copiously branching bush, not a ladder. Since our fossil record is so imperfect, we can't hope to find evidence for every tiny twiglet. (Sometimes, in rapidly evolving lineages of abundant organisms restricted to small areas and entombed in sediments with an excellent fossil record, we do discover an entire little bush—but such examples are as rare as they are precious.) In the usual case, we many recover the remains of side branch number 5 from the bush's early history, then bough number 40 a bit later, then the full series of branches 156-161 in a well preserved sequence of younger rocks, and finally surviving twigs 250 and 287.

Disagreement on Details

Whatever the arguments about the details of the causes of evolution, there is no disagreement among knowledgeable biologists that living things are descended from common ancestors. . . .

Evidence comes not only from the fossil record, . . . but from anatomical, embryological and molecular studies of living species.

One does not need historical documents to deduce that French and Spanish developed from Latin; nor does one need fossils to deduce the common ancestry of living things. The historical reality of evolution is accepted by the full spectrum of biologists, including cladists and geneticists, whatever their views of the theory of evolutionary processes may be.

Douglas J. Futuyma, *The New York Times*, October 12, 1986.

In other words, we usually find sequences of structural intermediates, not linear arrays of ancestors and descendants. Such sequences provide superb examples of temporally ordered evolutionary trends. Consider the evidence for human evolution in Africa. What more could you ask from a record of rare creatures living in terrestrial environments that provide poor opportunity for fossilization? We have a temporal sequence displaying clear trends in a suite of features, including threefold increase of brain size and corresponding decrease of jaws and teeth. (We are missing direct evidence for an earlier transition to upright posture, but wide-ranging and unstudied sediments of the right age have been found in East Africa, and we have an excellent chance to fill in this part of our story.) What alternative can we suggest to evolution? Would God—for some inscrutable reason, or merely to test our faith—create five species, one after the other (*Australopithecus afarensis, A. africanus, Homo habilis, H. erectus,* and *H. sapiens*), to mimic a continuous trend of evolutionary change?

Or, consider another example with evidence of structurally intermediate stages—the transition from reptiles to mammals. The lower jaw of mammals contains but a single bone, the dentary. Reptiles build their lower jaws of several bones. In perhaps the most fascinating of those quirky changes in function that make pathways of evolution, the two bones articulating the upper and lower jaws of reptiles migrate to the middle ear and become the malleus and incus (hammer and anvil) of mammals.

Creationists, ignorant of hard evidence in the fossil record, scoff at this tale. How could jaw bones become ear bones, they ask. What happened in between? An animal can't work with a jaw half disarticulated during the stressful time of transition.

The fossil record provides a direct answer. In an excellent series of temporally ordered structural intermediates, the reptilian dentary gets larger and larger, pushing back as the other bones of a reptile's lower jaw decrease in size. We've even found a transitional form with an elegant solution to the problem of remaking jaw bones into ear bones. This creature has a double articulation—one between the two bones that become the mammalian hammer and anvil (the old reptilian joint), and a second between the squamosal and dentary bones (the modern mammalian condition). With this built-in redundancy, the emerging mammals could abandon one connection by moving two bones into the ear, while retaining the second linkage, which becomes the sole articulation of modern mammals.

Pervasive Quirks

Third, and most persuasive in its ubiquity, we have the signs of history preserved within every organism, every ecosystem, and every pattern of biogeographic distribution, by those pervasive quirks, oddities, and imperfections that record pathways of historical descent. These evidences are indirect, since we are viewing modern results, not the processes that caused them, but what else can we make of the pervasive pattern? Why does our body, from the bones of our back to the musculature of our belly, display the vestiges of an arrangement better suited for quadrupedal life if we aren't the descendants of four-footed creatures? Why do the plants and animals of the Galapagos so closely resemble, but differ slightly from, the creatures of Ecuador, the nearest bit of land

600 miles to the east, especially when cool oceanic currents and volcanic substrate make the Galapagos such a different environment from Ecuador (thus removing the potential argument that God makes the best creatures for each place, and small differences only reflect a minimal disparity of environments)? The similarities can only mean that Ecuadorian creatures colonized the Galapagos and then diverged by a natural process of evolution.

Scientific Debate

The fossil record—the actual sequence of fossils—very much agrees with the overall notion that life has had a history, and that the forms of related organisms indeed do change as we trace them through the rock record. . . .

What constitutes honest scientific debate is often misconstrued outside of the relatively narrow confines of a scientific discipline: the nature of the dispute may not be thoroughly grasped—or far worse, the mere fact that there is disagreement is often used as evidence that scientists really do not know what the score is, and are perhaps even guilty of arranging the evidence to fit their preconceptions about the way the world really *ought* to be. Scientists, being human, are often prone to admit that such undetected biases can creep in, but they also know it is their job (and, especially, their colleagues' job) to make sure they keep on a straight and narrow path of objectivity.

Niles Eldredge, *Life Pulse: Episodes from the Story of the Fossil Record*, 1987.

This method of searching for oddities as vestiges of the past isn't peculiar to evolution, but a common procedure of all historical science. How, for example, do we know that words have histories, and haven't been decreed by some all-knowing committee in Mr. Orwell's bureau of Newspeak? Doesn't the bucolic etymology of so many words testify to a different life style among our ancestors? In this article, I try to "broadcast" some ideas (a mode of sowing seed) in order to counter the most "egregious" of creationist sophistries (the animal *ex grege*, or outside the flock), for which, given the *quid pro quo* of business, . . . [I am paid] an "emolument" (the fee that millers once received to grind corn).

I don't want to sound like a shrill dogmatist shouting "rally round the flag boys," but biologists have reached a consensus, based on these kinds of data, about the fact of evolution. When honest critics like Irving Kristol misinterpret this agreement, they're either confusing our fruitful consonance about the fact of evolution with our vibrant dissonance about mechanisms of change, or they've misinterpreted part of our admittedly arcane technical literature.

One such misinterpretation has gained sufficient notoriety that we crave resolution both for its own sake and as an illustration of the frustrating confusion that can arise when scientists aren't clear and when commentators, as a result of hidden agendas, don't listen. Tom Bethell argued in *Harper's* (February 1985) that a group of young taxonomists called pattern cladists have begun to doubt the existence of evolution itself.

This would be truly astounding news, since cladistics is a powerful method dedicated to reforming classification by using only the branching order of lineages on evolutionary trees ("propinquity of descent" in Darwin's lovely phrase), rather than vague notions of overall similarity in form or function. (For example, in the cladistic system, a lungfish is more closely related to a horse than to a salmon because the common ancestor of lungfish and horse is more recent in time than the link point of the lungfish-horse lineage with the branch leading to modern bony fishes, including salmon).

Cladists use only the order of branching to construct their schemes of relationships; it bothers them not a whit that lungfish and salmon look and work so much alike. Cladism, in other words, is the purest of all genealogical systems for classification, since it works only with closeness of common ancestry in time. How preciously ironic then, that this most rigidly evolutionary of all taxonomic systems should become the subject of such extraordinary misunderstanding—as devised by Bethell, and perpetuated by Kristol when he writes: ". . . many younger biologists (the so-called 'cladists') are persuaded that the differences among species—including those that seem to be closely related—are such as to make the very concept of evolution questionable."

Ill-Conceived Scientific Procedure

This error arose for the following reason. A small splinter group of cladists (not all of them, as Kristol claims)—"transformed" or "pattern" cladists by their own designation—have adopted what is to me an ill-conceived definition of scientific procedure. They've decided, by misreading Karl Popper's philosophy, that patterns of branching can be established unambiguously as a fact of nature, but that processes causing events of branching, since they can't be observed directly, can't be known with certainty. Therefore, they say, we must talk only of pattern and rigidly exclude all discussion of process (hence "pattern cladistics").

This is where Bethell got everything arse-backwards and began the whole confusion. A philosophical choice to abjure all talk about process isn't the same thing as declaring that no reason for patterns of branching exists. Pattern cladists don't doubt that evolution is the cause behind branching; rather, they've decided that our science shouldn't be discussing causes at all.

Now I happen to think that this philosophy is misguided; in unguarded moments I would even deem it absurd. Science, after all, is fundamentally about process; learning why and how things happen is the soul of our discipline. You can't abandon the search for cause in favor of a dry documentation of pattern. You must take risks of uncertainty in order to probe the deeper questions, rather than stopping with sterile security. You see, now I've blown our cover. We scientists do have our passionate debates—and I've just poured forth an example. But as I wrote earlier, this is a debate about the proper approach to causes, not an argument about whether causes exist, or even whether the cause of branching is evolution or something else. No cladist denies that branching patterns arise by evolution.

This incident also raises the troubling issue of how myths become beliefs through adulterated repetition without proper documentation. Bethell began by misunderstanding pattern cladistics, but at least he reports the movement as a small splinter, and tries to reproduce their arguments. Then Kristol picks up the ball and recasts it as a single sentence of supposed fact—and all cladists have now become doubters of evolution by proclamation. Thus a movement, by fiat, is turned into its opposite—as the purest of all methods for establishing genealogical connections becomes a weapon for denying the mechanism that all biologists accept as the cause of branching on life's tree: evolution itself. Our genealogy hasn't been threatened, but my geniality has almost succumbed. . . .

No Doubt

We can no longer doubt that biological evolution is a fact, or that the species presently found on earth have *not* been there from the start, continually existing, never changing, since the beginning of the story of terrestrial life. All these organisms are the (preliminary) result of a long history of development, still going on today, and no serious scientist questions this.

Hoimar von Ditfurth, *The Origins of Life: Evolution as Creation*, 1982.

What challenge can the facts of nature pose to our own decisions about the moral value of our lives? We are what we are, but we interpret the meaning of our heritage as we choose. Science can no more answer the questions of how we ought to live than religion can decree the age of the earth. Honorable and discerning scientists (most of us, I trust) have always understood that the limits to what science can answer also describe the power of its methods in their proper domain. Darwin himself exclaimed that science couldn't touch the problem of evil and similar moral conundrums: "A dog might as well speculate on the mind of Newton. Let each man hope and believe what he can."

There is no warfare between science and religion, never was except as a historical vestige of shifting taxonomic boundaries among disciplines. Theologians haven't been troubled by the fact of evolution, unless they try to extend their own domain beyond its proper border (hubris and territorial expansionism aren't the sins of scientists alone.). . .

Similarly, most scientists show no hostility to religion. Why should we, since our subject doesn't intersect the concerns of theology? I strongly dispute Kristol's claim that "the current teaching of evolution in our public schools does indeed have an ideological bias against religious belief." Unless at least half my colleagues are inconsistent dunces, there can be—on the most raw and direct empirical grounds—no conflict between science and religion. I know hundreds of scientists who share a conviction about the fact of evolution, and teach it in much the same way. Among these people I note an entire spectrum of religious attitudes—from devout daily prayer and worship to resolute atheism. Either there's no correlation between religious belief and confidence in evolution—or else half these people are fools.

A Shared Struggle for Wisdom

The common goal of science and religion is our shared struggle for wisdom in all its various guises. I know no better illustration of this great unity than a final story about Charles Darwin. This scourge of fundamentalism had a conventional church burial—in Westminster Abbey no less. J. Frederick Bridge, Abbey organist and Oxford don, composed a funeral anthem especially for the occasion. It may not rank high in the history of music, but it is, as my chorus director opined, a "sweet piece." (I've made what may be the only extant recording of this work, marred only by the voice of yours truly within the bass section.) Bridge selected for his text the finest biblical description of the common aim that will forever motivate both the directors of his building and the inhabitants of the temple of science—wisdom. "Her ways are ways of pleasantness and all her paths are peace" (Proverbs 3:17).

"The positive evidence for evolution is very much weaker than most laymen imagine, and than many scientists want us to imagine."

Evolution Is Not a Scientific Fact

Tom Bethell

Tom Bethell is a contributing editor of *Harper's* magazine and has written a book on evolution. The following viewpoint is based on interviews he conducted with scientists who study and classify animal species. These scientists, who work in the field of cladistics, argue that fossils do not prove that evolution occurred. Bethell argues that evolutionary biologists use incomplete data to arrive at conclusions. He contrasts this approach with that of the cladists, who contend that so little is known about the relationships between related species that it is impossible to prove that humans descended from other species.

As you read, consider the following questions:

1. According to the author, how does the approach of cladists differ from that of evolutionary biologists?
2. What is wrong with trying to prove evolution by looking at fossils, according to the cladists Bethell interviews?

The first time I saw Colin Patterson was at the American Museum of Natural History in New York City in the spring of 1983. He was in the office of Donn Rosen, a curator in the museum's department of ichthyology, which is the branch of zoology that deals with fishes. Patterson, a paleontologist specializing in fossil fishes, was staring through a binocular microscope at a slice of codfish. . . . I would later spend time with him in London, at the British Museum of Natural History, where he is a senior paleontologist, and at Cambridge University, where we attended a lecture by the famous Harvard paleontologist Stephen Jay Gould. He often conveyed an impression of moody rebelliousness: he is authoritative, the kind of person others defer to in a discussion; he is habitually pessimistic; and he seemed not at all sanguine about his brushes with other scientists—encounters that by the late 1970s had become quite frequent. Those with whom Patterson has been arguing are mostly paleontologists and evolutionary biologists—researchers and academics who have devoted their careers, their lives, to upholding and fine-tuning the ideas about the origins and the development of species introduced by Charles Darwin in the second half of the nineteenth century. Patterson, it seemed, was no longer sure he believed in evolutionary theory, and he was saying so. Or, perhaps more accurately, he was saying that evolutionists—like the creationists they periodically do battle with—are nothing more than believers themselves. . . .

The Cladists' Challenge

One of the least publicized and least understood challenges to Darwin and the theory of evolution—and surely one of the more fascinating, in its sweep and rigor—involves a school of taxonomists called cladists. (A "clade" is a branch, from the Greek *klados*; "cladist" is pronounced with a long *a*.) Particularly interesting—vexing, evolutionary biologists would say (and do)—are those who toil in what is called transformed cladistics, and who might be thought of as agnostic evolutionists. Like many who have broken with a faith and challenged an orthodoxy, the transformed cladists are perhaps best defined by an opponent—in this case, the British biologist Beverly Halstead. Asked not long ago in a BBC interview what he thought of transformed cladistics, Halstead replied: "Well, I object to it! I mean, this is going back to Aristotle. It is not pre-Darwinian, it is Aristotelian. From Darwin's day to the present we've understood there's a time element; we've begun to understand evolution. What they are doing in transformed cladistics is to say, let's forget about evolution, let's forget about process, let's simply consider pattern."

Since Darwin's time, biologists have been absorbed in process: Where did we come from? How did everything in nature get to be what it now is? How will things continue to alter? The transformed cladists—they are sometimes called pattern cladists—

are not concerned primarily with time or process. To understand why, it helps to know that they are trained in taxonomy: they are rigorous, scrupulous labelers. Their job as taxonomists is to discover and name the various groups found in nature—a task first assigned to Adam by God, according to Genesis—and put them into one category or another. Taxonomists try to determine not how groups came into existence but what groups exist, among both present-day and fossil organisms. To understand that cladists believe this knowledge must be acquired before ideas about process can be tested is to understand the natural tension that exists between taxonomists and evolutionary biologists. . . .

A Questionable Concept

The gradual transformation of the population of one species into another is a biological hypothesis, not a biological fact. . . .

Many younger biologists (the so-called "cladists") are persuaded that the differences among species—including those that seem to be closely related—are such as to make the very concept of evolution questionable.

So "evolution" is no simple established scientific orthodoxy, and to teach it as such is an exercise in dogmatism.

Irving Kristol, *The New York Times*, September 30, 1986.

[Transformed cladists] have come to think that it is the evolutionists who have the problem—the problem being slipshod methodology. Colin Patterson, perhaps the leading transformed cladist, has enunciated what might be regarded as the cladists' battle cry: "The concept of ancestry is not accessible by the tools we have." Patterson and his fellow cladists argue that a common ancestor can only be hypothesized, not identified in the fossil record. A group of people can be brought together for a family reunion on the basis of birth documents, tombstone inscriptions, and parish records—evidence of process, one might say. But in nature there are no parish records; there are only fossils. And a fossil, Patterson told me once, is a "mess on a rock." Time, change, process, evolution—none of this, the cladists argue, can be read from rocks.

A Matter of Faith

What can be discerned in nature, according to the cladists, are patterns—relationships between things, not between eras. There can be no absolute tracing back. There can be no certainty about parent-offspring links. There are only inferences drawn from fossils. To the cladists, the science of evolution is in large part a matter of faith—faith different, but not all *that* different, from that of the creationists. . . .

What evolutionary theory does, the cladists say, is make claims about something that cannot be demonstrated by studying fossils. They say that the "tree of life," with its paraphyletic branches, is nothing more than a hypothesis, a reasonable guess.

Nor do they believe it will ever be anything more than that. When asked about this in an interview, Patterson said: "I don't think we shall ever have any access to any form of tree which we can call factual." He was then asked: "Do you believe it to be, then, no reality?" He replied: "Well, isn't it strange that this is what it comes to, that you have to ask me whether I believe it, as if it mattered whether I believe it or not. Yes, I do believe it. But in saying that, it is obvious it is faith." . . .

I recently spent some time with two cladists on the staff of the Museum of Natural History. I first met with Gareth Nelson, who in 1982 was named chairman of the department of ichthyology. Nelson graduated from the University of Hawaii in 1966 and he joined the museum staff a year later. The walls of Nelson's office were lined with boxes of articles from scientific journals, and a large table was covered with papers and jars stuffed with small, silvery fish preserved in alcohol: anchovies. Nelson is just about the world's expert on anchovies, although he told me that the number of people studying them (three or four) is much smaller than the number of anchovy species (there are 150 known species, and Nelson believes there are many more). This disparity between the magnitude of the scientific "problem" and the number of people working on it is a commonplace in biology. Most laymen think that the experts have pretty exhaustively studied the earth's biota, when they have barely scratched the surface.

Meaningless Evidence

Nelson put the issue of evolution this way: in order to understand what we actually know, we must first look at what it is that the evolutionists claim to know for certain. He said that if you turn to a widely used college text like Alfred Romer's *Vertebrate Paleontology*, published by the University of Chicago Press in 1966 and now in its third edition, you will find such statements as "mammals evolved from reptiles," and "birds are descended from reptiles." (Very rarely, at least in the current literature, will you find the claim that a given species evolved from another given species.) The trouble with general statements like "mammals evolved from reptiles," Nelson said, is that the "ancestral groups are taxonomic artifacts." These groups "do not have any characters that are unique," he said. "They do not have defining characters, and therefore they are not real groups." I asked Nelson to name some of these allegedly "unreal" groups. He replied: invertebrates, fishes, reptiles, apes. According to Nelson, this does not by any means exhaust the list of negatively defined groups. Statements imputing ancestry to such groups have no real meaning, he said. . . .

A week or two after I met with Nelson I spoke to Norman Platnick, a curator in the museum's entomology department and an expert on spiders. . . .

Not far from the elevator I found Platnick's orderly office: spiders (dead) inside little labeled bottles; book-filled shelves; journal articles neatly stacked. It would seem that professional biologists spend at least as much time studying each other's work as they do the world around them. . . .

Spiders, which go back to the Devonian period, 400 million years ago, belong to the class Arachnida and the phylum Arthropoda. They are among the "invertebrates," in other words, and are not well preserved in the fossil record. About 35,000 species of spiders have been identified, Platnick said, "but there may be three times that many in the world." He thought there were perhaps four full-time systematists examining spiders in the United States, "and perhaps another dozen who teach at small colleges and do some research." There is an American Arachnological Society, with 475 members worldwide, some of them amateurs. They meet once a year and discuss scorpions and daddy longlegs, as well as spiders.

"Most of the spiders I look at may have been looked at by two or three people in history," Platnick said, adding that he would most likely be dead before anyone looked at them again.

Great Uncertainty

We are repeatedly told that evolution is "not a theory but a fact." This is little more than whistling in the dark. There has been a persistent campaign by evolutionists to bully the lay public into accepting evolution by adopting an authoritarian posture inappropriate to science. . . .

The truth is that there is great uncertainty about what (if anything) is known about evolution. Those who embrace controversy should be fearless in pointing this out.

Tom Bethell, *The Wall Street Journal*, December 9, 1986.

I asked Platnick what was known about spider phylogeny, or ancestry.

"Very little," he said. "We still don't know a hill of beans about that." We certainly don't know, he said, what species the animal belonged to that was the ancestor of the very first spider. All we know of such an animal is that it was *not* a spider. We don't even know of any links in the (presumed) 400-million-year chain of spider ancestry.

"I do not *ever* say that this spider is ancestral to that one," Platnick said firmly.

"Does anyone?"

"I don't know of a single case in the modern literature where it's claimed that one spider is the ancestor of another."

Some spiders have been well preserved in amber. Even so, Platnick said, "very few spider fossils have been so well preserved that you can put a species name on them." After a pause he added: "You don't learn much from fossils."

In view of Platnick's comments about our knowledge of spider ancestry, I was curious to know what he thought of the following passage from a well-known high school biology text, *Life: An Introduction to Biology,* by George Simpson and William S. Beck, first published in 1957 by Harcourt Brace Jovanovich and still in print.

> An animal is not classified as an arachnid because it has four or five pairs of legs rather than three. It is classified in the Arachnida because it has the same ancestry as other arachnids, and a different ancestry from insects over some hundreds of millions of years, as attested by all the varying characteristics of the two groups and by large numbers of fossil representatives of both.

At that he threw himself back in his chair, and burst out laughing.

In this passage, Simpson and Beck were practicing the verbal sleight of hand that has been common in evolutionary biology since the 1940s. All we know for sure is that there is a group of organisms (in this case spiders) that are identifiable as a group because they have certain unique characteristics. They have spinnerets for spinning silk, for instance, and thus we can say that all organisms with spinnerets are spiders. (They share other unique features, too.)

If we want to explain *why* thousands of members of a group have features uniquely in common, that is another matter entirely. We can, if we like, posit a theoretical common ancestor in the urspider, which transmitted spider traits to all its descendants. That is precisely what Darwin did in *On the Origin of Species.* But Simpson and Beck do something very different. They say that the composition of the class Arachnida was determined by examining not the features of spiders but their *ancestral lines.* But no such pedigrees are known to science—not just with respect to spiders but with respect to *all* groups of organisms.

Why Taxonomics Matters

The point stressed by the cladists is this: unless we know the taxonomic relationships of organisms—what makes each unique and different from the other—we cannot possibly guess at the ancestral relationships. Things in nature here and now must be ranked according to their taxonomic relationship before they can be placed in a family tree. Thus the speculations of evolutionists ("Do X and Y have a common ancestor?") must be subordinate

173

to the findings of taxonomists ("X and Y have features not shared by anything else"). If fossils came with pedigrees attached, this laborious method of comparison would not be necessary; but of course they don't. . . .

I decided it would be a good idea to talk with a scientist who believes strongly in evolutionary theory. I traveled to Boston to meet with Richard C. Lewontin, a geneticist, a one-time president of the Society for the Study of Evolution, a well-known writer on science, and currently Agassiz Professor of Zoology at Harvard. I had seen a quote from Lewontin used as a chapter head in a book titled *Science on Trial*, by Douglas Futuyma. The quote, as edited, read: "Evolution is fact, not theory. . . . Birds evolve from nonbirds, humans evolve from nonhumans." . . .

A Theory, Not a Fact

The majority of our biologists still accept, and our textbooks still teach, the "neo-Darwinian synthesis"—Darwin's original teaching as modified by modern genetics. We all know this theory: Living creatures emerged by evolution from inert matter, and the original species evolved over time into the species we are familiar with—including, of course, our own species, homo sapiens. The mechanism of this evolution is "survival of the fittest," speeded up by the occasional genetic mutation.

Though this theory is usually taught as an established scientific truth, it is nothing of the sort.

Irving Kristol, *The New York Times*, September 30, 1986.

What about these claims: evolution is fact; birds evolve from nonbirds, humans from nonhumans? The cladists disapproved, I said.

He paused for a split second and said: "Those are very weak statements, I agree." Then he made one of the clearest statements about evolution I have heard. He said: "Those statements flow simply from the assertion that all organisms have parents. It is an empirical claim, I think, that all living organisms have living organisms as parents. The second empirical claim is that there was a time on earth when there were no mammals. Now, if you allow me those two claims as empirical, then the claim that mammals arose from non-mammals is simply a conclusion. It's the deduction from two empirical claims. But that's all I want to claim for it. You can't make the direct empirical statement that mammals arose from non-mammals."

Lewontin had made what seemed to me to be a deduction—a materialist's deduction. "The only problem is that it appears to be based on evidence derived from fossils," I said. "But the cladists

174

say they don't really have that kind of information."

He reached for a copy of his 1982 book *Human Diversity*, and said: "Look, I'm a person who says in this book that we don't know anything about the ancestors of the human species." (He writes on page 163: "Despite the excited and optimistic claims that have been made by some paleontologists, no fossil hominid species can be established as our direct ancestor. . . .") "All the fossils which have been dug up and are claimed to be ancestors—we haven't the faintest idea whether they are ancestors. Because all you've got, and the cladists are right. . ." He got up and began to do his famous rat-a-tat-tat with a piece of chalk on the blackboard. "All you've got is Homo sapiens there, you've got *that* fossil there, you've got another fossil *there* . . . this is time here . . . and it's up to you to draw the lines. Because there *are* no lines. I don't think any one of them is likely to be the direct ancestor of the human species. But how would you know it's *that* [pat] one?

"The only way you can know that some fossil is the direct ancestor is that it's so human that it *is* human. There is a contradiction there. If it is different enough from humans to be interesting, then you don't know whether it's an ancestor or not. And if it's similar enough to be human, then it's not interesting."

He returned to his chair and looked out at the slanting rain. "So," he said: "Look, we're not ever going to know what the direct ancestor is."

What struck me about Lewontin's argument was how much it depended on his premise that all organisms have parents. In a sense, his argument includes the assertion that evolutionary theory is true. Lewontin maintains that his premise is "empirical," but this is so only in the (admittedly important) sense that it has never to our knowledge been falsified. No one has ever found an organism that is known not to have parents, or a parent. This is the strongest evidence on behalf of evolution. . . .

Evolutionary Agnostics

The theory of evolution has never been falsified. On the other hand, it is also surely true that the positive evidence for evolution is very much weaker than most laymen imagine, and than many scientists want us to imagine. Perhaps, as Patterson says, that positive evidence is missing entirely. The human mind, alas, seems on the whole to find such uncertainty intolerable. Most people want certainty in one form (Darwin) or another (the Bible). Only evolutionary agnostics like Patterson and Nelson and the other cladists seem willing to live with doubt. And that, surely, is the only truly scientific outlook.

"Evolution is Biblically unsound, theologically contradictory, and sociologically harmful."

The Bible Supports Scientific Creationism

Henry M. Morris

The following viewpoint is by Henry M. Morris, a well-known creation scientist who was formerly the chairperson of the civil engineering department at Virginia Polytechnic Institute. Morris is now president of the Institute for Creation Research in San Diego. In the viewpoint, Morris criticizes those who believe they can reconcile the teachings of Christianity with evolution's teachings. Evolution is wrong, Morris argues, and it challenges the Bible's message that God is the Creator.

As you read, consider the following questions:

1. How does creation, as recorded in the Bible, correspond to scientific evidence of how creation occurred, according to the author?
2. What is the main reason Morris gives to explain why Christians must oppose evolution?
3. What three fallacies of evolutionary thought does Morris cite?

Henry M. Morris, *The Troubled Waters of Evolution*. El Cajon, CA: Master Books, 1982. Reprinted by permission of Master Books, PO Box 1606, El Cajon, CA 92022.

Although the basic creation model offers a clear alternative to the evolution model, it can be made more specific by framing it around the Biblical revelation of earth pre-history. It will be found that this framework, when simply and consistently applied, also wonderfully coordinates and assimilates all known data of natural science.

According to the Bible, the period of special creation occupied six days, following which the Creator "rested from all His work which God created and made." Since that time, He has been "upholding all things." The present cosmos is being "kept in store" under the domain of *conservation*.

However, because of man's sin, God has placed a Curse "on the ground," so that the very "dust of the earth"—the fundamental elements out of which all things had been constructed by God—has been under the "bondage of decay." Thus it is that "the whole creation groaneth and travaileth in pain together until now." Everything, therefore, is heading downhill toward decay and death. The world is thus under the domain of *disintegration* as well as *conservation*.

Modern Science and the Bible

These two universal principles, so clearly set forth in the Bible, of course are now formally incorporated in the basic structure of modern science, as we have seen, and have come in the past century to be denominated as the Two Laws of Thermodynamics. The First Law is the Law of Conservation; the Second Law is the Law of Disintegration. The creation is constant in quantity, but deteriorating in quality. The total energy remains unchanged, but the available energy continually decreases.

Another facet of the Biblical model, of course, is the great Flood of the days of Noah. This is described in the Bible as a worldwide cataclysm of unprecedented and unequalled magnitude. "The world that was, being overflowed with water, perished."

The Flood was obviously primarily a hydraulic, and therefore sedimentary, phenomenon. Torrential waters poured down from the skies and gushed forth from the fountains of the great deep, for 150 days, all over the world. Accompanying these activities must necessarily have been a great complex of atmospheric violence, volcanic eruptions, earth movements, giant waves and other disturbances that profoundly altered the face of the earth. The world that emerged when the waters receded bore little resemblance to the beautiful antediluvian earth as created by God in the beginning.

The key to the innumerable evidences of catastrophism in the earth's crust and on its surface is found in the Flood and its after-effects. This is especially important in the proper interpretation of the record of the fossils in the earth's sedimentary rocks—a record which has mistakenly been appropriated by evolutionists as the chief evidence for their system.

The Biblical framework of pre-history also includes one other event of worldwide significance; namely, the confusion of tongues and dispersion of the nations of the tower of Babel. Although this event had little effect on the physical world, it did of course have profound effects on the world of mankind, and answers many questions in human history to which the evolution model has never provided any solution at all.

Steve Cardno. From The Lie by Kenneth Ham. El Cajon, Ca: Master Books, 1987.

The Biblical creation model is specifically outlined in the first eleven chapters of Genesis and is referred to in one way or another frequently throughout the entire Bible. It amplifies and particularizes the basic model of scientific creationism as discussed earlier. By way of summary and review, it centers around four great events of early history, each of *worldwide* significance, as follows:

(1) Special creation of all things in six days, by creative and integrative processes which no longer are in operation, following which God "rested."

(2) The curse on all things, by which the entire cosmos was brought into a state of gradual deterioration leading toward death.

(3) The universal Flood, which drastically changed the rates of most earth processes and the structure of the earth's surface.

(4) The dispersion of Babel, which resulted from the sudden proliferation of languages and other cultural distinctives among the nations and tribes of men.

The Biblical creationist maintains that all the real data of observation correlate perfectly with the above model. There are a great many measurable and observable phenomena in nature, and all of them, without exception, fit this Biblical model, evolutionary philosophers to the contrary notwithstanding. . . .

Evolution Undermines Christian Education

The evolutionary philosophy thoroughly dominates the curricula and faculties of secular colleges and universities today, as most people are well aware. It is not so well known, however, that this philosophy has also had considerable effect on many Christian colleges. . . .

On one occasion several years ago, the writer spent several hours discussing this problem with a professor of geology of one of the [Christian] Consortium colleges. This teacher insisted that Christians *must* accept the geological-age system as taught by evolutionary geologists. When asked how he, as professedly a Bible-believing Christian, reconciled the Genesis record of creation and the flood with this system, his reply was that he didn't know of any in which they *could* be reconciled. . . . When also asked how he reconciled Jesus Christ's acceptance of the literal Genesis record of creation and the flood with the geological ages, he replied that he didn't know how to reconcile that either. His final conclusion was that all of this was unimportant anyway. Only one thing apparently *was* important; namely, to accept the geological ages!

More recently, the writer had two opportunities to talk at some length with the present Head of the Geology Department at this same college on the same subject. He took much the same position, also adding that we would never be able to understand the meaning of the Genesis record of creation and the flood until we get to heaven! It is not important for us to understand it now, he felt.

Special Creation

One must confess a certain lack of patience with this type of logic. How can a Christian say the doctrine of special creation is unimportant when it is foundational to every other doctrine in Scripture? How can one say the evolutionary philosophy is not significant, when it has been made the basis of fascism, communism, animalism, racism, modernism, atheism, and practically every other harmful philosophy known to man? How can *Christian* college professors teach their students that evolution is an optional question when the Scriptures plainly teach otherwise?

"How long halt ye between two opinions? If the Lord be God, follow him: but if Baal, then follow him."

Real Understanding

Surely, as Christians blessed with the conviction that arises from the work of the Holy Spirit, we must accept the Bible as the infallible, authoritative Word of God—otherwise, we have nothing. If the Bible is to be questioned and cannot be trusted, and if it is continually subject to reinterpretation based on what men believe they have discovered, then we do not have an absolute authority. We do not have the Word of the One who knows everything, which means we have no basis for anything. Truth is spiritually discerned. Without the indwelling of the Holy Spirit there can be no real understanding.

Ken Ham, *The Lie: Evolution,* 1987.

Although evolutionism has most affected Christian higher education, this philosophy has also influenced numerous Christian elementary and secondary schools. Many leading Christian periodicals (*Eternity, Christianity Today, Christian Life,* etc.) have likewise been significantly infiltrated by evolutionary thinking. Many churches, missions, and other Christian institutions have been similarly affected.

Christian Cop-Outs

One of the most frustrating problems encountered in trying to encourage and strengthen belief in a Creator and in creationism is the indifference of so many professing Christian people to the urgent importance of this issue: "I don't believe in evolution anyhow, so why should I waste time in studying or promoting creationism?" "Why get involved in peripheral and controversial issues like that—just preach the Gospel!" "The Bible is not a textbook of science, but of how to live." "It is the Rock of Ages which is important—not the age of rocks!" "Winning souls is the principal thing—not the winning of debates."

Platitudes such as the above, however spiritual they sound, are really cop-outs. They tend to become excuses for avoiding serious thought and the offense of the cross. In the name of evangelism and of appealing to large numbers, a least-common-denominator emphasis on emotional experiences and a nominal commitment of some kind has become the dominant characteristic of most Christian teaching and activity today, and this is almost as true in fundamentalist and conservative circles as it is among religious liberals. . . .

The doctrine of special creation is the foundation of all other Christian doctrine. The experience of belief in Christ as Creator is the basis of all other Christian experience. Creationism is not peripheral or optional; it is central and vital. That is why God placed the account of creation at the beginning of the Bible, and why the very first verse of the Bible speaks of the creation of the physical universe.

Jesus Christ was Creator before He became Redeemer. He is the very "beginning of the creation of God." How then can it be possible to really know Him as Saviour unless one also, and first, knows God as Creator?

The very structure of man's time commemorates over and over again, week by week, the completed creation of all things in six days. The preaching of the Gospel necessarily includes the preaching of creation. ". . . the everlasting gospel to preach unto them that dwell on the earth . . . worship Him that made heaven, and earth, and the sea, and the fountains of waters."

If man is a product of evolution, he is not a fallen creature in need of a Saviour, but a rising creature, capable of saving himself. "The ethical human brain is the highest accomplishment of biological evolution."

The gospel of evolution is the enemy of the Gospel of Christ. The Gospel of Christ leads to salvation, righteousness, joy, peace, and meaning of life. Evolution's gospel yields materialism, collectivism, anarchism, atheism, and despair in death.

Evolutionary thinking dominates our schools today—our news media, our entertainment, our politics, our entire lives. But evolution is false and absurd scientifically! How long will Christian people and churches remain ignorant and apathetic concerning it?

The evolutionary system has been entrenched for so long that many people who otherwise accept the Bible as infallible have deemed it expedient to compromise on this issue. Thus, evolution has been called, "God's method of creation," and the Genesis record of the six days of creation has been reinterpreted in terms of the evolutonary ages of historical geology. These geological ages themselves have been accommodated in Genesis either by placing them in an assumed "gap" between Genesis 1:1 and 1:2 or by changing the "days" of creation into the "ages" of evolution.

Taking the Bible Literally

Theories of this kind raise more problems than they solve, however. It is more productive to take the Bible literally and then to interpret the actual facts of science within its revelatory framework. If the Bible cannot be understod, it is useless as *revelation*. If it contains scientific fallacies, it could not have been given by *inspiration*. . . .

181

Evolution is believed by its leading advocates to be a basic principle of continual development, of increasing order and complexity, throughout the universe. The complex elements are said to have developed from simpler elements, living organisms to have evolved from non-living chemicals, complex forms of life from simpler organisms, and even man himself to have gradually evolved from some kind of ape-like ancestor. Religions, cultures, and other social institutions are likewise believed to be continually evolving into higher forms.

Evolution's Fallacies

Thus, evolution is a complete world-view, an explanation of origins and meanings without the necessity of a personal God who created and upholds all things. Since this philosophy is so widely and persuasively taught in our schools, Christians are often tempted to accept the compromise position of "ethistic evolution," according to which evolution is viewed as God's method of creation. However, this is basically an inconsistent and contradictory position. A few of its fallacies are as follows:

(1) It contradicts the Biblical record of creation. Ten times in the first chapter of Genesis, it is said that God created plants and animals to reproduce "after their kinds." The Biblical "kind" may be broader than our modern "species" concept, but at least it implies definite limits to variation. The New Testament writers accepted the full historicity of the Genesis account of creation. Even Christ Himself quoted from it as historically accurate and authoritative.

A Clear Teaching

The Bible clearly teaches that God created the heavens and the earth and all that is in them in six days of approximately 24 hours. Believers have accepted this clear teaching of Scripture for thousands of years, with very few exceptions (mainly those who were influenced by the world's thought on the matter of origins). . . .

Not only is the Bible clear about creation, but science itself, properly done, will *never* deny the Creator. It is men's *conclusions* and *beliefs* about the created world which challenge the Biblical account of creation, not the facts. Thousands of good scientists today, many of them famous, are creationists.

Bible-Science Association, *Our Miraculous World*, 1987.

---

(2) It is inconsistent with God's methods. The standard concept of evolution involves the development of innumerable misfits and extinctions, useless and even harmful organisms. If this is God's "method of creation," it is strange that He would use such cruel, haphazard, inefficient, wasteful processes. Furthermore, the idea

of the "survival of the fittest," whereby the stronger animals eliminate the weaker in the "struggle for existence" is the essence of Darwin's theory of evolution by natural selection, and this whole scheme is flatly contradicted by the Biblical doctine of love, of unselfish sacrifice, and of Christian charity. The God of the Bible is a God of order and of grace, not a God of confusion and cruelty.

(3) The evolutionary philosophy is the intellectual basis of all anti-theistic systems. It served Hitler as the rationale for Nazism and Marx as the supposed scientific basis for communism. It is the basis of the various modern methods of psychology and sociology that treat man merely as a higher animal and which have led to the misnamed "new morality" and ethical relativism. It has provided the pseudo-scientific rationale for racism and military aggression. Its whole effect on the world and mankind has been harmful and degrading. Jesus said: "A good tree cannot bring forth evil fruit." The evil fruit of the evolutionary philosophy is evidence enough of its evil roots.

Thus, evolution is Biblically unsound, theologically contradictory, and sociologically harmful.

"To rush biblical statements into this arena [of science] . . . is to be very confused about what it is the Genesis materials are teaching."

The Bible Does Not Support Scientific Creationism

Conrad Hyers

In the following viewpoint, Conrad Hyers argues that the Bible should not be used as a science text. Old Testament writers were not trying to present a scientifically accurate account of creation similar to modern science books, Hyers contends. He maintains that creationists actually detract from the Bible's spiritual meaning by attempting to use it as a basis for scientific fact. Hyers is the chairperson of the religion department at Gustavus Adolphus College in Minnesota. He has written *The Meaning of Creation: Genesis and Modern Science.*

As you read, consider the following questions:

1. How does Hyers characterize creation scientists?
2. Hyers argues that the purpose of Old Testament writers was not to scientifically describe the physical nature of the universe. What was their purpose?
3. According to Hyers, what is the true opposite of creation as written in the Bible?

Conrad Hyers, "The Fall and Rise of Creationism." Copyright 1985 Christian Century Foundation. Reprinted by permission from the April 24, 1985 issue of *The Christian Century.*

Until recently, controversy over creation and evolution sounded like something from the dusty archives of the past, safely shelved somewhere in Tennessee in the records of the Scopes "Monkey Trial" in 1925. The issues have been smoldering ever since, however, and in the past decade have erupted with renewed fury. The celebrated trials in Arkansas and Louisiana rudely awakened public consciousness to a phenomenon more widespread and tenacious than most had imagined. . . .

The Energetic Ultraright

While mainline publishers of religious books and church-school curricula have been virtually silent on the subject, there are currently in print more than 350 books challenging evolutionary science and advocating a "creation science" based on six 24-hour days of creation, a "young-earth" dating, and a worldwide "flood geology." A considerable, well-financed effort has been made to inundate the Christian bookstore and mail-order markets with similar literature. . . .

When one adds to the picture the literature and influence of groups such as the Moral Majority and the many fundamentalist radio and television programs reaching multimillions weekly, it is clear that the ultraright has been energetically at work in all aspects of lobbying, publishing and mass media, while those representing a moderate and presumably normative position on the Bible and science have been napping. Most mainline churches, seminary professors, college and university religion teachers and denominational publishing houses have not taken the creationists very seriously. It is as if everyone thought that the issues had been settled by the Scopes trial in the '20s and certainly put to rest by the intervening decades of biblical and scientific study. Creationists are often dismissed with disdain as so unworthy of the effort of a rejoinder or so hopelessly dogmatic that a careful reply would be a waste of time or beneath the dignity of biblical scholarship.

This attitude has also been held among scientists until recently, when the creationist pressures on public education and policy became so threatening that some scientists founded a new journal, *Creation/Evolution*, a "Committee of Correspondence" and a *Creation/Evolution Newsletter*, aimed at defending evolutionary science and dismantling creationist arguments. The American Civil Liberties Union, the National Education Association, lawyers, legislators and judges have been similarly forced to deal with the issue because of the numerous bills and civil suits demanding equal time for creationism. . . .

The average church member, who is usually a layperson in both science and religion, finds the situation confounding. Most have only a Sunday school knowledge of the Bible and perhaps a high school equivalency in science. While members of fundamentalist churches are very clear about their approach to such issues—namely, a simplistic, militant either/or mind-set—most members of nonfundamentalist churches are unsure how to respond to creationist challenges and evolutionist counter-challenges. This uncertainty is borne out by polls, which show that as many as 75 percent of those surveyed thought it only fair to give class time to the biblical accounts of creation, or a "creation model" derived from them—as if they were of the same order as contemporary scientific accounts. . . .

Sheer Humbug

When the "Scientific Creationists" speak of divine creation in Genesis, they fail to mention to which creation story they are referring. With respect to the creation of humankind there are three separate creation stories in Genesis. . . . In the first story God creates man and woman (1:27), whereas in the second he forms man alone of the dust of the earth (2:7), and in the third he creates woman from one of man's ribs (2:21-22).

As a student of biblical literature I see these three different creation stories as probably derived from three distinct traditions, combined by the authors of Genesis into a single chapter, without fusing the stories into a single consistent narrative. To folklorists and ethnologists this is not an unfamiliar turn of events; in many creation myths, and whatever the historical antecedents of Genesis, it represents but one of innumerable creation myths which different people at different times have invented in order to account for the manner in which Earth and everything upon it came into being. That supernaturals formed the first men and women out of dust or clay forms a part of the creation myths of many peoples. . . . It is the sheerest humbug to claim that such stories have anything to do with science. It should, of course, be understood that a great deal more than simple cosmological explanation is involved in creation myths, for they usually have deep emotional and individually meaningful significances for the lives of the believers.

Ashley Montagu, *Science and Creationism*, 1984.

The creationists have done a service in calling attention to the tendencies in science and evolutionary theory to transform methodologically self-limited statements into all-encompassing metaphysical judgments. The problem, however, is that instead of forcefully challenging all these conclusions—which do not directly and necessarily follow from science or from evolutionary theory—the scientific creationists *encourage* them. They accept the either/or of evolution and creation, and they not only accept but insist on the thesis that evolutionary teaching logically and necessarily leads to naturalism, materialism, reductionism, positivism, secularism, atheism and humanism. . . .

The scientific creationists also give further aid and comfort to the philosophies they so vehemently protest by proposing to offer instead a "scientific" interpretation of creation. This then places the biblical affirmations of creation, or supposed "scientific models" derived from them, on the same level as modern scientific theory and natural history, inviting their evaluation and rejection in the very same terms. Most of the 350-plus books written by "creation scientists" consist in large part of discussions of the supposed errors of evolutionary teaching, reviewing vast amounts of technical scientific data and theory, challenging this or that piece of evidence, method of dating or use of data, while producing evidences and counterarguments of their own in favor of a young earth, recent humanity, worldwide flood, etc. Little attention is devoted to a correspondingly careful study of the specific type of biblical literature being interpreted, or the ways this literature is different from scientific literature. Neither is time spent on the original issues that the creation texts were addressing and the original meanings of the words for those first using them.

A Different Type of Literature

"Scientific creationism" is hardly identical with biblical creationism. The creation texts represent a very different type of literature and concern from modern scientific discourse. To rush biblical statements into this arena, as though they were of the same order as Charles Darwin's *Origin of Species* or Stephen Jay Gould's *The Panda's Thumb*, or as though scientific conclusions could be drawn from them, is to be very confused about what it is the Genesis materials are teaching. One also plays directly into the hands of those who would dismiss them as quasi-scientific explanations of things for which we now have more sophisticated explanations.

Neither those who would set aside Genesis as primitive science nor those who would try to defend it as the true science of origins seem to grasp the differences between modern scientific and ancient cosmological literatures. What is more critical is that neither side seems to comprehend the relationship between biblical and other ancient cosmologies. The biblical teaching, after all, was not aimed at one or another of the various theories developed in the history of modern science but at the cosmological understandings of origins found among surrounding peoples. The question, then, is: In what senses was the Bible critiquing and rejecting these pagan cosmologies with which it had so immediately to do?

Ancient cosmologies were developed on the basis of *phenomenal* observations of the world—that is, things as they appeared to everyday observation. In this respect their descriptions of natural occurrences were similar to our own expressions, such as "sunrise" and "sunset." Early cosmologies also pictured the cosmos *relative* to the human observer, as we continue to do when we speak of sending a rocket "upward" into space or refer to Australians as living "down under." The ancients imagined the universe in terms of four directions or quarters horizontally, laid out relative to the society doing the mapping, with the center of the world located in the holy city and/or capital of each nation in turn. There were also three major zones vertically (heavens above, earth at the center, underworld and abyss beneath), with their subdivisions. We thus find the typical ancient picture of a domed canopy over the sky, supported by pillars, with a flat earth below floating on a watery abyss, with sun, moon and stars moving in the heavens relative to the earth, and with the world axis intersecting the sacred center of one's nation.

Understanding the Bible

It is a naive and futile exercise to attempt to reconcile the biblical accounts of creation with the findings of modern science. Any correspondence which can be discovered or ingeniously established between the two must surely be nothing more than mere coincidence. Even more serious than the inherent fundamental misconception of the psychology of biblical man is the unwholesome effect upon the understanding of the Bible itself. For the net result is self-defeating. The literalistic approach serves to . . . obscure the elements that are meaningful and enduring, thus distorting the biblical message and destroying its relevancy.

Nahum M. Sarna, in *Is God a Creationist?*, 1983.

These representations of the cosmos were not being questioned in the Bible or even discussed. They were not the point of contention between Jewish cosmology and the cosmologies of Egypt, Canaan, Assyria, Babylonia, Greece or Rome. The Bible simply *uses* the same general cosmological patterns and expressions familiar to all within and without Israel. Offering a superior cosmology in a *physical* sense was not a matter of theological concern, nor would it have made any particular religious difference. A few pre-Socratic Greeks in the sixth century B.C. were beginning to speculate about the physical nature and arrangements of the natural order, but in Israel these were not issues. In fact, to have made an issue of physical cosmology would have detracted from, if not subverted, the religious message.

In the biblical texts the concern was to affirm the radical difference between a polytheistic and a monotheistic cosmology. All the surrounding cosmologies identified the major regions of the cosmos with their various gods and goddesses. Genesis, over against this viewpoint, affirms (1) that there is only one God; (2) that this God is not identified with or contained by any region of nature; (3) that the pagan gods and goddesses are not divinities at all but creatures, creations of the one true God; and (4) that the worship of any of these false divinities is idolatry. This is what is being taught and celebrated by the creation texts, not any particular cosmological picture that may then be placed in contention with existing or subsequent physical pictures of the cosmos.

What is often ignored in all this, however, is that the *temporal* as well as the spatial aspects of ancient cosmology were employed in the Bible: the physical progression from chaos to cosmos. This progression and its sequence were not a point of contention either. Most of the cosmologies in the ancient world began with a cosmic ocean, darkness and a generalized formlessness—just as Genesis does: "And the earth was without form and void, and darkness was upon the face of the deep." Elements are introduced which give shape to the shapeless: light into darkness; a domed sky (firmament) dividing waters above from waters below; the earth with its vegetation separated from the waters; the sun, moon and stars to regulate the days, months and seasons. The specific order may vary, depending on which chaotic problem is resolved first, but the general pattern and progression is the same. It is a perfectly logical way of proceeding, though it is hardly identical with what we have come to call science or natural history. Its logic is *cosmo*logical, not geological or biological or astronomical.

Pagan Creation Myths

The fundamental difference between the Genesis progression from chaos to cosmos and that of pagan cosmologies lies along the physical plane not in its chronological order but rather in its *theological* order. Here too the issue is religious: a radical contrast is made between a monotheistic creation and a polytheistic cosmogony ("birth of the cosmos"). The pagan myths commonly depicted the origins of natural phenomena in terms of the marriages and births of various gods and goddesses. In Babylonian myth the saltwater goddess (Tiamat) mated with the freshwater god (Apsu) and begat the gods and goddesses of silt and the horizon, which in turn begat heaven (Anu), who begat the earth (Enki). Genesis, on the other hand, portrays the One God who has created all that which surrounding people worship as the divinities of nature. The theological order, therefore, is a genealogy not of the gods (*theogony*) but of creator and creature: "In the beginning God created the heavens and the earth." The true opposite of creation, thus, cannot be any scientific model of origins, evolutionary or otherwise, but is this *procreation* model of polytheistic myth.

The creation accounts were not attempting to present a more cosmologically, let alone scientifically, correct way of representing physical relationships in space or time. Genesis is not offering or supporting a "creation model" that can be placed in competition with other physical models, any more than it is offering a "flat earth model" in competition with geological models or a "geocentric model" in competition with astronomical models. To put Genesis on the level of a physical discussion of the natural order is to *secularize* it—while complaining loudly about secularism in modern culture!

An Irrelevant Question

It must be pointed out that the ancient Hebrew pursued a religious rather than scientific mode of thinking. He was intensely concerned with the purpose and destiny of mankind, and his descriptions of nature were in these terms. The question of how natural phenomena occurred was simply not meaningful except as it was related to the steadfast love and purpose of Jehovah. . . .

The biblical basis of creationism is unacceptable theologically. It is based on a biblical interpretation that has long been discredited.

Stanley D. Beck, *Bioscience*, October 1982.

The fundamental mistake made by creationists is the same as that made by defenders of the *spatial* cosmology employed by the Bible: a flat-earth and earth-centered cosmos. Creationists have simply shifted the argument to the *temporal* side of the cosmology the Bible uses: the spatial cosmology may now be taken metaphorically, but the temporal side must still be taken literally. A century ago John Hampden was defending "the clear and unmistakable flat-earth teaching of the Bible," and insisting that "no one can believe a single doctrine or dogma of modern astronomy, and accept Scripture as divine revelation." Note the very similar words of creationist Henry Morris in defending six literal and recent days of creation: "The creation account is clear, definite, sequential and matter-of-fact, giving every appearance of straightforward historical narrative. . . . Belief in evolution leads usually and logically to rejection of the trustworthiness of the Bible."

If Christians, school boards and God must be eternally committed to preserving the temporal side of biblical cosmology, then to be consistent there should be a return to preserving the spatial side as well. Both form a whole cloth. Some creationists have tried to avoid such consistency by arguing that the temporal aspects are of a different order than the spatial. Spatial relations within the universe are presently observable, whereas temporal relations in the matter of origins are not. So we are forced to take the spatial references poetically, but there is not enough evidence to force us to take the temporal references as anything but literal statements of simple historical truth. It is clear from such a dodge that the principles of biblical interpretation derive from modern scientific issues rather than from the issues which led the biblical writers to use this particular cosmological form.

Secular Creationists

The creationists think of themselves as staunch conservatives, engaged in a loyal defense of biblical teaching. To some extent they are, inasmuch as they are seeking to preserve a doctrine of creation vis-à-vis secularism and scientism. In other respects, however, they are themselves very influenced by secularism and scientism. They confuse what is being taught theologically with the cosmological garb in which the teaching is being presented. They are conserving the right things in the wrong ways. In so doing most of the attention gets focused on the physical issues of modern science—which were not issues at all in the Bible. Endless forays must be made on all scientific fronts—geology, biology, paleontology, astronomy, chemistry, physics, meteorology, genetics, sedimentology, radiometry and the like—either to try to discredit evolution or to defend creation.

Recognizing Deceptive Arguments

People who feel strongly about an issue use many techniques to persuade others to agree with them. Some of these techniques appeal to the intellect, some to the emotions. Many of them distract the reader from the real issues.

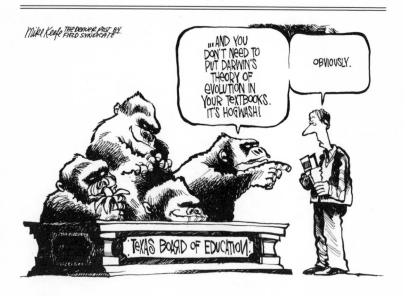

Mike Keefe, reprinted with permission.

The cartoon above illustrates one type of deceptive argument—the personal attack. The cartoonist portrays those who oppose evolution as apes with low intelligence. This cartoon does not consider their arguments, but instead insults them on a personal level.

Below are listed a few common examples of argumentation tactics. Most of them can be used either to advance an argument in an honest, reasonable way or they can deceive and distract readers from important issues that may weaken the author's arguments.

It is helpful for critical thinkers to recognize these tactics in order to rationally evaluate an author's ideas.

a. *bandwagon*—the idea that "everybody" does this or believes this

b. *personal attack*—criticizing an opponent *personally* instead of rationally debating his or her ideas

c. *scare tactic*—the threat that if you don't do this or believe this, something terrible will happen

d. *slanter*—trying to persuade through exaggerated and inflammatory language instead of through reason

e. *strawperson*—distorting or exaggerating an opponent's arguments to make one's own seem stronger

f. *testimonial*—quoting or paraphrasing an authority to support one's own viewpoint

The following activity will allow you to sharpen your skills in recognizing deceptive arguments. The statements are derived from the viewpoints in this chapter. *Beside each one, mark the letter of the type of deceptive appeal being used. More than one type of tactic may be applicable.*

1. How can a Christian say evolution is not harmful, when its philosophy has led to fascism, communism, animalism, racism, atheism, and practically every other harmful philosophy?

2. Colin Patterson, a well-known and respected paleontologist, doubts that evolution can ever be proven as a fact.

3. The fact of evolution is as well established as anything in science (as secure as the revolution of the earth about the sun).

4. Members of fundamentalist churches approach the Bible and science with a simplistic, either-or mindset.

5. Creationism reverses the scientific process. It accepts as authoritative a conclusion and then tries to support that conclusion by whatever means possible.

6. Darwin did not base his ideas on observation of scientific data. He began with a belief system and then looked for data to support his beliefs.

7. Teaching the creationist doctrine in a science class

compromises public education and threatens the advancement of science.

8. Christ Himself quoted from the Genesis account of creation as historically accurate and authoritative.

9. I'm used to the militant fundamentalists' dishonest misquotations, their constant repetition of arguments even they must recognize as nonsense.

10. It is surely true that the evidence for evolution is very much weaker than most laypersons imagine, and than most scientists want us to imagine.

11. The Gospel of Christ leads to joy, peace, and meaning in life. Evolution's gospel yields materialism, atheism, and despair.

12. Today there is no significant scientific doubt about the close evolutionary relationship between apes and humans.

13. Evidence for relation by common descent has been provided by rigorous study in the biological fields of paleontology, comparative anatomy, biochemistry, and molecular genetics.

14. Evolution is not adequate for the big questions. It does not agree with facts and reality. Creation science offers a fully acceptable and satisfying alternative.

15. How did Darwin get around the obvious discrepancy between his theory and scientific facts? Rather than admit his theory was wrong, he blamed the fossil record for being incomplete.

Should Ethical Values Limit Scientific Research?

Chapter Preface

Many of the benefits of modern science are obvious—people live longer, have machines to make many tasks easier, and have more leisure time because tasks are less time-consuming. Yet profound ethical questions are raised by many of science's technologies, such as nuclear weapons, genetic engineering, and machines that pollute the environment. The conflict between science's benefits and its risks is the basis of the following chapter.

If science can produce both harm and good, what values should be used to determine what to research and develop? Some philosophers believe that the values of ancient societies are a useful guide. Ancient cultures deified natural forces and adapted themselves to their environment. In contrast, in modern scientific societies, most people have far less contact with nature. As a result, the sense of awe people once felt toward the power of the universe has been destroyed, these philosophers contend. Science's risks could be considerably reduced, they argue, if the modern world had more respect for nature. Before developing a technology, its impact on the environment should be assessed. Neither nuclear energy nor nuclear weapons should be produced because of the problem of toxic wastes and the danger of contamination. And expensive and potentially dangerous technologies such as genetic engineering should not be researched at all. This money, they believe, could be better used to provide basic health care for all. Although it is probably impossible and undesirable to live without technology, these philosophers admit, using ancient values as an ethical guide would lead to safer technology and more responsible science.

Many scientists and philosophers disagree with this position, however. To them, it seems absurd to criticize science's success in making life easier, more efficient, and more pleasant. The dangers of genetic engineering and pollution are exaggerated, according to some scientists, while others argue that although these technologies pose serious problems, more scientific research will reduce their risks. Further research is promising, they contend, because science itself offers useful ethics. Its ethics are implicit in the scientific method—honesty, thoroughness, objectivity, and accuracy. With these four criteria guiding scientists' work, both risks and benefits are taken into account before a new technology is developed.

The four authors in the following chapter present their views on where society should derive its moral values for assessing the paradox of science's benefits and risks.

"Scientists fail to take note of the possible ill effects that could follow from their work; they make the . . . vague assumption that all science is good."

Ethical Values Should Limit Scientific Research

Liebe F. Cavalieri

In the following viewpoint, Liebe F. Cavalieri argues that society faces several problems as a result of unbridled technology—genetic engineering, a deteriorating environment, and depleted resources. According to Cavalieri, many scientists have traditionally believed they are not responsible for the technology that results from their research. This view is short-sighted and dangerous, he argues. Scientists should use ethical values as a guide in their research. Cavalieri is a member of the Sloan-Kettering Institute for Cancer Research and teaches biochemistry at Cornell University Medical College.

As you read, consider the following questions:

1. What assumptions have scientists traditionally made about their work, according to Cavalieri?
2. What conflict does the author see between science that serves industry and science that serves humanity?
3. What technological disaster does the author predict and what does he believe scientists could do to avert the disaster?

Liebe F. Cavalieri, *The Double-Edged Helix: Genetic Engineering in the Real World* (Volume 2 in the Convergence Series, founded by Ruth Nanda Anshen, Praeger Publishers, New York, 1985). Copyright © 1985 by Liebe F. Cavalieri. Reprinted with permission of author, Dr. Anshen, and publisher.

Modern scientific research in this country has become increasingly mission-oriented. When the research is economically important, its results are often applied with little loss of time; such was the situation with the transistor, the heart of modern electronics. In that case, and in many others, science acted as an arm of technology. It is foolish for scientists to close their eyes to this reality, when they should be guarding science against abuse and exploitation for commercial purposes that have little to do with either human needs or the acquisition of pure knowledge. In traditional fashion, . . . most scientists have not felt the need to become involved in the application of their discoveries; indeed, they have carefully avoided any such intervention, arguing that this is not their domain. This simplistic notion, which came into vogue about 150 years ago, is irrelevant and even dangerous in modern times. In the face of recombinant DNA technology, which will most certainly affect the lives of future humans, this archaic view of the pursuit of knowledge is especially in need of substantial updating, for if the scientific community will not guard the public interest when a powerful but highly esoteric new scientific technique is discovered, who will?

Contrary to prevailing fears, the acceptance of public accountability and responsibility by the scientific community would not preclude the pursuit of knowledge for its own sake. In fact, . . . that pursuit is currently being phased out with no good justification.

Genetic Engineering

Recombinant DNA technology has immense societal implications, embodying applications to medicine, agriculture, and industry; its possible influence on ecological systems and future generations of humans is incalculable. It will permit manipulation of the gene pool of the earth, and thus manipulation of the nature of all life. At this time, techniques have already been developed by which genes, which are composed of DNA, can be shuffled about so that DNA from any source—say, animals or viruses or fruit flies—can be inserted into living bacteria. Inside the bacteria these genes can be made to perform their normal functions, if all goes according to Hoyle, even though they are outside their normal habitat. . . . Recombinant DNA presents scientists with a new and uniquely powerful means for altering living cells according to their design. One Nobel laureate has said: "We can outdo evolution." The biological scientists' responsibility is therefore immense; it is as great, or greater, than that which fell upon physicists a few decades ago. I suspect that many of the implications of this technology have been cast aside by the scientific community because a more enlightened view would require a general examination of societal problems, and the solutions to those problems might place constraints on the scientific enterprise.

Meanwhile, although the public awe of science continues, there is a growing uneasiness about technology. Someday, as the nuclear, ecological, and now genetic hazards and threats grow larger, this unease is likely to erupt with destructive force as a full-scale antiscientific and antiintellectual movement. . . .

Integrating Values with Science

The social consciousness of most scientists does not extend to their own sphere of activities. This is not a criticism; it is an observation. For example, many molecular biologists take pride in their "liberal" political views: they marched in protest of the Southeast Asia war; they fought against the use of chemical and biological warfare; they decry radioactive contamination by nuclear wastes; they abhor pollution. In brief, their values seem to be related to the bettering of the human condition. Yet in their own realm many of the same scientists fail to take note of the possible ill effects that could follow from their work; they make the implicit, vague assumption that all science is good, as though its beneficent application were foolproof. This leads to the illogical conclusion that any and all goals are equally desirable in the search for knowledge, and this is somehow connected with freedom of inquiry. Scientists are rightly concerned about freedom of inquiry. But when it is discussed, insistence upon the neutrality of science often

Ed Gamble, reprinted with permission.

aborts rational analysis. Some scientists hold up the specters of Galileo or Lysenko at any suggestion of public accountability, although their histories are not relevant to the issues of public and environmental safety raised, for example, by recombinant DNA technology. Scientists still feel comfortable with seventeenth-century arguments concerning knowledge and truth, arguments that take no account of modern technological society and the accelerated impact of science on everyone.

Science and the Industrial System

A common feature of technologies is that they respond first to the needs of the industrial structure that spawned them and second, if these do not interfere with the first, to human needs. This is the immutable contradiction of our industrial system; it is a system that, by design, depends on production and growth. The physical realities of finite energy supplies, the limited ability of the environment to absorb pollution, population growth and the finite potential for food production, and, ultimately, the projected thermal instability of the planet force the inevitable conclusion that growth must cease within a few decades. By anyone's calculus there can be no setting aside of this dilemma. The choice is clear: let matters proceed in a more or less random fashion to the natural and ominous end point; or try to transform the present socio-economic structure based on unrestrained technology, by developing appropriate controls. The practice of science as we know it cannot continue unrestrained, in the present milieu, for its results are bound to be applied by the industrial establishment in the name of progress. But, as the scientist Bentley Glass asks, ". . . can we honestly set aside the conclusion that *progress*, in the sense of ever-growing power over the environment, must soon come to an end?"

In attempts to maximize the best and minimize the worst, technocrats place a high degree of confidence in cost-benefit (or risk-benefit) analysis. But such analysis becomes more irrelevant as time goes on; indeed in many areas, such as the alteration of the landscape for industrial reasons, cost-benefit analysis is completely inadequate. Aesthetic, ethical, and moral questions involve value judgments, to which the "hard" numbers required for cost-benefit analysis cannot be assigned. Decisions involving those questions must therefore be political, not technical.

Alternative Technology

It is not so much technology, itself, as its present vast scale, that creates the problems. The application of science to the development of intermediate and alternative technologies could be highly beneficial. Such technologies emphasize natural processes, the use of renewable resources, labor-intensive instead of energy-intensive production, and minimal waste. . . . Giant technological approaches are in general renounced. Philosophically this approach is capable of achieving a state of human fulfillment not possible with a surfeit of material goods. We have already proved that a plethora of hardware, drugs, and consumer goods have not achieved this aim. The convergence of so many technologies has reduced the public to a listless, frustrated mass of humanity without a meaningful function. Another technology will not solve the problem; that will require a monumental and courageous political decision, backed by the determination of all of us.

A Scientific Reformation

Science-and-technology has produced so much dirt and smog and ugliness, so many explosions and crashes in fail-safe systems, so much wasted weaponry and undisposable waste, that popular resistance to the "inner logic" of the scientific method grows louder every year. . . .

Three hundred years after Newton, we the people seem determined to take science and technology off "automatic pilot" and steer them toward the fulfillment of human aspirations—beginning with what Samuel Gompers, a pioneer of the U.S. labor movement, called the most basic needs of all: bread, work and peace.

If science is the religion of modern governance, a new kind of Reformation is now at hand. It's about time.

Harlan Cleveland, *Minneapolis Star Tribune*, August 30, 1987.

In the face of such fundamental problems, cries by scientists for freedom of inquiry seem banal, self-serving, and irrelevant. The cries are a result of what Theodore Roszak has called the "single vision" of science—the view that the content of human life can be comprehended only through a scientific understanding of its inner machinery, by a complete dissection and analysis. This reductionist philosophy has created and nurtured the technological state, and it has done so at the expense of the value of wholeness. This is an unfortunate outcome for science, which does not inevitably demand application as technology; nor is science incompatible with other, more humane philosophies. It is the emotional and commercial content of science, put there by our culture, that has led directly to the problems. Science practiced in a newly responsible way could play a vital role in extricating society from the impending crisis. But this means that scientists will have to develop a social conscience, convey this to the people, and above all, teach their newly acquired wisdom to the technocrats.

To call for an awakening of scientists, technocrats, and the masses on whom technology is practiced sounds all but hopeless, to be sure. But there is no other way to halt the impending technological disaster. Scientists have had freedom from account-ability and responsibility for a very long time. They have the knowledge and the qualifications necessary to recognize the dangers of our present technological course, and they cannot escape from the moral responsibility of acting to change it—even at the sacrifice of cherished prerogatives.

"Ethical questions do not have answers in the sense that scientific questions do; scientists show good sense in not using science to try to answer them."

Ethical Values Should Not Limit Scientific Research

Gerald Feinberg

Gerald Feinberg is a physics professor at Columbia University in New York who has also worked at the CERN laboratory in Geneva, Switzerland. CERN is the principal European center for research in particle physics. In the following viewpoint, Feinberg argues that religious values should not limit scientific inquiry. It is impossible to predict how most scientific findings will be applied, he contends, which makes limiting the questions scientists may probe pointless and potentially harmful.

As you read, consider the following questions:

1. How does the author describe the relationship between religion and modern science?
2. Why does Feinberg believe it is wrong to impose social controls on science?
3. According to Feinberg, why is it important to continue to fund scientific research that is not targeted to develop a specific technology?

The role that science plays in the overall intellectual life of society has changed significantly over the years. At the dawn of modern science, in the seventeenth century, it was common, even for scientists like Newton, to think of science as subordinate to other intellectual pursuits, such as religion. Scientists now consider that scientific inquiry dominates the human intellectual adventure. This change of view is largely a response to the unparalleled success that scientists have had in solving the problems that they pose. The contrast between science, where the answers to questions are often found quite rapidly, and fields such as philosophy, where definitive answers are almost never found, has acted as a powerful influence in convincing scientists of the intellectual preeminence of their work.

Scientific Prestige

This supremacy meets with very little challenge from nonscientists. When something new or unexpected happens in the world, such as a summer cold spell or a new disease, the immediate reaction among many is to ask what science has to say about it. This attitude is not really based on an understanding of what a scientific explanation is, or how scientists go about trying to understand new phenomena. Instead, it comes from some general aura of prestige that is based vaguely on the past achievements of science.

Yet there are exceptions to the perceived intellectual predominance of science, especially in the areas of ethics and religion. Many scientists believe that science has no way to answer ethical questions, such as whether abortion is morally justifiable. All science can hope to do is help clarify some of the factual matters related to these questions, such as whether a fetus can feel pain. Many nonscientists and some scientists consider it a fault of science that ethical matters are beyond its grasp; after all, ethical questions are at least as important to the lives of people as are factual ones. This type of criticism goes back at least as far as Socrates. Yet many philosophers argue, as do I, that ethical questions do not have answers in the sense that scientific questions do; scientists show good sense in not using science to try to answer them.

The relation between science and religion is more complex, and the final lines between the two have not yet been drawn to everyone's satisfaction. Many of the topics that were once matters of religious faith have been transferred to the purview of science. This change has not happened without bitter arguments, over, for example, the evolution of species, molecular biology, and in some places, over the whole outlook of science.

It has been demonstrated over a long history of conflict that religion has nothing to teach science about the matter that most concerns science, that is, the way the universe works. Accordingly, it would be best if religious believers abandoned their efforts to influence the content of science. The long-term trend is certainly in that direction, and despite a flurry of legal activity among those calling themselves creation scientists, it is not from religious believers that the most serious challenges to science will come in the future.

It is more common for religious believers to preach to scientists about the moral aspects of science, particularly when its technological applications are as far-reaching in their impact as some forms of biotechnology, which could literally change the human species. Everyone should bring whatever sources of moral inspiration they have to bear on such critical questions. But even here, religion has no more claim on the attention of nonbelievers than any other source.

Progress or Suicide?

In Western societies, the power and productivity of science has sprung largely from its pluralism and its consequent freedom. History reminds us that constant vigilance is required if we are to avoid the perilous consequences of attempts by society or a misguided few to determine what is permissible to know and what is illicit to learn. Attempts to restrain the search for knowledge have often proved to be more frightening than the scenarios constructed by the prophets of doom and gloom themselves. To cut off research because of fear of the possibilities inherent in knowledge is to condemn our society to a life without creativity, without new capabilities. It would be a suicidal policy.

Gerald D. Laubach, *USA Today*, July 1980.

If religion has nothing useful to say to science, does it follow that science has nothing useful to say to religion? Much early religious belief offered explanations, such as those in the book of Genesis, of aspects of the universe that are now explained by science. To the extent that this motive still plays an important role in religious belief, the results of science are relevant, and when understood by the believers, could lead to a modification or abandonment of the belief. Scientists in non-Marxist countries rarely try to systematically explain the consequences of their work for religious belief, and I do not expect this to change.

The Scientists' Image

On the whole, nonscientists in developed countries have had positive attitudes toward scientists, at least in the past fifty years or so. Opinion surveys among adults in the United States tend to give scientists very high ratings as desirable contributors to society.

This endorsement derives mostly from the technological applications of scientific research, rather than from any real understanding of what scientists do. In fact, a strong case can be made that the public at large has little sympathy for what motivates scientists in their work. As long as there is a continued appreciation of the technological by-products of this work, this is not a serious situation. But continued appreciation is by no means assured, especially since some technological developments—nuclear reactors, means for prolonging life, and computers, for example—have been denounced by many. . . .

There is the threat of social control over the type of research to be carried out as well as over the conclusions of research. There is the threat of severe cutbacks in the level of financial support. Both of these threats have become real in some recent cases, and the experience has conditioned many scientists to a state of alertness about their recurrence.

Social Controls Are Harmful

I believe that the only serious threat from society to the continuation of science comes from the will to exercise social controls over science. This will is to be found in various places in society. It exists among some of those who feel threatened by the discoveries of science, such as the believers in fundamentalistic religion. It exists among those whose passion for social justice blinds them to the possibility that there are other human impulses whose gratification is equally desirable. It exists among those who do not believe that some pursuits are justified in their own terms rather than as means to some other social ends. And most seriously, it exists among those who are fearful of the possible consequences of trying to use applied scientific knowledge to modify the human condition. These are very distinct rationales for limiting the activities that scientists can pursue, and the degrees to which they can be justified vary significantly. But for the purpose of predicting future restrictions on science, what matters more is the strength of the impulse, and how it may manifest itself.

I believe that there is no valid reason for any society to limit the type of questions that scientists may investigate, or to constrain the type of answers that scientists may find to the questions that interest them. Society should only restrict scientific research that would directly harm other human beings. A society is no more justified in regulating the curiosity of its scientists than it would be in regulating their eating habits, or regulating the expression of its artists.

Controversial Areas

A serious problem for science today is posed by the actions of those people both inside and outside science who wish to forbid research in certain controversial areas. Scientists working on the

206

inheritance of intelligence, and on recombinant DNA have met with sometimes violent opposition. As a result, many interested scientists have decided to avoid these fields altogether. One prominent researcher on the heritability of intelligence has said that if her work showed that intelligence was largely a matter of heredity, she would be tempted to leave the United States because of the controversy that this result would generate.

Fear of Progress

There are countless instances throughout history where science, even with its imperfections, was right and human instincts were wrong. Passionate fears were aroused with the advent of steam power and electricity, surgery and immunology, and the automobile and air travel. Those who fear the unknown have been all too willing to repeat the Inquisition's sins against Galileo. Fortunately, since the Age of Enlightenment, reason has, for the most part, prevailed.

These caveats aside, I believe the steady stream of alarmist, anti-science news of recent years nourishes, as much as it reflects, a growing anti-science cast in society as a whole—one that bodes ill for both science and society.

Gerald D. Laubach, *USA Today*, July 1980.

The aims of science are never served by this type of coercion. Though there may be valid reasons for trying to persuade scientists of the inappropriateness of certain lines of research, and though sharp intellectual criticism is well within the bounds of acceptable relations among scientists, violent harassment of fellow scientists of whose research one disapproves lies far outside those bounds. Scientists as a group should take steps to discourage such coercion when it arises inside of science. Those scientists who regularly engage in it should be regarded with the same contempt as those scientists who falsify research. Whatever their other merits, they should be penalized professionally by their colleagues. If we allow anyone, whatever their motives, to repress scientific curiosity by force, then one of the great lessons that science has taught mankind will have been lost: Unless we are all free to express our curiosity to seek the truth, wherever it leads us, then none of us are truly free.

Control Technology, Not Research

One area in which I believe that society does have a legitimate concern is over the technological consequences of scientific research, but this concern is not a justification for forbidding a certain type of research. We cannot know very well what new technology can emerge from scientific research until after the research has been done, often not until long after, so that trying to control technology by controlling science is likely to be ineffective, unless we restrict all research. It is much more effective to control the technology itself, after its possibility has been demonstrated, but before it has been developed or implemented on a large scale.

"[Scientism] asked man to sacrifice a good part of that which made for him the reality of the world—its beauty [and] its holiness."

Science Has Corrupted Religious Values

Huston Smith

In the following viewpoint, Huston Smith argues that science, which takes a quantitative view of the world, can only explain part of reality. An explanation for the other part is offered by religions, which have traditionally celebrated the sacred, mysterious aspects of nature. The modern West has lost much of its spirituality, he concludes, because it has ignored the traditional religious view and accepted misinterpreted science that claims to offer a complete worldview. Smith has taught philosophy at the Massachusetts Institute of Technology (MIT) and at Syracuse University. He is the author of the widely-acclaimed *The Religions of Man*.

As you read, consider the following questions:

1. Why does the West's outlook differ from all others, according to Smith?
2. How does Smith define "scientism"?
3. What contrast does the author see between the way Native Americans viewed the American continent and the way Europeans viewed it?

Excerpts from *Forgotten Truth: The Primordial Tradition* by Huston Smith. Copyright © 1976 by Huston Smith. Reprinted by permission of Harper & Row Publishers Inc.

Man has a profound need to believe that the truth he perceives is rooted in the unchanging depths of the universe; for were it not so, could the truth be really important? Yet how can he so believe when others see truth so differently? Archaic man, wrapped in his tribal beliefs like a chrysalis in a cocoon, did not have this problem. Even civilized man on the whole has been spared it, for until recently the various civilizations have been largely self-contained. It is we—we moderns, we worldly wise—who experience the problem acutely.

Twenty years ago I wrote a book, *The Religions of Man*, which presented the world's enduring traditions in their individuality and variety. It has taken me until now to see how they converge. The outlooks of individual men and women (the militant atheist, the pious believer, the cagey skeptic) are too varied even to classify, but when they gather in collectivities—the outlooks of tribes, societies, civilizations, and at the deepest level the world's great religions—these collective outlooks admit of overview. What then emerges is a remarkable unity underlying the surface variety. When we look at human bodies, what we normally notice is their surface features, which of course differ markedly. Meanwhile on the insides the spines that support these motley physiognomies are structurally very much alike. It is the same with human outlooks. Outwardly they differ, but inwardly it is as if an "invisible geometry" has everywhere been working to shape them to a single truth.

The West's Deviation

The sole notable exception is ourselves; our contemporary Western outlook differs in its very soul from what might otherwise be called "the human unanimity." But there is an explanation for this: modern science and its misreading. If the cause were science itself, our deviation might be taken as a breakthrough: a new departure for mankind, the dawning of an age of reason after a long night of ignorance and superstition. But since it derives from a misreading of science, it is an aberration. If we succeed in correcting it, we can rejoin the human race. . . .

That the scientific outlook should, in Carl Becker's word, have "ravished" the modern mind is completely understandable. Through technology, science effects miracles: skyscrapers that stand; men standing on the moon. Moreover, in its early stages these miracles were in the direction of the heart's desire: multiplication of goods and the reduction of drudgery and disease. There was the sheer noetic majesty of the house pure science erected, and above all there was method. By enabling men to agree on the truth because it could be demonstrated, this method produced a knowledge that was cumulative and could advance. No wonder man converted. The conversion was not forced. It did not occur because scientists were imperialists but because their achievements were so impressive, their marching orders so exhilarating, that thinkers jostled to join their ranks.

A Limited Instrument

We ourselves were once in their number and would be so today were it not for a fact that has become increasingly unblinkable. Strictly speaking, a scientific world view is impossible; it is a contradiction in terms. The reason is that science does not treat of the world; it treats of a part of it only. One world at a time, one hears. Fair enough, but not half a world, which is all that science can offer. . . .

Warfare Upon Joy

More and more the spirit of "nothing but" hovers over advanced scientific research: the effort to degrade, disenchant, level down. Is it that the creative and the joyous embarrass the scientific mind to such an extent that it must try with might and main to degrade them? Consider the strange compulsion our biologists have to synthesize life in a test tube—and the seriousness with which this project is taken. Every dumb beast of the earth knows without thinking once about it how to create life: it does so by seeking delight where it shines most brightly. But, the biologist argues, once we have done it in a laboratory, *then* we shall really know what it is all about. Then we shall be able to *improve* upon it!

What a measure of our alienation it is that we do not regard that man as a fool who grimly devotes his life to devising routine laboratory procedures for that which is given to him like a magnificent gift in the immediacy of his own most natural desire.

Theodore Roszak, *The Making of a Counter Culture*, 1968.

As a probe toward the way things are, science is a powerful but strictly limited instrument. One wonders if it was during the Battle of Britain that Karl Popper of the University of London, ranking philosopher of science in our generation, hit upon an image that has become standard in making this point. His image likens science to a searchlight scanning a night sky for planes. For a plane to register, two things are required: it must exist, and it must be where the beam is. The plane must *be*, and it must be *there* (where the beam is).

The point of this image is, of course, to make plain the restricted nature of the scientific quest. Far from lighting up the entire sky, it illumines but an arc within it. Norbert Wiener used to make the point by saying: "Messages from the universe arrive addressed no more specifically than 'To Whom It May Concern.' Scientists open those that concern them." No mosaic constructed from messages thus narrowly selected can be the full picture. . . .

The triumphs of modern science went to man's head in something of the way rum does, causing him to grow loose in his logic. He came to think that what science discovers somehow casts doubt on things it does not discover; that the success it realizes in its own domain throws into question the reality of domains its devices cannot touch. In short, he came to assume that science implies scientism: the belief that no realities save ones that conform to the matrices science works with—space, time, matter/energy, and in the end number—exist.

The Effect of Reductionism on Values

It was not always so, but today a sadness comes over us as we think back over the way this *reductio* leveled the world view that preceded it. Traditionally men had honored, even venerated, their ancestors as being essentially wiser than themselves because closer to the source of things. Now forefathers came to be regarded as "children of the race," laboring under children's immaturity. Their *ens perfectissimum* was a mirage, a wish-fulfilling security blanket spun of thin air to compensate for the hardships of real life. Or alternatively, their convictions regarding the human soul were opiates invented by the privileged to quiet, as if by lobotomy, those who without them might press for a fair share of the world's prerequisites.

Reviewing the way the new evicted the old—myopia parading as vision, eternity-blindness as enlightenment and the dawn of a brighter day—we find our thoughts turning to the Native Americans. They too watched a landscape dismantled, in their case a physical landscape of almost magical richness. Untapped, unravaged, its gains of soil had been to them beads in the garment of the Great Spirit; its trees were temple pillars, its earth too sacred to be trodden save by soft skin moccasins. Across this unparalleled expanse of virgin nature there poured hordes possessing a capacity so strange that they seemed to the natives they dispossessed to represent a different breed: the capacity to look on everything in creation as material for exploitation, seeing trees only as timber, deer only as meat, mountains as no more than potential quarries. For the victims of this "civilizing mission," as the predators chose to call their conquest, there could only be, in the words of a former U.S. Commissioner of Indian Affairs, a "sadness deeper than imagination can hold—sadness of men completely conscious, watching the universe being destroyed by a numberless and scorning foe." For the Indians "had what the world has lost . . . the ancient, lost reverence and passion for human personality joined with the ancient, lost reverence and passion for the earth and its web of life."

[John] Collier's account emphasizes the quality of sadness rather than anger in the Indians' response. Inasmuch as humanity is in some way one, the response may have included an element of pity for us all. In any case, it appears of a piece with our wistfulness as we think of the destruction of the primordial world view that occurred concurrently and relatedly through scientism's reduction of its qualitative aspects to modalities that are basically quantitative. This ontological strip mining asked man to sacrifice a good part of that which made for him the reality of the world—its beauty, its holiness and crucial expanses of truth—in return for a mathematical scheme whose prime advantage was to help man manipulate matter on its own plane. The discontinuous character of number ordained in advance that such a predominantly quantitative approach would miss the immense tissue of being, its side that consists of pure continuity and relations kept necessarily in balance.

"'Man's chief end is to glorify God and to enjoy him forever.' . . . [This is] the rubric under which the Christian must practice his science."

Science Has Not Corrupted Religious Values

Donald M. MacKay

Physicist Donald M. MacKay founded and directed the department of communications and neuroscience at the University of Keele in Great Britain. He has written several books on Christianity and science. In the following viewpoint, MacKay argues that the purpose of science meshes with the Bible's teachings. The Bible commands humans to subdue nature and use it responsibly for their benefit, he contends. This message overturned the pagan view of nature as something to be feared, MacKay believes. In marked contrast to the pagan world, the modern world has science and Christianity to improve human life and fulfill God's commands.

As you read, consider the following questions:

1. What does the author describe as the pagan view of nature?
2. What place does God want humans to have in the universe, according to the author?
3. In what way does MacKay believe Francis Bacon challenged the medieval view of nature?

Donald M. MacKay, "Christian Priorities in Science." *Journal of the American Scientific Affiliation*, June 1986. Reprinted with permission.

The scientist is by profession a map-maker; and like other map-makers he is pledged to allow his own particular values to distort as little as possible the representation he makes of the state of affairs. "Whether I like it or not, or you like it or not, that's the way it is as far as I can see." In this sense, he strives to make scientific knowledge "value-free." His maps are meant to be reliable guides to other people, of whose values he can know nothing; so "scientific detachment" and "depersonalization," far from being arbitrary eccentricities of the trade, are all part of his duty as an honest craftsman. . . .

Ethical Standards

Once we think of science as a human enterprise, questions of value crowd thick and fast upon us. To list just a few examples, science demands of us evaluation, explicit or implicit,

1. In accepting the obligations, both ethical and social, of map-making;

2. In choosing what to map;

3. In choosing the categories in terms of which to map (e.g., geological, agricultural, etc.);

4. In assessing relative costs and benefits in relation to identified "needs";

5. In deciding where and in what terms to apply for financial support;

6. In assessing the ethical/moral acceptability of research methods;

7. In the creative process of inventing hypotheses to test;

8. In noticing and reporting data adverse to a chosen hypothesis;

9. In selecting *what* to publish, and *when* and *where*;

10. In encouraging/discouraging specific applications of scientific discoveries;

11. In accepting/rejecting new scientific problems that may be raised by given applications;

12. In presenting to the general public, including any fellow-Christians who have to make pronouncements in the name of the Church, the implications (practical, theoretical, philosophical, religious if any) of scientific discoveries. . . .

Christian Priorities

"Man's chief end is to glorify God and to enjoy him forever." So the shorter Catechism sums up the rubric under which the Christian must practice his science. Not only must he seek to live to that end, but in all his efforts to serve his fellow men he must aim to further, and not to hinder, their own prospects of doing the same. This already constitutes quite a severe filter, as a glance at our twelve examples of evaluation will show. We glorify God first and foremost by establishing love (in its strongest sense) as the ruling spirit of our whole enterprise—love to him as our Master

215

and Redeemer, and as the Giver of being to all our data and all our powers; and love to our neighbor which must never fall short of the love we have, or ought to have, for ourselves.

Love of God involves grateful and obedient service with all our heart (enthusiastic commitment), mind (scrupulous acceptance of the rational implications of God's data) and strength (diligence in action). Though God can be glorified by mere admiring contemplation of his works, full obedience, especially for the scientist, demands precisely those emphases on accuracy, objectivity and rationality that (in most disciplines claiming the name of "science") are recognized as professionally essential. . . .

Shaped by Each Other

Historical investigation to date has revealed a rich and varied interaction between science and Christianity. People of assorted scientific and theological persuasions and varieties of knowledge and commitment have, with varying degrees of skill and integrity, gone about the business of understanding themselves and their world, building institutions, creating careers, and pursuing sundry satisfactions. In the process, Christianity and science—as intellectual systems, as institutions, and as objects of personal commitment— have rubbed against each other, sometimes comfortably, sometimes with destructive force. In the future, we must not simply ask "Who was the aggressor?" but "How were Christianity and science affected by their encounter?". . .

We will uncover as much struggle and competition within the Christian and scientific communities as between them. Most important, we will see that influence has flowed in both directions, that Christianity and science alike have been profoundly shaped by their relations with each other.

David C. Lindberg and Ronald L. Numbers, *Perspectives on Science and Christian Faith*, September 1987.

Already we see a strong contrast between the Biblical concepts of nature and man and a variety of pagan ideas. Many people in our day, as in previous ages, suppose the typically "religious" attitude toward natural science to be that embodied in the ancient Greek legend of Prometheus, who stole the sacred fire. Nature is thought of as semi-divine; she has her secrets. The gods would like to keep some of these to themselves, and jealously resent any advances in man's knowledge of them. Science is thus thought of as an irreverent and dangerous pursuit in which sinful man aspires unto the place of God. If disaster results from attempts to apply man's scientific knowledge, this is considered to be what he deserves for prying into the sacred mysteries of the Creator. . . .

The Bible sets man in perspective as a creature of God, a part of the vast created order that owes its continuance in being to the divine upholding power. Unlike the rest of the natural world known to us, however, human beings have powers of foresight, planning and action that make us especially responsible in the eyes of our Creator. With these powers, according to the Bible, goes a special obligation toward the Creator. Men are commanded, not merely permitted, to "subdue the earth." This is to be done not, indeed, in a spirit of arrogant independence, but as the stewards of God's creation. Human beings are answerable to Him for the effectiveness with which they have fulfilled His mandate.

The Christian ethos is thus in complete contrast to the pagan caricature with which it is so often confused. In place of the craven fear that haunts the unwelcome interloper, we are meant to enjoy the peaceful confidence of a servant-son at home in his Father's creation. We know that we are on our Father's business no less when investigating His handiwork than when engaged in formal acts of worship. In place of jealously secretive gods we have One whose very nature is Truth and Light, Himself the giver of all that is true, who rejoices when any of His truth is brought to the light and obeyed in humility.

Responsible Freedom

The Bible encourages man to roam the domain of the natural world in responsible freedom, showing all of it the respect due to his Father's creation, but none of it the superstitious reverence that would deny its status as a created thing like himself. . . .

The contrast between biblical and pagan theologies of nature is at no point more decisive than where science comes to inspire technology. "What right has man to improve upon nature; aren't we beginning to usurp the prerogatives of the Creator?" Such questions are often asked rhetorically, backed by observations of the kind parodied by Flanders and Swann: "If God had meant men to fly, he would never have given us the railways."

There is of course a sober warning for all ages in the story of the Tower of Babel, where men sought to build "a tower whose top may reach unto heaven." What the context makes clear, however, is that their sin consisted not in the building but in the motivation for it—an arrogant desire to be independent of God. Nowhere in the Bible is technological achievement disapproved, except where it expressed human pride and vainglory. More relevant is the reiterated biblical teaching that "He that knoweth to do good and doeth it not, to him it is sin." From the biblical standpoint whatever needs to be done to alleviate the lot of our fellow men is a duty from which we can excuse ourselves only for good cause.

The contrary pagan notion that it is both impossible and illicit for man to compete with or improve upon nature has had a long and fascinating history from ancient times. The Greek concept of the Golden Age, when men were supposed to have lived healthy and contented lives without technological aids, colored much classical and medieval thinking. The supposed divinity of nature was taken to imply that man would be claiming divine prerogatives if he attempted to copy or improve upon it. The general belief of the Middle Ages was that feats of nature could be surpassed only by magic.

A More and More Christian World

The idea that there is any inherent opposition between religion and technology founders on two brute facts: the historical reality that one particular religion, namely Christianity, has been the sponsor of modern technology; and the sociological truth that technology is creating a world which is manifestly more and more Christian. For Christianity, at least, there is no opposition to modern technology. Far from being opposed, the two are intimately, even mystically, intertwined.

Wilhelm E. Fudpucker, in *Theology and Technology*, 1984.

The most powerful biblical arguments against this pessimistic view were advanced by Francis Bacon:

If there be any humility towards the Creator, if there be any reverence for or disposition to magnify His works, if there be any charity for man, (we should) dismiss those preposterous philosophies which have led experience captive, and approach with humility and veneration to unroll the volume of creation.

As [Professor R.] Hooykaas puts it, Bacon

blew the trumpet in the war against the sins of laziness, despair, pride, and ignorance; and he urged his contemporaries, for the sake of God and their neighbors, to re-assume the rights that God had given them and to restore that dominion over nature which God had allotted to man. His ideal was a science in the service of man, as the result of restoration of the rule of man over nature. This to him was not a purely human but a divinely inspired work: "The beginning is from God . . . the Father of lights."

a critical thinking activity

Understanding Words in Context

Readers occasionally come across words which they do not recognize. And frequently, because they do not know a word or words, they will not fully understand the passage being read. Obviously, the reader can look up an unfamiliar word in a dictionary. However, by carefully examining the word in the context in which it is used, the word's meaning can often be determined. A careful reader may find clues to the meaning of the word in surrounding words, ideas, and attitudes.

Below are excerpts from the viewpoints in this chapter. One or two words are printed in italics. Try to determine the meaning of each word by reading the excerpt. Under each excerpt you will find four definitions for the italicized word. Choose the one that is closest to your understanding of the word.

Finally, use a dictionary to see how well you have understood the words in context. It will be helpful to discuss with others the clues which helped you decide on each word's meaning.

1. Humans' chief goal is to glorify God. This is the *RUBRIC* under which the Christian must practice science.

   RUBRIC means:

   a) cube
   b) established rule
   c) religion
   d) laboratory

2. Humans have a profound need to believe that the truths they *PERCEIVE* are founded in unchanging, universal factors; were it not so, could the truth be really important?

   PERCEIVE means:

   a) to disagree with
   b) to ask
   c) to mock
   d) to sense or understand

3. In the face of fundamental social problems caused by unlimited science, scientists' cries for freedom of research seem *BANAL* and self-serving.

BANAL means:

a) interesting
b) thoughtful
c) boring
d) trite

4. Scientism's *ONTOLOGICAL* strip mining asked man to sacrifice his reality of the world—its beauty and holiness—in return for a mathematical view which would allow him to manipulate matter on its own plane.

ONTOLOGICAL means:

a) coal
b) stupid
c) scientific
d) metaphysical

5. The final lines between science and religion have not yet been drawn. Many topics that were once matters of religious faith have been transferred to the *PURVIEW* of science.

PURVIEW means:

a) deviant
b) range
c) college
d) ignorance

6. The practice of science as we know it cannot continue unrestrained; for in the present *MILIEU* its results will be carelessly applied by industry in the name of progress.

MILIEU means:

a) setting
b) city
c) French factory
d) century

7. To Native Americans, trees were temple pillars, the earth too sacred to be *TRODDEN* save by soft skin moccasins.

TRODDEN means:

a) walked upon
b) gardened
c) driven on
d) harvested

8. These observations can be easily *PARODIED*; for example, "If God had meant humans to fly, he would never have given us railways."

PARODIED means:

a) taken seriously
b) ignored
c) made fun of
d) forgotten

Organizations To Contact

The editors have compiled the following list of organizations which are concerned with the issues debated in this book. All of them have publications available for interested readers. The descriptions are derived from materials provided by the organizations themselves.

American Association for the Advancement of Science
1333 H St. NW
Washington, DC 20005
(202) 326-6400

The Association represents all fields of science. It works to improve the effectiveness of science in the promotion of human welfare, and for a better understanding of the role of science and technology in society. It publishes the weekly magazine, *Science*, as well as books, newsletters, and quarterlies.

American Atheists
PO Box 2117
Austin, TX 78768-2117
(512) 458-1244

American Atheists is an educational organization dedicated to the complete and absolute separation of state and church. Its purpose is to stimulate freedom of thought and inquiry concerning religious beliefs and practices. It publishes *American Atheist* magazine, numerous books, and reprints of articles through American Atheist Press.

American Humanist Association
7 Harwood Drive
PO Box 146
Amherst, NY 14226-0146
(716) 839-5080

The Association's members are devoted to humanism as a way of life. They do not acknowledge a supernatural power. They believe that scientific advances can help humanity use its natural and social resources more effectively. The Association publishes numerous brochures, books, and journals, including the bimonthly *The Humanist* and the quarterly *Creation/Evolution*.

American Scientific Affiliation (ASA)
PO Box 668
Ipswich, MA 01938
(617) 356-5656

ASA members are scientists who subscribe to the Christian faith. The Affiliation investigates the relationship between science and technology and Christian beliefs. Its numerous publications include a source book and a journal, *Perspectives on Science and Christian Faith*.

Americans United for Separation of Church and State
8120 Fenton St.
Silver Spring, MD 20910
(301) 589-3707

The organization's purpose is to protect the right of Americans to religious freedom. Litigation, education, and advocacy are the principal means it has used to oppose the passing of state creation science laws and other threats to the separation of church and state. In addition to numerous brochures and pamphlets, the organization publishes a monthly newsletter, *Church and State*.

Associates for Religion and Intellectual Life (ARIL)
College of New Rochelle
New Rochelle, NY 10805
(914) 632-8852

ARIL is comprised of Jews and Christians involved in academic and intellectual pursuits. It strives to aid members in resolving conflicts that arise between religious beliefs and continuing advances in science and other academic fields. ARIL publishes a quarterly journal, *Religion and Intellectual Life*.

Bible-Science Association
2911 E. 42nd St.
Minneapolis, MN 55406

Association members adhere to a strictly literal understanding of the Biblical account of creation. The Association promotes and defends this understanding in its work. It publishes *Catalog of Creationism Resources* and a supplementary textbook series, *Our Science Readers*.

Billy James Hargis' Christian Crusade
PO Box 977
Tulsa, OK 74102
(918) 836-2206

The Crusade is a Christian educational ministry whose stated purpose is to safeguard and preserve the conservative Christian ideals upon which America was founded. It opposes socialism and federal infringement of states' rights. Its monthly *Christian Crusade Newspaper* has published many articles on evolution and other scientific advances that threaten Christian values.

Creation Research Society
2717 Cranbrook Road
Ann Arbor, MI 48104
(313) 971-5915

The Society is an organization of scientists. They are Christians who believe that the facts of science support the revealed account of creation in the Bible. The Society is one of the major publishers of creation research materials. Their books include *The Argument: Creationism vs. Evolutionism, Why Not Creation?* and *Design and Origins in Astronomy*.

Freedom from Religion Foundation (FFRF)
PO Box 750
Madison, WI 53701
(608) 256-8900

FFRF is a politically active organization of "free thinkers." Its purpose is to promote separation of church and state, educate the public on nontheistic matters, and combat fundamentalism. Its extensive publications include books, brochures, pamphlets, and the only freethought paper in the US, *Freethought Today*.

The Hastings Center
360 Broadway
Hastings-on-Hudson, NY 10706
(914) 478-0500

Since its founding in 1969, the Hastings Center has played a central role in raising issues as a response to advances in medicine and the biological sciences. The Center has three goals: advancement of research on ethical issues, stimulation of universities and professional schools to support the teaching of ethics, and public education. It publishes *The Hastings Center Report*.

Institute for Creation Research
10946 Woodside Ave. N.
Santee, CA 92071
(619) 448-0900

The Institute is a science research organization that promotes creationism. It operates a graduate school in science and a multi-media ministry. Its publications list, which includes the Creation-Evolution Series, is available by mail. It also publishes a monthly newsletter, *Acts and Facts*.

National Council on Religion and Public Education (NCRPE)
1300 Oread
Lawrence, KS 66045
(913) 843-7257

The Council is comprised of schools, organizations, and individuals who believe religion should be studied in public education in ways that do not promote the values or beliefs of one religion over another. It publishes the *Religion and Public Education* magazine and resource materials such as "Teaching About the Bible" and *A Compact Guide to Bible Based Beliefs*.

New York Academy of Sciences
2 E. 63rd St.
New York, NY 10021
(212) 838-0230

The Academy disseminates information, educates scientists and the public, and promotes the role of science in human welfare concerns. Its Educational Programs Department sponsors science fairs, a Science Research Training Program, and the Junior Academy, an organization of high school students interested in science and technology. The publications of the New York Academy of Sciences includes *Annals of New York Sciences*, and the bimonthly *The Sciences*.

Science for the People (SFTP)
897 Main St.
Cambridge, MA 02139
(617) 547-0370

SFTP works to create a society based on human needs rather than profit, and to support science that serves all people. Its bimonthly magazine, *Science for the People*, includes articles on science and ethics, and the role of science in society.

United Ministries in Education (UME)
8900 Whispering Pines Lane
Charlotte, NC 28210
(704) 588-2182

UME is an organization of seven Protestant churches which provides ministry related to every level of public education. The seven constituent churches have diverse beliefs about the roles of science and religion. One constituent, the United Church Board for Homeland Ministries, believes that scientific concepts can enrich religious understanding. UME has a variety of project areas including one on science and technology. It publishes a resource listing, books, and monographs, including, *Science, Technology and the Christian Faith*.

Appendix of Periodicals

Many periodicals that frequently address the science and religion issue are not widely available. Below is a list of relevant publications and information about where to obtain them.

Acts & Facts
Institute for Creation Research
PO Box 2667
El Cajon, CA 92021

A brief monthly periodical that disseminates information on creation and evolution. Written from a creationist perspective, *Acts & Facts* is edited by Henry M. Morris.

American Atheist
American Atheist Press, Inc.
PO Box 2117
Austin, TX 78768-2117

A monthly journal of atheist news and thought, edited by R. Murray-O'Hair.

Creation/Evolution Quarterly
7 Harwood Drive
PO Box 146
Amherst, NY 14226-0146

Published by the American Humanist Association, this pro-evolution quarterly carries technical articles on creation and evolution.

Daedalus
Business Office
PO Box 515
Canton, MA 02021

A quarterly journal of the American Academy of Arts and Sciences. *Daedalus* publishes scholarly articles on political, philosophical, cultural, and historical topics.

Eternity
Subscription Department
PO Box 611
Holmes, PA 19043

A monthly Christian newsmagazine published by Evangelical Ministries, Inc. The magazine features articles on politics, economics, religion, the arts, and sciences.

Free Inquiry
Box 5
Buffalo, NY 14215-0005

A quarterly journal published by the Council for Democratic and Secular Humanism. The journal offers agnostic and atheist views on the philosophies of science and religion.

The New American
395 Concord Ave.
Belmont, MA 02178

A biweekly conservative newsmagazine published by the John Birch Society. *The New American* has a fundamentalist religious perspective.

Perspectives on Science and Christian Faith
American Scientific Affiliation
55 Market St.
Ipswich, MA 01938

A quarterly journal published by a Christian organization of scientists. Its articles focus on the interaction between science and Christian faith.

The Sciences
2 E. 63rd St.
New York, NY 10021

A bimonthly journal published by the New York Academy of Sciences. *The Sciences'* contributors include many of the nation's most prominent scientists.

The World & I
2850 New York Ave. NE
Washington, DC 20002

A monthly chronicle of politics, arts, science, and world culture, published by *The Washington Times,* an influential conservative Christian newspaper.

Zygon: Journal of Religion and Science
Rollins College
Box 2764
Winter Park, FL 32789

A quarterly philosophical journal. *Zygon's* view is that new scientific concepts should be integrated into religious beliefs.

Periodical Bibliography

The following articles have been selected to supplement the diverse views presented in this book. They are divided by chapter topic.

Are Science and Religion Compatible?

Joel I. Friedman — "The Natural God: A God Even an Atheist Can Believe In," *Zygon*, September 1986.

Langdon Gilkey — "Religion and Science in an Advanced Scientific Culture," *Zygon*, June 1987.

Stephen Jay Gould — "Justice Scalia's Misunderstanding," *Natural History*, October 1987.

Stanley L. Jaki — "Science: From the Womb of Religion," *The Christian Century*, October 7, 1987.

Jon G. Murray — "Science—Unabridged," *American Atheist*, October 1986.

National Forum — "Science and Religion," Spring 1983. Available from The Honor Society of Phi Kappa Phi, PO Box 16000, Louisiana State University, Baton Rouge, LA 70893.

Madalyn O'Hair — "Comets and Religion," *American Atheist*, August 1987.

Harold P. Nebelsick — "Theological Clues from the Scientific World," *Journal of the American Scientific Association*, June 1986.

Tim Stafford — "Cease-Fire in the Laboratory," *Christianity Today*, April 3, 1987.

Deane Starr — "The Crying Need for a Believable Theology," *The Humanist*, July/August 1984.

Lionel Tiger — "Survival of the Faithful," *The Sciences*, March/April 1985.

Origins of the Universe

John D. Barrow — "The Anthropic Cosmological Principle," *The World & I*, August 1987.

Robert P. Crease and Charles C. Mann — "How the Universe Works," *The Atlantic Monthly*, August 1984.

Paul Davies — "New Physics and the New Big Bang," *Sky & Telescope*, November 1985.

Paul Davies — "Relics of Creation," *Sky & Telescope*, February 1985.

Allen Emerson

"A Disorienting View of God's Creation," *Christianity Today*, February 1, 1985.

A.K. Finkbeiner

"The Puzzling Structure of the Universe," *The World & I*, November 1987.

Fred Hoyle

"The Big Bang Under Attack," *Science Digest*, May 1984.

Eugene F. Mallove

"Cosmologists Are Asking a Lot of Creative Questions," *The Washington Post National Weekly Edition*, November 11, 1985.

Heinz R. Pagels

"A Cozy Cosmology," *The Sciences*, March/April 1985.

Holmes Rolston III

"Science & the Way to God," *Commonweal*, May 22, 1987.

Roy Abraham Varghese

"The Religious Dimensions of Modern Physics," *The World & I*, April 1987.

M. Mitchell Waldrop

"Before the Beginning," *Science 84*, January/February 1984.

Origins of Life

Richard A. Baer Jr.

"They *Are* Teaching Religion in the Public Schools," *Christianity Today*, February 17, 1984.

Sharon Begley

"Science Contra Darwin," *Newsweek*, April 8, 1985.

Sarah Boxer

"Will Creationism Rise Again?" *Discover*, October 1987.

Christianity Today

"Debate: Should Public Schools Teach Creation Science?" September 18, 1987.

Frederick Edwords

"Question Marks," *The Humanist*, July/August 1985.

Norman L. Geisler

"Monkey Trials, Part II: This Time the Apes Win," *Eternity*, October 1987.

Stephen Jay Gould

"The Verdict on Creationism," *The New York Times Magazine*, July 19, 1987.

Jack Hitt

"What *Did* Noah Do with the Manure?" *The Washington Monthly*, February 1987.

William F. Jasper

"Creation Research Expanding," *The New American*, December 16, 1985.

Henry M. Morris

"Is Creationism Scientific?" *Acts & Facts*, December 1987. Available from Institute for Creation Research, PO Box 2667, El Cajon, CA 92021.

Neil Postman and Marc Postman	"Teach Creationism," *The Nation*, January 11, 1986.
Charles E. Rice	"Evolutionism Is a Religion," *The New American*, August 3, 1987.
Pat Shipman	"Baffling Limb on the Family Tree," *Discover*, September 1986.
Huston Smith	"Evolution and Evolutionism," *The Christian Century*, July 7-14, 1982.
Kathleen Stein	"Censoring Science," *Omni*, February 1987.
Tikkun	"Creationism vs. Evolution: Radical Perspectives on the Confrontation of Spirit and Science," November/December 1987.
James M. Wall	"Supreme Court on 'Flat Souls,'" *The Christian Century*, July 1-8, 1987.

Ethics

Joe Edward Barnhart	"The Relativity of Biblical Ethics," *Free Inquiry*, Summer 1987.
Daniel J. Boorstin	"Science as Mythology," *Science Digest*, December 1984.
Bernard D. Davis	"Science, Objectivity, and Moral Values," *The World & I*, November 1987.
Marjorie Hall Davis	"Beliefs of a Christian Minister in Light of Contemporary Science," *Zygon*, September 1987.
Lucia K.B. Hall	"The Irrational Basis of Ethics," *The Humanist*, July/August 1986.
Gerald Holton	"The Advancement of Science and Its Burdens," *Daedalus*, Summer 1986.
Paul MacCready	"An Evolutionary Perspective," *Free Inquiry*, Spring 1987.
Julie Ann Miller	"The Clergy Ponder the New Genetics," *Science News*, March 24, 1984.
R.C. Sproul	"Clock-Maker Myths: God in the Here and Now," *Eternity*, October 1987.
Jim Swan	"Sacred Ground: Myth and Science Investigate the Powers of the Earth," *Utne Reader*, September/October 1987.

Bibliography of Books

A.G. Cairns-Smith — *Seven Clues to the Origin of Life.* Cambridge, UK: Cambridge University Press, 1985.

Bertrand L. Conway — *The Condemnation of Galileo.* New York: The Paulist Press, 1913.

Tess Cosslett, ed. — *Science and Religion in the Nineteenth Century.* Cambridge, UK: Cambridge University Press, 1984.

Paul Davies — *God and the New Physics.* New York: Simon and Schuster, 1982.

Richard Dawkins — *The Blind Watchmaker.* New York: W.W. Norton, 1986.

Hoimar von Ditfurth — *The Origins of Life: Evolution as Creation.* San Francisco: Harper & Row, 1982.

Stillman Drake — *Galileo at Work: His Scientific Biography.* Chicago: The University of Chicago Press, 1978.

Alfred Einstein — *Out of My Later Years.* Secaucus, NJ: Citadel Press, 1956.

Niles Eldredge — *Life Pulse: Episodes from the Story of the Fossil Record.* New York: Facts on File Publications, 1987.

Niles Eldredge — *Time Frames: The Rethinking of Darwinian Evolution and the Theory of Punctuated Equilibrium.* New York: Simon and Schuster, 1985.

Gerald Feinberg — *Solid Clues: Quantum Physics, Molecular Biology, and the Future of Science.* New York: Simon and Schuster, 1985.

David E. Fisher — *The Birth of the Earth.* New York: Columbia University Press, 1986.

Harald Fritzsch — *The Creation of Matter: the Universe from Beginning to End.* New York: Basic Books, 1985.

Ludovico Geymonat — *Galileo Galilei: A Biography and Inquiry into His Philosophy of Science.* New York: McGraw-Hill Book Company, 1965.

Duane T. Gish — *Evolution: The Challenge of the Fossil Record.* San Diego: Creation-Life Publishers, 1985.

Derek Gjertsen — *The Classics of Science: A Study of Twelve Enduring Scientific Works.* New York: Lilian Barber Press, Inc., 1984.

Sheldon Norman Grebstein — *Monkey Trial: The State of Tennessee vs. John Thomas Scopes.* Boston: Houghton Mifflin Company, 1960.

Ken Ham — *The Lie: Evolution.* El Cajon, CA: Master Book Publishers, 1987.

Robert W. Hanson, ed. — *Science and Creation: Geological, Theological & Educational Perspectives.* New York: Macmillan Publishing Company, 1986.

Charles P. Henderson Jr. — *God and Science: The Death and Rebirth of Theism.* Atlanta: John Knox Press, 1986.

Fred Hoyle — *The Intelligent Universe.* New York: Holt, Rinehart and Winston, 1983.

Richard H. Jones	*Science and Mysticism.* Cranbury, NJ: Associated University Presses, 1986.
Kenneth Korey, ed.	*The Essential Darwin.* Boston: Little, Brown and Company, 1984.
Mary Midgley	*Evolution as a Religion.* London: Methuen, 1985.
Carl Mitcham and Jim Grote, eds.	*Theology and Technology: Essays in Christian Analysis and Exegesis.* Lanham, MD: University Press of America, 1984.
Jacques Monod	*Chance and Necessity.* New York: Alfred A. Knopf, 1971.
Ashley Montagu, ed.	*Science and Creationism.* New York: Oxford University Press, 1984.
Clive Morphet	*Galileo and Copernican Astronomy.* London: Butterworths, 1977.
Henry M. Morris, ed.	*Scientific Creationism.* San Diego: Creation-Life Publishers, 1974.
Henry M. Morris	*The Troubled Waters of Evolution.* San Diego: Creation-Life Publishers, 1974.
Virginia Stem Owens	*And the Trees Clap Their Hands: Faith, Perception, and the New Physics.* Grand Rapids, MI: William B. Eerdmans Publishing Company, 1983.
David M. Raup	*The Nemesis Affair.* New York: W.W. Norton, 1986.
Jeremy Rifkin	*Declaration of a Heretic.* Boston: Routledge & Kegan Paul, 1985.
Theodore Roszak	*Person/Planet: The Creative Disintegration of Industrial Society.* Garden City, NY: Doubleday, 1984.
Peter Russel	*The Global Brain: Speculations on the Evolutionary Leap to Planetary Consciousness.* Los Angeles: J.P. Tarcher, Inc., 1983.
John T. Scopes and James Presley	*Center of the Storm.* New York: Holt, Rinehart and Winston, 1967.
Andrew Scott	*The Creation of Life.* New York: Basil Blackwell, 1986.
Robert Shapiro	*Origins: A Skeptic's Guide to the Creation of Life on Earth.* New York: Summit Books, 1986.
Harold S. Slusher	*The Age of the Solar System.* El Cajon, CA: Institute for Creation Research, 1982.
Huston Smith	*Forgotten Truth: The Primordial Tradition.* New York: Harper & Row, 1976.
Pamela Weintraub, ed.	*The Omni Interviews.* New York: Ticknor & Fields, 1984.
David B. Wilson, ed.	*Did the Devil Make Darwin Do It?* Ames, IA: The Iowa State University Press, 1983.

Index